God Who Dares to be Man

BONNELL SPENCER

Order of the Holy Cross

GOD WHO DARES TO BE MAN

Theology for Prayer and Suffering

Foreword by PAUL MOORE, Jr.
Bishop of New York

SEABURY PRESS / NEW YORK

1980
The Seabury Press
815 Second Avenue
New York, N.Y. 10017

Printed in the United States of America

Library of Congress Cataloging in Publication Data

Spencer, Bonnell.
  God who dares to be man.

  Includes bibliographical references and indexes.
  1. Theology, Doctrinal—Popular works. 2. Spiritual life—Anglican authors. I. Title.
BT77.S7I3   230'.3   80-16833
ISBN 0-8164-0478-X

To
Ellen Stephen OSH
Bede Thomas OHC
and
James Robert OHC
without whose help
this would have been
a poorer book.

Contents

OMEGA / The Call to Hope

Foreword

God Who Dares to be Man is a book shot through with reason and common sense. The very insistence on eliminating physical magic or intellectual tricks from the understanding of the gospel story emphasizes the full humanity of Jesus and makes more glorious the *kenosis*, the self emptying of God entering human history. This reasonableness in no way reduces Jesus to being just a good man, but rather "earths" the compassion of God firmly in the world which is to be redeemed.

This book is theology, tough theology, but it is theology wrested out of personal and pastoral experience, theology written to be used by one who has used it to draw intelligent doubters to the Lord, to bring the comfort of Christ to minds and hearts which would be disgusted at a God who forced them to belie their experience in order to believe.

But the author is clearly well read in the modern theologians: process theology, the theology of hope, and so forth. The thought of these contemporary theologians grows out of the changing intellectual soil of our time, but few of us have the time or competence to draw from their wells. By the same token it is difficult to keep up with biblical scholarship. And yet we need to be given the best of modern thought for our own theologizing. Father Spencer gives us this opportunity.

I am most appreciative, however, for the author's courage, which is grounded in the rock of a faith lived out in the discipline of the religious life. No one can doubt his catholicity, even though he casually states that Jesus probably was married and just as easily affirms the ancient tradition of the feminine quality of the Holy Spirit by referring to the Spirit as "she." And no one can doubt his working faith in the healing power of prayer, buttressed by his own experience, when he denies the likelihood of God interfering with the natural order he has created.

The book is a loving book. Again and again the theme of God's love emerges. Again and again theological principles stand or fall against the criterion of infinite love. This loving, active, moving, suffering God is a portrait of the Mystery of Being appropriate to our day — this Hebrew God who moved across the desert, who thundered from the mountain, who redeemed the fall of Jerusalem, who felt pain through his son on Calvary. This God is our God. Such a loving God is exciting, and in his integrity allows us our integrity. He urges us to think and study and pray and live and love with all our autonomous mind and heart and soul, without fear of tripping over some frozen archaic syllogism or fundamentalist text, torn out of the whole word of God.

Ours is a time to test and pull and tug at the tough fiber of our faith so that we can be sure it will hold us strong, whatever may happen. This is a book of action which gives a pattern for such testing.

I first met Father Spencer when I was seventeen years old, some forty-two years ago. Then his bright human and restless spirit attracted young persons by the hundreds to try the Catholic faith. This book shows that same attractive restless spirit after a long and strenuous life of prayer within the monastery walls, and a vigorous far-reaching ministry in God's world outside.

Paul Moore, Jr.
Bishop of New York

Preface

The spiritual life is a subject in which there is great interest today. Many of the books on it, however, content themselves with discussing its nature, purpose, and techniques. They take for granted the underlying concepts of God, creation, human nature, Jesus as the Word made flesh, the church as the extension of his humanity, and so forth. As a result, the reader must assume these concepts are to be understood in their traditional form.

But the popular understanding of that traditional form conflicts at many points with the insights of modern knowledge. The spiritual life then becomes unrelated to it. It exists in and for itself apart from the presuppositions of everyday life. It may even be used as an escape from the problems of the contemporary world.

This should not and need not be. Because the Christian faith is true, it can be reconciled with the truths discovered by modern natural and social sciences. And the gospel itself is enriched when it is so interpreted. That is what this book aims to accomplish. It is not a theological treatise. I am simply trying to restate the basic Christian concepts in terms that are credible to the men and women of today, as the basis for their life of prayer and a support in time of suffering.

The book reviews the conclusions I have reached after forty years of teaching at the parish and high school level. For that reason I have written it frankly in the first person. I want it to be constantly clear that I am stating my understanding of the gospel in faith and practice. I hope it is consonant with Christianity and may help to relate the gospel to the modern world.

In the five years that the book has been in preparation I have read as widely as I could. Admittedly, the selection has been somewhat hit and miss, being often determined by what books were available in libraries. Perhaps what has impressed me most is how frequently I have hit on just the book I needed at that moment in the development of my thought, apparently quite accidentally. It has not been possible to trace back to its source every idea I have incorporated. In order to give credit to some of those who have helped or stimulated me, I refer to their works in the notes.

It has been pointed out to me that the title, because it used the word "man" in the generic sense, will by some be considered sexist. I am sorry about that. Jesus was a man, and the basic concept of the book rests on the parallel between the incarnation and the creation of mankind on the one hand and the use of mankind for Christ's continued work through the church on the other. That can be clearly and crisply indicated only by using the word "man" in the three contexts. Anyone who reads the book will discover that I am committed not only to the equality of men and women, but also to the need for recognizing the feminine element in God.

I want to express my gratitude to several members of the Order of the Holy Cross and the Order of St. Helena, and to other friends outside the orders, who have read my manuscript in whole or in part. Their advice and criticisms, and especially their enthusiastic encouragement, have meant much to me. I am also grateful to Clarice Case for her help with the proofreading.

A

ALPHA

THE CALL TO FAITH

Chapter 1 / **CREATOR**

To dare is not usually predicated of God. That verb implies facing danger or risk in a situation the outcome of which is uncertain. Can God be involved in anything like that?

Certainly not the God of popular theology. Its basic concept is that God is almighty. He controls and determines everything that happens. For he either causes each event directly or allows it to occur through secondary causes when he could always intervene and prevent it. Furthermore, he knows, and has known from all eternity, everything that has happened or can happen, down to the smallest details. All, therefore, is foreordained.

Only a God who exercises such complete control will satisfy the demand for a deity who can be depended upon to work everything out right for his adherents. Nothing is able successfully to oppose him. Such a God cannot dare because he is incapable of taking a risk that could even for a moment put his unalterable will into jeopardy. He operates, overrules, or tolerates everything in terms of his unchangeable purpose. He is a comfortable God to have on your side.

But there are problems. If we concentrate on God's almightiness as his chief characteristic, do we not turn him into an oriental despot? In worshiping him are we not exalting brute force? And is it not true of God as it is of man that "power corrupts; absolute power corrupts absolutely"?

To such a God we can only surrender in fear and trembling as abject slaves. No, we cannot even do that. For if God foreknows and predestines our acts from all eternity, how can we have any power of self-determination, of self-surrender? Are we not puppets whom he manipulates by pulling the strings? But if so, why then does he hold us responsible for our actions and punish us for our sins?

A God of absolute power who either causes or deliberately permits everything that happens must take full responsibility for it himself. Nothing can take place unless he wills it. That includes Auschwitz and our devastation of Vietnam. Can a God who willingly tolerates such outrageous suffering be called good? Is he not callously indifferent to both the integrity and the welfare of his creatures? A God like that cannot be worshiped by thinking people today. Any man or woman who has a modicum of human decency is morally superior to him.

Admittedly, I have been describing a popular concept in its crudest terms. But the question is whether these crudities and inconsistencies are inherent in the idea of God itself. Atheists contend that they are and reject belief in God altogether. Theologians of the traditional schools have been aware of these difficulties, of course, and have maintained that they have successfully resolved them. But there is a growing number of Christian thinkers who have found their arguments unconvincing in themselves and incompatible with the insights of modern knowledge derived from other fields of research.[1]

Now the conclusions of the sciences—natural, social, behavioral—must be taken seriously. Christianity should respect the integrity of all disciplines of investigation. They, and they alone, can determine what is true or false in their fields. It is not the function of theology either to endorse one of several competing theories and discard the others on some criterion of its own, or to dictate to any other discipline the limits or acceptable conclusions of its investigations.

It must be recognized, however, that these other disciplines leave no room for God in their explanation of reality. He is never used to bridge a gap in the process of cause and effect. If at present they cannot account for the origin of a phenomenon, they hope that further research will discover it, as has been their experience so often in the past. Only insurance companies are content to call the inexplicable an "act of God." The sciences have no tolerance for a God of the gaps in their knowledge.

Furthermore, the sciences, each conducting its researches independently, have produced the welter of conflicting opinions which make this a pluralistic age. Many contend that no unified and significant concept of reality is feasible today or will ever be possible again. This skepticism is probably justified if it refers to an all-inclusive and integrated system of propositions that can be proved. Not only is the current situation too fluid for any final conclusions, but it is equally unlikely that an all-embracing logical formula will again be found.

What then? Has modern knowledge crowded out God both as an overall explanation of reality and as a factor in its operation? Must we abandon the hope of formulating a concept of God? Should we just accept the current conclusions in the various areas of a pluralistic universe and operate in terms of them for practical results without worrying about their mutual consistency? Many today are content to settle for that.

But the issue then becomes a matter of meaning. Human beings want life to be significant. We hear much nowadays about the problem of identity. What is it but the difficulty many are having in finding any real reason for their existence? We can, of course, concoct purposes and goals for ourselves. But are these after all only products of our own imaginations, projections of our hopes? Have they any basis in reality?

They cannot have any if reality itself is meaningless, a mere conjunction of blind forces grinding themselves out by happenstance. For there to be purpose and meaning in the universe as a whole there must be something akin to a mind expressing itself through it. That, however conceived, is what down the ages has been called God. But it will not be a healthy solution of our dilemma to assert his existence by blind faith unrelated to the rest of our experience. That would turn God into an emotional escape from the reality of life, not its ultimate foundation.

If we cannot account for that reality in a neatly logical system of theological doctrines, what then can we do? We can employ a device frequently used by other disciplines these days. We can suggest a model, or rather, since we want it to give a basic framework for the whole of reality, what is usually called a paradigm.[2] That approach is sound on two counts.

First, reality is confrontation. It presents itself to us in concrete particularity that is not logically deduced but simply given. Its significance, insofar as we can perceive it, is expressed better in narrative or picture form than in abstract propositions. That does not mean a paradigm may be inconsistent or unreasonable. It must not take refuge in paradoxes that are flat contradictions, or seek escape into mystery when the exposition gets tough. On the other hand, a paradigm does not attempt to prove itself. It seeks to focus the relevant facts into a picture that clarifies their interrelationships and total significance.

Second, the Judeo-Christian revelation is presented to us in narrative and practical form. In the Bible God manifests himself mainly in mighty acts and in rules of conduct. There is surprisingly little doctrinal interpretation and no theological speculation. We shall be faithful to that tradition if we seek, not a logical exposition but a paradigm that will picture reality in such a way that it finds cohesion in a being who expresses himself through it, and at the same time does not contradict, but rather uses to the full, the insights achieved by all the other contemporary disciplines of research. So we shall begin our search for the paradigm with the Bible itself.

He Who Acts

"In the beginning God created the heavens and the earth." The opening sentence of the Bible asserts our basic relationship to God. We creatures can know only a God who has created. We experience him as he is revealed in and through the already existing universe. For us creation is the beginning.

Creation is an activity of God. In the later of the two accounts (Gen. 1), God successively calls into being the various items of the universe. The earlier story (Gen. 2) is more naïve. God plants a garden, forms man out of a lump of clay, and woman out of Adam's rib. Like a true craftsman, God puts himself into his work. Then, the first account tells us, he rested on the seventh day. But he did not retire. He keeps right on working in creation for the rest of the Bible.

Creation itself is a continuous activity. Genesis asserts that the universe as we know it came into being all at once. Until the nineteenth century science itself accepted that view. But Genesis does not mean that God stopped creating once he had started the universe. If all things depend on God for their existence, then he must be constantly creating to continue them in it. This sustaining work of God is sometimes called his providence, but it is fundamentally creative. At every moment he gives creation the power to be.

If God is always creating, there is no reason why he cannot always have been creating. No doubt this universe had a beginning, and that is all Genesis says. Some cosmologists think it originated about five billion years ago in an immense explosion that scattered the galaxies at the enormous speed by which they are still retreating from each other. But presumably it was an explosion of something that already existed. The initiation of this universe need not have been the beginning of creation.

Even Thomas Aquinas admitted that it was logically possible that

God has always created. To me it seems most probable. If creation is the work of God's eternal love, as the Christian believes, has not God always so expressed himself? Did God change, if not his nature at least his functioning, to become a creator? I do not mean by this to suggest that God is only a creator. There is more to God than that. Doubtless he has an infinite variety of other activities by which he shows forth his love. Though continuously creating, he also transcends creation.

The Judeo-Christian tradition has always had a strong sense of the otherness of God. Creation is not a form of God or an emanation from him. He is not a world soul struggling with intractable matter. He stands over against creation as the one who makes it. But as creator he is not wholly other. He is constantly involved in sustaining and governing its development. This is God's immanence, which is the necessary complement of his transcendence, not its contradiction.

The recognition that God eternally creates underlines the important truth that he is the sole source of all that exists. He creates out of nothing. He gives to every moment, to every aspect of creation, the power to be. It makes no difference if these moments extend from eternity to eternity. As we hope to enjoy everlasting life with God, the infinite extension into the future is already assumed. Why cannot there be a similar extension into the past?

The explicit assertion that God creates out of nothing first occurs in 2 Maccabees 7:28. In the New Testament it is echoed only in Romans 4:17 and Hebrews 11:3. This reflects the Bible's lack of interest in doctrinal statements. But the idea underlies its whole concept of God, who does not share the universe with any opposing or resisting power which he has not himself created. Nothing exists independently of him.

A dualistic concept of the universe is always a temptation. It seems to account more easily for the presence of evil in the cosmos and its opposition to the good. But it means conceiving of God as externally limited, not completely in control. It gives no assurance of the ultimate triumph of love. The Judeo-Christian tradition has always resisted that temptation. It insists on the sole and unlimited sovereignty of God. "You shall have no gods except me" (Ex. 20:2).

This is essential to the belief that God freely creates. Nothing other than himself constrains or induces him to do so. Creation is an act of pure and disinterested love on God's part. He wants to create solely because he is love. His aim is to produce lovers, beings capable of enjoying his love by receiving it and making a self-determined response to it. To achieve that purpose he must not only give himself to creation; he must also wait upon its response and be affected by it.

So he gives the cosmos authentic existence and the autonomous exercise of real power. He limits himself by setting up that which can genuinely oppose him, and respects its integrity when it does. This is required by the very process of creation itself. A creator cannot keep all power to himself without making the universe a mere figment of his imagination. If it is to be real, it must have independent integrity, even though all its innate power is constantly derived from God's loving creative act.

His respect for the integrity of creation means further that he will not arbitrarily terminate it. Again the constraint is not an external force but his own inexhaustible love. No matter how persistently or outrageously creatures resist his will, he continues their existence, respecting their independence, and striving to entice them into union with him. Such is the measure, the infinite patience, of his love.

That love is the basis of the Judeo-Christian conviction that God is good. Although it recognizes both that God is almighty, the source of all existence and power, and that there is evil in the universe, nevertheless God can say of his completed handiwork, "It is very good" (Gen. 1:31). The origin of evil can be found in God's self-limitation which, because it is an expression of love, is a greater good than mere absence of evil in a predetermined universe would be. The reality of evil can be admitted and reconciled with a good God. But the reconciliation depends on conceiving of him as more than the ultimate, transcendent source or reality, its initial creator. He must be constantly involved, acting and reacting within it, so that in the end his love can utilize and overcome evil in the production of the highest good.

The God of the Bible is the living God. The Old Testament does not hesitate to portray him in the most anthropomorphic terms. Despite his perfect wisdom, he has to come down to earth to find out what is going on. He gets angry, repents, and changes his mind. He cares, suffers, and loves. He is thoroughly alive. Today we find much of this excessively naïve. But in our efforts to be more sophisticated we must not lose the dynamic quality. God acts within the universe, he struggles with evil, he redeems, he triumphs through his unremitting love. This note must be retained if our paradigm is to be faithful to the deepest insight of our Judeo-Christian heritage. It should, indeed, be its primary feature. It brings the picture to life. It conceives of God as a vibrant reality not a logical abstraction. He acts, he works, he suffers, he conquers, he lives, he loves.

The Absolute

When the Christian gospel entered the Greco-Roman world, it had to adapt to the prevailing philosophical climate. This included a concept of God which had been logically deducted from consideration of the world as we experience it. Everything in the universe is contingent; that is, it depends on something else. But what does the whole process depend on, what causes it, what starts it moving? There must be, it was argued, an absolute being that exists in itself, dependent on nothing but itself. This being is the first cause, the uncaused origin of all causation, the unmoved mover from whom all motion is derived.

So God is omnipotent, the source of all power and potentiality. This attribute could be linked with the biblical concept of God as almighty. But there was a difference. The Judeo-Christian God created out of nothing. The philosophers' God need not do so. He had only to give form to pre-existing inchoate matter. To the latter the defects of the world as we know it could be ascribed. This was a dualistic solution of the problem of evil. Plato thought the ultimate was the Good. But significantly, when he considered the possibility of creation, he attributed it, not to that ultimate reality but to a demiurge, a world soul that is doing its best with somewhat intransigent matter.

Christianity refused to accept that dualism. It declared the absolute of the philosophers to be the creator of all that exists. That undermined the logical consistency of the Greek concept. But in other matters the abstract, philosophical attributes were transferred to the living God. The result was a hybrid with glaring inconsistencies.

Adjustments had to be made somewhere. It is easier to be consistent when dealing with logical concepts than with a dynamic personality. Theologians like to be consistent. So most of the adjustments were made at the expense of the biblical God. If the logical integrity of the Greek concept of deity was somewhat impaired by its adjustment to moral monotheism, the vitality of the God whom Abraham served and Jesus called Abba, Father, was diminished far more drastically when he was characterized by logical abstractions.

But the great damage was done by the further deductions. Absolutes are essentially static. God's perfection became unchanging, but any change would necessarily be for the worse. In particular, it was held impossible for God to suffer. Indeed, it is hard to see how he could do anything except be what he already is, the eternal I AM, as in the beginning, so now, and forever. Could it be said in any meaningful way that such a God is alive?

Worse still, he becomes unrelated to the universe, or at least he is unaffected by it. This is sometimes expressed in the formula, "Creation minus God equals zero; God minus creation equals God." But if creation makes no difference to God, if what creatures do has no effect on him, if he does not rejoice in their joys or suffer with and over their sorrows, to call him love is incongruous. For supreme indifference and uninvolvement are not love. A God who does not in some sense suffer with us could neither be loved nor admired. He is simply insufferable.

Here is the source of the difficulties in declaring the God of traditional theology to be good. It is fashionable today to blame all our theological ills on the interpretation of our biblical faith in terms of Greek philosophy because it has led to such concepts as an impassible God. That is more unfair. If the early theologians had not expressed Christianity in the thoughtworld of the Roman Empire, it would have remained a Jewish sect. There was such a Jewish-Christian church; it died out in the second century.

Furthermore, the logical attributes of God are not false in themselves. They express important truths about the relationship of the universe to God, and the absoluteness of his attributes and potentialities in their abstract form.[3] That they are abstract does not diminish their reality. They constitute the eternal and unchanging character of God. What we designate as a person's character is always an abstraction. We have to infer it from his acts and attitudes. Because God's attributes have to be deduced from the logical implications of a contingent and finite universe they are not to be despised as unreal or unimportant.

They are the recognition that reality must ultimately be grounded in a transcendent, infinite being. And that being must be other than his creation. Therefore, we must not limit his otherness to his creative activity. We are all too prone to confine God within the bounds of human analogies, moral principles, and spiritual usefulness. We make gods for ourselves out of our adjustments to our environment. Freud was right when he recognized that the father god who disciplines and punishes or condones and comforts is a projection of the father image. Or the despotic god of absolute power is the deification of the law and order by which the rulers in church and state maintain their control. We contrive gods after our likeness as objects we can use.

So we must recognize that God is beyond creation, beyond good and evil, beyond being and nonbeing. The absolute attributes are the great safeguard of this transcendence. They assert that God in himself is not dependent on creation, not limited by it, not subject to mortality or temporal change. This provides the theological basis for the negative approach to God that experiences his ineffable mystery, his numinous aspect, in the "cloud of unknowing," into which the great mystics of east and west penetrate to a slight degree, and which they designate with equal propriety as "the All" or "the Nothing."

The problem arises when the absolute attributes are used to isolate God from his creation. A favorite text for the otherness of God is Isaiah 55:8: "My thoughts are not your thoughts, my ways not your ways." This is too often quoted without the counterbalancing passage three verses later: "The word that goes forth from my mouth does not return to me empty, without carrying out my will and succeeding in what it was sent to do." The latter is as essential as the former.

A God who is wholly other, of whom no experience is possible, and who is not perceptibly involved in creation, could not by definition be known. Only through his immanence can God's transcendence be recognized. If our paradigm is to be inclusive, therefore, it must make provision for the absolute attributes of God and at the same time bring him into living and mutual relationship with creation.

Process of Creation

When we call God a creator we are using a human analogy. Dorothy Sayers in *The Mind of the Maker*[4] analyzed artistic creation to throw light on what we mean by that analogy. She finds three elements in the process which I shall designate the idea, its formulation, and its actualization.

The idea is the basic concept of the work in its totality. This is the artist's inspiration, which he intuits as a whole. It is an abstraction which he cannot know as an idea; he simply has it and the urge to express it. If he loses interest in the idea or finds its expression too difficult, he can discard it. But because it is an abstract unity, he cannot change it. To do so would make it a new and different idea.

In order to know the idea it has to be formulated. This involves, in a drama for instance, the determination of the characters, the working out of the plot, the devising of episodes, scenes, and situations. All this formulation is controlled by the basic idea even though the idea cannot be expressed except by that process. A truly creative artist, however, is intuitively aware of whether or not the formulation as it develops is remaining faithful to the basic idea.

The third aspect is its actualization in the drama itself. At some point this should eventuate in the writing of the play and, if the author is so fortunate, in its production on the stage. This process is the response to the formulation by which the author, as well as the readers and audience, discovers what the basic idea is, provided both the formulation and the actualization are commensurate with it.

Although the production is potentially the full actualization of the playwright's intention, the process of actualization begins in the author's mind before a word is written. The formulation is verbalized or visualized by the author as fast as it occurs, and it is only in this way that he is aware of the idea and its content. Idea, formulation, and actualization are simultaneous and coexistent. They are coordinated aspects of a single whole, which can be distinguished but not separated. The whole can, and indeed often does, exist initially in the mind of the maker.

While the idea is unchangeable, the formulation is in a state of constant adaptation as the author sees how it is being actualized. This is because a truly creative author produces real characters. They have, as it were, a life of their own. So it may be that in the course of the development of a play some action which the author had planned for them turns out to be not in character. Then some adjustment has to be made.

Faced with this situation, the author may do one of three things. First, if the basic idea is sound and the artist has the skill, he works out the plot in such a way that the characters remain true to themselves. Second, if he cannot find a way to do that, he may abandon the idea as unworkable or lay it aside until the inspiration becomes clear enough to enable him to solve the problem. But third, human nature being what it is, he may manipulate the plot to bring it to his intended termination in spite of the characters.

An example of this in Shakespeare is *The Merchant of Venice*, in which Shylock becomes so real that we begin to empathize with his feelings. To leave him defeated and crushed would have turned the play into a tragedy. So to give it a happy ending Shakespeare provides his forced "conversion" to Christianity, which destroys the integrity of Shylock's character and of the play itself. Such human failings, however, serve only to point up the distinction between the three elements in creation—the idea, its formulation, and its actualization—and the necessity for them to be in perfect harmony with each other.

Sayers sees in this an analogy for the Trinity. The Father conceives creation as a whole—its fundamental purpose and objective. In this general concept all the ways by which these can be accomplished are included as abstract possibilities. The Father is omniscient and omnipotent in that he knows all the potentials of creation. His basic idea is a dynamic, living concept, not a rigidly preconceived and predetermined plan. It can develop in innumerable ways. And there are vast reaches of it that can never be actualized because finite creation cannot fully include the infinite. This transcendent overplus of God has been well designated "the darkness of excess of light."

But although the basic idea is neither static nor fixed, it does not change. No matter how many adjustments and limitations occur in its process of actualization, they are all derived from its anticipated possibilities, and its loving purpose will eventually be realized. Precisely because it is abstract and infinitely adaptable, it can remain constant. In the end God's love will prevail.

The Father, then, preserves the absolute and eternal attributes of God. They originate solely in his love. Here also is his freedom and goodness. He is not persuaded or constrained by any external power or principle, least of all by a superior moral standard. He is good because he is love and creates love. In this unchanging purpose all finite contingency is based. He is all knowledge and all potentiality, the unmoved mover and the uncaused cause, the self-derived source of all that is—"the love that moves the sun and the other stars."[5]

His basic idea is formulated through the Son, the Logos, the Word. "No one knows the Father except the Son and those to whom the Son chooses to reveal him" (Mt. 11:27). But it is not enough for the Word to be spoken. To become operative a word must be heard, heeded, and responded to. So in response to the Logos the Spirit hovers over the face of the deep bringing order out of chaos (Gen. 1:2), breathes life into man (Gen. 2:7), and leads into all truth (Jn. 16:13). By the cooperation of the Father, Son, and Holy Spirit creation is actualized.

The limitations of Sayers's analogy become apparent here. A human creator uses concepts already in his mind, whereas God creates out of nothing. Although human artists try to let their characters live their own lives, they never fully succeed. God can and does give creatures their integrity because he bestows on them the power of self-realization. A philosophical and psychological scheme by which we can picture this process is suggested in the writings of Alfred North Whitehead, Charles Hartshorne, and their disciples.[6] It is not my intention to expound or defend their position as such, but to use it for the clarification of the paradigm I am proposing.

Process of Becoming

Whitehead postulates that reality does not consist of substances — entities that have a stable being and nature for longer or shorter periods of duration, but is made up of actual occasions of becoming. These occasions are very brief; in human experience it is estimated there are between four to ten a second. The psychologist William James called them the specious present. These occasions, however, are not limited to human beings. Entities from electrons on up are characterized by them. In themselves they are imperceptible. We experience them as they are strung together in continuous sequences like the frames of a motion picture.

Each occasion is regulated by a subjective aim that seeks to become itself. Whitehead prefers the phrase "subjective aim" to the word "subject" in order to emphasize that the I, the self, the subject, is not an entity separate from the experience. It is that which determines the active process of self-formation and exists only within it.

The occasion synthesizes itself by incorporating or rejecting the influences that impinge upon it from its environment. The principal source of this data is the state of being achieved by the occasion's immediately preceeding becoming and its content. Adjacent frames of a motion picture are for the most part identical. But new sensations and memories can be received and their incorporation effects the slight change that produces the motion.

In handling this data the subjective aim is striving for a harmonious satisfaction in the present. It also projects itself toward the future in the being it becomes, which can influence its own and other subsequent becomings. Being is always a thing of the past, that which has already become. Becoming alone is the active present.

We cannot experience other becomings directly. They have already become before they can influence us. With most objects of our experience the interval between their becoming and our perception of them as beings is too short to be noticeable. We can recognize it, however, in the case of a star which, let us say, is a thousand light years away. What we see is the star as it had become a millennium ago. It is possible that the star exploded three centuries later and there is now no star at that spot in the heavens to be seen.

We have direct experience only of our own becomings. This, however, is a subjective experience. While they are happening they cannot be objects of knowledge any more than we can see our eyes. Even our own becomings must have eventuated into beings before they can provide the data for our present occasion of experience.

Occasions of becoming form themselves but they cannot generate themselves. They are started by what Whitehead calls an "initial aim." I prefer to call it an "initiating aim" to emphasize that it enables the becoming as well as motivates it. In brief, the initiating aim creates the creativity by which the creature creates itself. This is the work of the Holy Spirit. In determining the inititating aim three factors are involved.

First, the Spirit is the repository in whom is stored the memory of all beings. This is taken into account when the initiating aim is formulated so that each occasion is coordinated with and fits into the ongoing development of all reality. In this way the Spirit maintains the integrity and continuity of the past, which gives the present the foundation and structure it needs for its thrust into the future.

Second, the Spirit directly intuits the basic idea of the Father, "for the Spirit reaches the depths of everything, even the depths of God. After all, the depths of a man can only be known by his own spirit, not by any other man, and in the same way the depths of God can only be known by the Spirit of God" (1 Cor. 2:10f). This enables the Spirit to work constantly for the harmony of creation which is the ultimate will of God.

Third, the specific objective of the initiating aim is the highest potential that can be achieved by that particular occasion. This potential is proffered to it by the Son, the Logos, the Word. It is determined by the circumstances and capacities of the occasion itself. It is specifically designed for it. It is adjusted to the situation even though its previous becoming failed, in whole or in part, to achieve its potential. In this way the integrity of each becoming is respected. Its past shortcomings are taken into account when the opportunity for a slight yet possible improvement is offered to the current occasion. So on a minute scale evil can be overcome by good.

The potential is always derived from and consonant with the basic idea of the Father. But in formulating it the Logos is affected by the self-determined condition of the creature, and adapts the unchanging purpose to it. It is a real two-way relationship between God and creation. This contradicts the denial of God's relatedness that traditional theology makes on the grounds that to be related would be a limitation that would make God finite.

Now it is true that relatedness is a limitation for creatures, because each is linked to only one specific time, place, and set of circumstances. But God is not limited in that way. As traditional theology itself recognizes, he is omnipresent. He is related to each and every instance of reality. His relatedness is absolute and infinite. The Logos has "an unlimited capacity to adapt, without loss of integrity, to everything whatsoever."[7]

Absolute relatedness does not infringe on the infinitude of God. But to deny that relationship would be an intolerable limitation. It would mean he could not love. A lover is affected by the beloved. A lover adjusts himself to the needs of the beloved at whatever cost to himself. That is just what God does through the initiating aim and the proffered potential of each occasion of becoming. Because God is constantly and universally so related, creation is the work of his love.

The great value of this paradigm is that it depicts the continuity of divine creation. Because God is related to each and every becoming he does not have to interfere from time to time in the cosmos in order to direct it. He needs no gaps through which to enter since he is constantly involved in the process. But because he creates self-determined creativity, the integrity of each becoming is fully respected. He governs the cosmos, not by force but by persuasion. The Logos lures toward the highest potential and the Spirit initiates the subjective aim toward it. But the response of the subjective aim is not compelled. God creates by love in order to create the capacity for love.[8]

The Work of Love

The response of love, at least at the conscious level, requires some degree of deliberate self-determination. The beloved must freely give or withhold a surrender to the lover. God bestows on his creatures that capacity to respond. The subjective aim, in receiving the power to become itself, can resist the accompanying motivation and direction supplied by the Spirit. There is the possibility of discontinuity between the initiating and subjective aims. Accordingly, the latter can be more or less responsive to the lure of the potential proffered by the Logos.

This is beautifully illustrated in Michaelangelo's central panel of the Sistine Chapel ceiling — the creation of Adam. God is portrayed with his hand stretched out toward the recumbent Adam, who is lifting his hand somewhat limply toward God's. But their fingers just fail to touch. In that gap lies the power of self-determination.

The subjective aim is the determinant of its instant of becoming. It exists and functions only in that instant. A subject is the continuity of a series of subjective aims. It does not operate from outside them, having the experiences or directing the process. It is the becoming. I fully agree with Whitehead in rejecting the concept of an independent, substantive subject — self, mind, or soul.[9]

The continuity of the subject consists of the sequence of its subjective aims. In Whitehead's process theology this is maintained by the objective influence on its successor exerted by the being that eventuated from the previous occasion of becoming. I agree that this objective influence is the principal source of continuity. But I also think that the subjective aim of the previous occasion can influence its successor subjectively, that is, directly.

After all, the writing of a single word requires a number of actual occasions through which one's intention remains unchanged. It does not have to, of course. An occasion can determine its degree of conformity to the previous subjective aim. It can alter its intention. It can be distracted. But even so, it starts off to some extent from where it was. The influence of its previous subjective aim is a factor that must be taken into account.

Although, let me repeat, the subject does not exist outside the series of subjective aims, I think the persistence of a subjective as well as an objective relationship between them helps us conceive how a living subject develops character. Its successive aims have a tendency to be more or less responsive to the lure of the potential or, to put it in ordinary terms, to be more or less selfish. I find this easier to picture if the living process of one occasion of becoming can have a subjective influence on its successor.[10]

The subjective continuity of the subject is also an important factor in the love relationship of human beings to God. Love is always subject-to-subject, not subject-to-object. In choosing the potential for a human occasion of becoming, the Logos takes into consideration not only the objective achievement of its previous occasion, but also the tendency and character of the past subjective aims. It presents the potential in the form that will most enticingly lure the current one.

Because this luring toward the good takes into account the evil of human selfishness and sin, yet respects the free will of the sinner, constant adjustment of the Father's loving purpose is necessary. That has its price. For the self-conscious creature it means the acceptance and endurance of suffering. Because the Logos is love, he shares the cost. Ultimately he takes the evil upon himself and it brings him to Calvary.

The persistence of the Logos in enticing men and women to move in the direction of love opens the future to change. We do not need to be enslaved either by our own past selfishness or by the limitation and corruptions of the heritage and current mores of our environment. The Logos offers us freedom from history, our own personal history and that of society, so that we can make history. And because both the Logos and the Spirit are constantly adjusting the unchangeable purpose of the Father to the self-determinations of the creatures, there is a sense in which God himself is involved in the process of becoming.[11]

In our search for a paradigm that will express God's creative relationship to the cosmos, we have come, with the aid of Sayers, a modern author, and Whitehead, a contemporary philosopher, to the traditional Christian concept of God as a Trinity of Father, Son, and Holy Spirit. But we are interested in it not as a theological doctrine but as a myth; that is, a story based on a human analogy. It is a love story, and an exciting one at that.

It tells us how the Father from all eternity purposes to bring forth creatures who will be united to him in love. It tells how the Spirit initiates and enables a process whereby the creature can make a self-determined response of love. It tells how the Son, at infinite cost to himself, continually adjusts the abiding purpose to the integrity of the creature's self-determinations. It portrays God as intimately involved in the process of creation, yet eternally transcendent to it. Above all, it affirms that God is in himself love, the mutual self-giving of the Father, Son, and Holy Spirit.

Creation is one expression of God's love. We experience it in this cosmos of time and space. So far we have been considering God's relationship to it mostly from his side. We must now approach the question from another angle and see whether our paradigm is compatible with our scientific knowledge. Can the universe be conceived as the product of the continuous activity of divine creation? And can human beings provide an analogy for God because they are created in his image?

Chapter 2 / **EVOLUTION**

If God is creator of the universe, there must be some sense in which "the heavens declare the glory of God, and the firmament shows his handiwork" (Ps. 19:1).[1] This need not, however, imply Paley's argument from design.[2] He held that because the universe is a machine which fulfills a purpose, like a watch, it therefore demands a watchmaker. Apart from the debated question whether the universe has a purpose, the argument is unacceptable today because to describe the universe as a machine attributes to it more determinism than contemporary science is prepared to grant.

Paley's argument rests on Newtonian science with its tidy and stable little universe. Having been properly manufactured and wound up, it could proceed to run itself efficiently and predictably. As late as the beginning of the nineteenth century it was believed that, if one could know the position and velocity of every atom, it would be possible to predict the exact state of the universe two hundred years later. Although that information was not available, it was held theoretically knowable.

Furthermore, Bishop Ussher's chronology that dated creation at 4004 B.C., with every species of flora and fauna determined "in their several kinds" from the start, was still accepted in scientific circles despite the embarrassing questions being raised by geologists and biologists. Darwin's theory of evolution by natural selection caused the first disturbance of this complacency in the popular mind. The discrepancy between that theory and the first and second accounts in Genesis was not the real problem. Theologians quickly worked it out that the Bible records the fact of God's creation, and evolution explains how he accomplished it.

But creation by evolution is different from creation by fiat. God is no longer immediately responsible for the universe as we know it if he did not create it directly as it is according to a predetermined plan. The past hundred and fifty years have seen continued advances in the sciences and with them a surprising decrease in the determinism ascribed to the universe. The concept of a static, transcendent God who orders things into being from outside the cosmos is no longer relevant. It hardly fits an open-ended universe that has been developing in terms of discernible natural laws for billions of years. If there is a creator, his involvement in it must be very different.

Dynamic Universe

Whitehead, the originator of process theology, was a mathematician and scientist before he became a philosopher. His principal concern was to give a metaphysical basis for the dynamic universe we know today. In order to account for both the novelty and the order we find in it, he found it necessary to postulate a God who lets the universe become itself and at the same time guides and persuades it to achieve its potential. So the paradigm I have expounded is based on concepts explicitly designed to incorporate the results of modern science.

Evolution is one factor that has contributed to the idea of a dynamic universe. It supplemented the old cyclical concept of time, which was derived from the annual round of the seasons—the death of winter and the rising again of spring. That expressed a truth which is still valid. But it is not the whole story. Life has not just gone on being as it has always been from the beginning. Nature as well as human society has a history. Time does not only go round in circles. It moves toward a future. It is even conceivable that is has an objective.

If evolution brought home the dynamic character of time, the principle of relativity has done the same for space. The static three-dimensional framework which Newton believed extended unchanged throughout the universe can no longer be accepted. This, far more than Copernicus's discovery of the solar system, and even than the terrifying expansion of the sidereal universe with which modern astronomy confronts us, has removed the earth from the center of reality. We can no longer take it as an absolute fixed point to which we can relate the whole framework of space.

Atomic physics has been another factor in destroying a static concept of the universe. The solid little atoms, considered to be irreducible to anything less, have been exploded. At first the model of a miniature solar system with the electrons revolving around a nuclear proton was suggested. But that in turn proved to be too stable. Electrons have been recognized as quanta of energy and subject to apparently random jumps between discernible orbits. The nucleus has been broken up into components which again are observable effects of energy. All matter is therefore the objectification of energy and energy can be known only in its effects.

The most recent major factor in the current world view of science is the contribution of biochemistry. Research in the DNA genetic code has shown that all life is grounded in and controlled by four small molecules or bases. In sexual organisms their arrangement is the result of the conjunction of the ovum and sperm of the parents. It is reproduced in all the cells of the new body. This assures that the species and the individuals will maintain the same nature. Yet there are occasional (and apparently random) mutations and variations in combination of the genes. Most of these are detrimental to the organism and do not survive. But a few may be beneficial and eventually become dominant through natural selection.

Finally, there is Heisenberg's principle of indeterminacy. This recognizes that the position and velocity of an electron cannot both be known with full accuracy. Bronowski prefers to call this the principle of tolerance because the area of uncertainty is circumscribed. A degree of it must be tolerated. To that extent complete predictability is impossible. Again, although a certain percentage of quantum jumps will occur, it cannot be determined in advance which electrons will make them and when. Genetic mutations are likewise unpredictable in terms of their individual instances.

In other words, at least as far as contemporary knowledge in many areas goes, not everything can be accounted for by strict cause and effect. Events occur to which no cause can be assigned. They apparently happen by chance. Sometimes people seem to think that to attribute an effect to chance is to account for it. That is not so. To attribute it to chance is to admit that it cannot be accounted for. It is a random occurrence.

The recognition of these areas of uncertainty does not make the formulation of natural laws impossible. The laws are statistical. They are not less accurate for that reason. They can be used as the basis for prediction and be verified by it. But although the general outcome can be anticipated, individual instances are not predetermined.

For example, before a major holiday the traffic department often predicts the number of fatal accidents that will occur. The predictions turn out to be amazingly accurate. Yet, although the hundred, let us say, deaths do occur, not a single one of them could have been predicted in advance. Each accident happened in terms of its own set of circumstances which could not have been foreknown and could presumably have been avoided.

The indeterminacy of individual instances makes the determinism that was compatible with the Newtonian universe no longer possible. Chance seems to be an inherent element in the universe. It opens the door to the introduction of novelty which our conception of the developing universe requires. It also leaves room for the self-synthesis of the actual occasions of experience. The whole universe is in the process of becoming something different, which is accomplished because some individual becomings successfully opt for that which had not been before.

Does this also open the way for the control of the process by God? We must be cautious here. To attribute something to chance is to recognize that in terms of the empirical situation we do not know its cause. This may be because there is in fact no cause to know. Random events may be inherently inexplicable.[3]

We must not be hasty in attributing chance occurences to God lest we fall into the old error of trying to fit him into the gaps in our knowledge. But it is also true in terms of our paradigm that God is related to every occasion of becoming by providing its initiating aim and the lure of its potential. It is at least conceivable that it is in response to these that certain occasions synthesize themselves in novel ways.[4]

Life

The universe we know is, or at least has been, evolving. Its development from the simplest atoms to the varied and complicated forms of life on this planet can be accounted for in no other way. The relationships between the various stages can be traced sufficiently to make a continuous process the most plausible explanation. It cannot be absolutely demonstrated. There are still major gaps in the picture and it can be maintained that an impulse from outside the process must be introduced to bridge them. Three such gaps are the origin of life, of consciousness, and of reflection.

The line between organic and inorganic matter, between life and nonlife, has generally been considered an impassable divide. Many still argue that life could not possibly have generated spontaneously from nonliving material. The failure of the best efforts so far to produce it artificially is seen as confirmation of this. It is claimed that life must have come originally from outside this planet. Few today believe that it came from elsewhere in the universe. But there are still those who maintain that it must have originated in a supermundane life force or in the living God.

Modern genetics, however, has demonstrated not only the chemical basis of the living cell, but also that the cell reproduces and maintains itself through its chemical consistency. Furthermore, laboratory reproductions of the conditions that are known to have prevailed on the earth four billion years ago have succeeded in forming amino acids from which proteins are made, and they in turn are the building blocks of life as we know it. The first such experiments simulated the sultry oceans. But more recently experiments involving freezing conditions have produced adenine, one of the four molecular bases in the DNA genetic alphabet.

It is a long way from the formation of these constituents to the living cell itself. In terms of evolution it probably took a billion years or so. It is not surprising, therefore, that it is taking a while to bridge that gap in the laboratory, if indeed that can ever be accomplished. But the ability to simulate the first steps in the process that could lead from inorganic matter as it once existed to the production of life has convinced some scientists that it did in fact at one time evolve from nonliving matter.

It is therefore a scientifically tenable hypothesis to hold that there is a single continuous evolution from the simplest forms of matter through its more complex structures — through the crystals, amino acids, and proteins to macromolecules capable of reproducing themselves and unicellular life, and then through the ever more complex organisms to humankind itself. There are no gaps which could not conceivably have been bridged by a natural development.

In particular, there is no need for life to have been intruded from an uncreated source outside the universe. To those who are looking for places where God's intervention can be required this is a blow. But in the paradigm I am suggesting God is in constant relation to the whole process and does not have to intrude into it.

It is to the process as a whole that we must look to determine whether there is any need for, or at least possibility of, divine guidance and control. A notable characteristic of evolution is that it has moved in the direction of more and more complex forms. This has been accomplished in the teeth of two opposing forces: homeostasis, the tendency of entities to maintain the same form; and entropy, the tendency of an energy system to run down. Does the persistence of evolution in the direction of complexity encourage, if not actually require, the hypothesis that there is something or someone to maintain it?

The question can also be asked in regard to the origin of the phyla, the major divisions of the forms of life. Natural selection and geographical or other barriers are sufficient to account for the differentiation of species in terms of slight variations which prove beneficial. But the development from a reptilelike creature to a bird requires the coordination of many complex changes persisting simultaneously over long periods. It is difficult to see how they can constantly have been of sufficient advantage to the individuals that had them to assure their survival by natural selection. To my mind it would help if there were something or someone pressing toward the evolution of major groups.

But these problems must be solved by the scientists and by no one else. The advantage of the paradigm I am proposing is that it leaves the question open. The Logos' lure of each occasion of becoming toward its highest potential could encourage the mutations and developments that maintain the upward trend if that were necessary. On the other hand, it could have been left to the natural selection of random variations if that proves to be a suffficient explanation of the evolution of complexity.

In leaving the question open, however, I want to make three further comments. First, it is possible for process theology to assign a reason for the preference of more complex forms of matter and life. Whitehead defines the good and desirable in terms of harmony, which has two components. One is the absence of discord. The other is the advance beyond triviality.

Harmony is the coordination of the many into one. The self-synthesis of every occasion of becoming accomplishes this to the degree that it is successful. But it makes a difference whether only a few simple things or a rich and diversified variety are coordinated. The latter, when achieved, is a higher and more significant harmony. The difference in value is that of the old contrast between the well-being of an oyster at the mouth of a sewer and the struggles of

Socrates with the misunderstanding and opposition of his wife, his students, and the state, in his pursuit of truth. Most people would admit that Socrates' was the higher achievement. Complexity is of positive value in the production of richer harmony.

But second, it must be emphasized that the analysis of the evidence in the actual functioning of evolution does not give any indication of purpose. Each individual form of life, except occasionally human beings, is concerned only with its own survival and the satisfaction of its instincts. It is not interested in the continuance, let alone the improvement, of the species. And evolution has produced some phyla, as well as innumerable species, that have flourished for longer or shorter periods and have become extinct.

Finally, although there is, of course, a continuous development from the simplest forms of life to mankind as we find ourselves today, it is only from our point of view that we can single this out as the intended main line. Man may at the moment be the highest form of life on this planet, but it is hard to prove that the whole evolutionary process was designed to bring him forth. It can be maintained with at least equal cogency that he just happened naturally like the bacteria, the termites, the eagles, and the chimpanzees.

Consciousness

So far we have been considering nature as it can be studied objectively. The evidence has come through our senses or the extension of them by the sophisticated equipment of modern scientific laboratories. But there is another form of knowledge which each of us experiences. It is of ourselves as conscious subjects. We know that as subjects we are intimately related to our bodies and through them to the external world. Most of us are equally sure, however, that there is a difference between ourselves as directly experiencing subjects and ourselves and other things as the objects of experience.

Now the only subject I can know is myself. It is logically possible to adopt the philosophical position known as solipsism, by which I maintain that I alone exist and everything else is a figment of my consciousness. No one can argue me out of that contention because in terms of it I refuse to admit that anyone else exists. It is a logically impregnable but rather lonely position.

Most of us assume that objective reality does exist independently of our minds in the varied forms which we experience it, and indeed in many others which we do not know. And a considerable accumulation of evidence has convinced us that there are other human persons who have similar subjective experiences. Be it noted, however, that this is a hypothesis for which we have no direct evidence. We cannot experience another subject experiencing. We can only assume from the actions of his or her body that the other person is functioning as a conscious subject.

How far down the scale of life does consciousness go? The answer depends on how we define consciousness. Certainly in the higher mammals, especially those that have lived in close association with us, we see many aspects of it. If consciousness is defined as awareness of the environment and ability to adapt to it, it must surely be attributed at least to all animals with a central nervous system. Today much is being made of the sensitivity of plants. And does not even an amoeba move toward what attracts it and away from what repels it? Perhaps we should equate consciousness in some rudimentary form with life itself.

But can we stop there? If we do we shall have to attribute to consciousness what we hesitated to assert about life; namely, that it is an intrusion from outside the process of evolution. On the other hand, if life was gradually developed from inorganic matter over a billion years, presumably the consciousness that seems to go with life was also. A number of respectable thinkers, including scientists, have reached this conclusion, in addition to Whitehead who attributes a subjective aim to every occasion of becoming.[5]

It is probably confusing to call this consciousness below the level of life, and even in the simpler forms of life itself. But it is a capacity for self-synthesis which pervades all reality. It is the power of creation to be itself, which must be bestowed upon if it is to have genuine existence. Perhaps it is better to call it the "inwardness" of things. But even if we restrict consciousness to the higher forms of life, it is still impossible to determine the exact point at which it emerges. Awareness of environment increases so gradually in the evolutionary process that we find no gap that justifies the conclusion that consciousness was inserted at that point.

On the other hand, the inwardness of things fits in well with atomic physics. The principle of indeterminacy is not just that if we know the exact velocity of an electron we cannot know its exact position. Rather it is that the electron does not have an exact position. It is not a solid object that is there. It is a quantum of energy becoming matter. Is not this saying in terms of physics that it is an occasion in the process of becoming a being? Energy is the inwardness of matter, the subjective aim that becomes itself in the electron.

We are not required to maintain that everything we can distinguish and name is a subject of self-synthesis. Stones are not. They are merely collections of molecules with no internal principle of organization. Parts of a stone can be chipped off or worn away without affecting its nature. It can be broken in half without becoming two separate subjects of experience. In this it differs from a living cell which, when it divides, becomes two independent organisms each functioning as a subject. So we must distinguish between mere collections and entities that have some internal principle of unity.

Among the latter process philosophy includes electrons, atoms, molecules, crystals, macromolecules, living cells and microscopic organisms. At the upper end of the evolutionary scale it includes at least those animals with a central nervous system. There are some differences of opinion about things that come in between. Has a tree sufficient internal unity to function through a subjective aim or is it just a society of cooperating living organisms? My own guess is that trees have enough coordination to suggest that they are in some sense subjects, but for the purpose of my paradigm the question can be left open.

It should be noted that entities both living and nonliving usually function in terms of two frames of reference. Each becomes itself and is also taken up into and contributes to a higher complex. Thus electrons are incorporated into atoms, atoms into molecules, some molecules into living cells, and cells into more complicated forms of life. This dual reference can be a source of conflict, the individual becoming itself in a way that is detrimental to the organism of which it is part. Our bodies, for instance, are composed of living cells some of which may become cancerous.

A further question may be raised at this point. Do the major organs of our bodies operate through their own subjective aims? If so, and if it is possible for a conscious subjective aim to influence the subjective aims of its organs, that might account for the amazing control over these organs that some people seem to have, being able to reduce the frequency of their heartbeats and so forth. The occurence of such phenomena is well attested. That this paradigm can suggest an explanation of them is another point in its favor.

But its greatest advantage is that it can attribute the origin of life and consciousness to a living and conscious creator without having to find a gap in the natural process through which he can intrude them. The initiating aim and the lure of the potential put the Spirit and the Logos into contact with every occasion of experience. They make possible the novelty that the evolutionary process requires without disturbing the statistical natural laws. The creator can work constantly to fulfill his purpose without his guidance and persuasive control being detectable. He is truly a God who hides himself (Is. 45:15) and so leaves us free to ignore or to deny his governance.

The hypothesis of a hidden God may be useful in accounting for life and consciousness, but is it a mere speculation or is it a call to faith? The answer, I believe, is to be found in the consideration of human beings. In order to preserve the integrity of self-determination in inorganic matter, which has little if any freedom of choice, the pressure of the motivation and lure must be kept very low. It may be increased in organisms with a central nervous system that, because they are more aware of their environment, can make a more deliberate response. When we get to men and women, who have the capacity for self-conscious reflection, the relationship of the Logos and Spirit can be more direct. To them we now turn.

Reflection

In terms of this paradigm life has developed naturally from inorganic matter and consciousness is present throughout creation, at least in rudimentary form as the inwardness of things. Both the objective and subjective aspects of evolution can be accounted for without having to introduce a new element from outside at any point in the process. In mankind a new capacity is found — self-conscious reflection. Does it require a new creative act? The Christian tradition has asserted that it does. In addition to a body and mind, each human individual is believed to be a soul created directly by God.

Two general comments may be made at once. First, this is the final resort of the God of the gaps. All the rest of creation, including human bodies and minds, are the product of evolution, but because men and women are created in the image of God, they are held to have an added endowment provided individually and directly by God. This hypothesis is safe from biological or psychological refutation because the soul is discernible only in our capacity to make deliberate, self-conscious choices, which is the basis for our ability to love, and thus to reflect the image of God who is love.

But second, is the hypothesis necessary, or even likely? Our experience of self-consciousness is precisely that which leads us not only to attribute a similar consciousness to other human beings, but also to extend consciousness in some form to animals, and ultimately to suggest a continuous inwardness of things right down to the electron. Self-conscious reflection, therefore, would seem not to be an entirely new factor introduced at the level of mankind, but rather the awareness of what was potentially present all along. It parallels on the subjective side the scientific discernment of the objective functioning of nature, which is also a unique capacity of the human species.

Furthermore, when we consider what we already know about the evolution of hominids, it is hard to find a gap for the introduction of an entirely new factor direct from the hand of God. The fossil evidence is far from complete, of course. Yet in the last few years enough has been found to convince many paleoanthropologists that a continuous sequence of development is highly probable.[6]

A general sketch of what seems to be the current thesis is that somewhere between fifty and thirty million years ago in the order of primates a separation occurred between the ancestors of modern monkeys and the ancestors of the hominoids, that is, apes and man. A further separation of apes from hominids, the forerunners of the genus *homo*, is usually dated from twenty-five to ten million years ago, with the earlier date preferred.

The first fossil evidence of the hominid line may be the *ramapithecus*, of which remains have been found in east Africa and India. They are dated about twelve million years ago, perhaps earlier in Africa. The remains are so fragmentary that they are hard to classify. It has apelike characteristics but it apparently stood erect.

From it we jump to the *australopithecus*, of which the fossil record goes back to around five million years ago. In one form or another it survived nearly four million years. Africa seems to have been the locus of its earliest forms, but its spread eventually extended as far as Java.

Perhaps as long as three million years ago a line emerged, sometimes called *homo habilis* because its members manufactured "pebble tools" by striking flakes off a small stone to provide a sharp edge. The tools were used for the butchering, and perhaps the hunting, of animals. These cultural advances were made possible by the increased size of the brain, which is indicated by the fossil skulls of *homo habilis*. Whether they should be considered a species distinct from the *australopithecus* and given the designation *homo* is still a matter of dispute. But the important thing is that there were hominids of about two million years ago who had developed communication and skill to the point required for the making and using of stone tools.

The next species of hominids, the *homo erectus*, emerged about a million, three hundred thousand years ago and lasted for about a million years. They used fire and had a more sophisticated collection of stone tools. Their technique for hunting large animals involved skillful planning and cooperation. Considerable proficiency in the use of language would have been needed to accomplish this.

They were followed by the *neanderthals*, who flourished a hundred thousand to forty thousand years ago. It is not certain what their relation was to the *homo erectus*, or to their contemporaries, the *cro-magnons*, who alone have survived as modern man (*homo sapiens*). In western Europe it seems that the more advanced *cro-magnons* encountered the more primitive *neanderthals* and largely exterminated them. It was the *cro-magnons* who produced the cave paintings of France and Spain. Among them about twelve thousand years ago agriculture and permanent settlements began to develop.

In spite of major gaps in the evidence, the picture that is emerging is of a slow, gradual development over millions of years. Undoubtedly there were cleavages from time to time when a species divided into distinct lines. One such cleavage may have occurred in the *australopithecus*, with one branch increasing in physical size and becoming largely vegetarian (*a. robustus*), and the other remaining small in body but with larger brains that enabled them to procure and prepare meat for their diet (*homo habilis*). Such cleavages, however, can be accounted for by genetic mutations that provided the opportunity for the species to move into an available ecological niche.

The process has been so natural and so continuous that paleoanthropologists are not yet in agreement at which point it can be asserted that mankind originated. No break in the sequence, therefore, is of sufficient magnitude to justify the belief that at that generation God began directly creating and inserting human souls. Since there also is no empirical evidence for them, I find no basis for postulating their existence.

I accept the position taken by process philosophy that the subject which we experience directly exists only in the subjective aims of successive occasions of becoming. I do hold that such subjective aims are linked subjectively, but I see no need or grounds for a substantial subject that exists independently of its experiences, still less for an immortal soul individually and directly supplied by God.

A question equally difficult to answer is when men and women were first able to make deliberate conscious choices. Presumably it would not be possible until the individual had enough capacity for reflection to distinguish himself or herself from the group. Fossil evidence is not much help in indicating when this might have happened. But if to a certain degree the development of the race is recapitulated in the experience of an infant, there would seem at first to be no real distinction between the self and the environment. That also may be the experience of animals, which our ancestors shared when they were close to the animal state.

The first indications of the hominids functioning beyond the level of mere instinct point to their acting as a group in passing on the skills needed to make tools and in the cooperation needed for hunting big game. Occasions for conscious choice would then arise as the individual found his largely instinctivce urges at variance with the actions demanded of him by the group. It seems to me likely that this recognition of conscious choice and the further development of a sense of moral obligation must have been a gradual, long-drawn-out process extending over thousands of years.

So even if the whole sequence of generations were fully known to us, we could not point to the first sin. The transition from innocence to sin did not occur in a single act. Rather the consciousness of conflict between selfishness and duty grew imperceptibly. Mankind had a tendency toward wrongdoing and had yielded to it many times before the possibility of a clear-cut sense of moral resonsibility had developed. Indeed, it was only out of such a premoral struggle that a sense of obligation could have originated.

Yet originate it did, and self-conscious reflection is the specific characteristic that enabled the hominids not only to survive in their primal habitat in competition with the other forms of life, but also to spread over the whole land mass of the earth, to adjust to conditions ranging from the tropics to the arctic, and to dominate, if not threaten with extinction, all other species. It enabled mankind to distinguish between himself and the rest of nature and to explore the latter objectively. Little by little, painfully slowly at first and even more painfully rapidly in the last few years, the human species has learned how nature operates, how to conform to it, how to use it, and finally how to control, adapt, and exploit it.

This increased knowledge has its terrifying aspects, partly because our power over nature, ourselves, and society may lead to the destruction of the possibility of life on this planet. That will be considered later. Here I want to face the frightening insignificance we experience in a vast and apparently indifferent universe. The expanse of space that we have been able to explore, with its millions of galaxies and billions of stars in each, is likely to give us earthlings an inferiority complex. In the other direction lies the vastly complicated world of atoms and electrons. All this seems to function without any concern for the human species.

A possible answer is indicated in the old story of the astronomer who ended a popular lecture on the sidereal universe by working down from the galaxies to the tiny planet earth and the funny little two-legged creatures on it. "So," he concluded, "astronomically speaking, man is infinitesimal." Whereupon a member of the audience stood up and said, "Begging the speaker's pardon, but astronomically speaking, man is the astronomer." That is the other side of the picture. Man may be small in relation to the universe but, so far as we know, he is the only creature who knows how small he is.

However, to be genuinely consoling, this must be real knowledge about the universe as it exists. There are many today, especially among the scientifically minded, who question whether we have any objective insight into the functioning of creation, or at least whether our insights indicate an intelligible and meaningful universe.

Purpose

One reason why modern science no longer seems to be giving an objective account of reality is because it operates largely in terms of mathematical equations. When science pictured the universe as atoms in a static frame of space, as in Newtonian physics, or as a miniature solar system, as in early atomic physics, the impression was of a solid concrete reality. Mathematics, on the other hand, is an abstract science. Its formulae are worked out in terms of arbitrary symbols which the mathematicians have devised and which they alone can understand and manipulate. So to the layman the scientific universe seems no longer to be an objective reality, but instead a figment of the scientist's imagination. Some scientists themselves are content so to consider it.

But other scientists, including Einstein, have been impressed not only by how well their equations work as descriptions of the functioning of the universe, but also how elegant and harmonious the equations are in themselves. The universe seems to be designed in a most satisfying way in terms of higher mathematics. So, although it is not a machine that requires a watchmaker, does it not appear to be the achievement of a master mathematician? But even so, is it anything more than an ingenious contrivance of his mind devised for his passing amusement?

The contrary would seem to be indicated by the emergence within the universe of minds capable of perceiving its mathematical basis, and of using it to predict and even to control its functioning. This suggests that the master mathematician wants to share the fun with other minds. One result of the mathematical formulae that express the motions of the heavenly bodies, the internal structure of the atom, and the genetic code of life has been the production of beings capable of formulating them.

Now it might be conceivable, though I personally think it unlikely, that an entirely random universe might by chance produce beings with the capacity for self-conscious reflection. But that such reflection could devise formulae that work as means of explaining and operating the process, and nevertheless work entirely by chance, is pushing coincidence to a point of credulity I cannot attain. I find easier a faith that a mind deliberately designed the universe to produce minds similar enough that they could understand its functioning and from it infer his authorship.

In other words, because I find the universe comprehensible, and therefore meaningful, I believe it must also have a purpose. For meaning, if it is significant, exists to be discerned. God wants the design to be known and himself to be known through it. Such knowledge establishes a personal relationship that moves from cognition to appreciation. In the King James Version of the Bible a deep insight is reflected in the use of the verb "to know" to signify "to love". That the creator can be known through his work implies that he wants to share himself with us. So it is possible to argue from the mathematical equations in which modern science is couched to the origin of the universe in a God of love.

But it cannot be proved. It cannot even be demonstrated. At best it can only be inferred. It requires a leap of faith and it must require one if it really is a manifestation of love seeking the response of love. God in himself is so overwhelmingly wonderful that he would stun into passive submission any creature to whom he revealed himself directly. A creaturely response of love is possible only if God is hidden by, as well as implied in, creation. We must be shielded from the fire of God's love by the intervention of the universe.

That means it must be possible to view the universe as having no objective, as fulfilling no purpose, as being without meaning except for such meanings and purposes as we create for ourselves. That many profound thinkers so interpret the world of nature, of mankind, and of human society as we know them, shows that the possibility is real. To their satisfaction they can demonstrate that the universe is indifferent to man. In producing the human species, nature accidentally outdid itself and evolved a monstrosity, a misfit — a being capable of understanding when there is nothing to know, with a sense of obligation when there are no duties, with a yearning for eternal love that can find only a fleeting satisfaction.[7]

We owe a great debt to the school of the absurd for pointing out this dilemma so vividly. It brings home to us what is at issue in believing that the universe is designed and controlled by God in so constant and unobtrusive a way that it cannot be demonstrated or proved, or in rejecting that faith. Without it man is an anomaly. Since the universe is meaningless, there can be no possibility of ultimate truth or falsehood. Neither can there be right or wrong, because there is no purpose to fulfill. Each individual may determine for himself what is true and what is good, and no one can say him nay, because there are no objective criteria in reality by which he may be judged.

Rather inconsistently, those who deny meaning and purpose in the universe resent what they hold to be its actual (though not deliberate) hostility to man. This, they insist, is the clinching proof that the world could not be the work of a good and loving creator. If my paradigm is sound, it must honestly face and answer that problem.

At this point we shall consider the so-called evils in natural creation, and them alone. A sound handling of the problem demands that we deal with the various types of evils and alleged evils separately since a favorite device of those who cite them as proof against the possibility of a God is to lump them all together. This is much to their advantage. As fast as an answer in terms of one type of evil is given, they shift their ground to another type and declare the answer inadequate because it does not account for that as well. But as I hope to show, the various types each have their own explanation, and I shall deal with each in its appropriate place in this exposition.[8]

It is essential from the start to insist that the phrase "natural evils" is a misnomer. The word evil connotes something bad. If we allow the forces of destruction, conflict, and decay in the natural world, together with the resulting pain and death, to be called evils, we have already conceded the case to our opponents. Unfortunately it is almost impossible to find another designation for them. The best I can come up with is the violence of nature. At least liberation theologians, who insist that violence is sometimes necessary and therefore justified, will not consider the word synonymous with bad.

Natural Violence

We definitely do find violence in the natural world. The question we must answer is whether that violence is justified in a universe created in order to evolve the human species. For the problem of theodicy — that is, the justification of the ways of God to man — can arise only in a world created by God to produce man. So the question can be rephrased: Is the violence of nature inherent in the evolution of the genus *homo*? The answer in terms of the universe as we know it can only be yes.

Let us begin with the natural upheavals such as earthquakes, hurricanes, tidal waves, forest fires, and the like. For billions of years the planet earth has been cooling and shrinking. Earthquakes and volcanic eruptions have been and still are the result. But another consequence, some modern scientists hold, is the production of conditions that have allowed the emergence and persistence of life. We have noted that laboratory experiments simulating conditions at one stage of the earth's development have produced the first steps in the path toward life. We have every reason to believe that the geological and meteorological conditions that have prevailed since, including our own day insofar as we have not upset them by our exploitation of the environment, are those that are suited to the evolution of life into more complex, sensitive, and conscious forms. The proof lies in the fact that they have evolved.

Another factor in the process of evolution is natural selection. This operates through competition, conflict, pain, and death. It must be remembered that it is the species, not the individual, that evolves. A species is able to maintain itself or improve its adaptation to its environment because the inferior individuals are killed off before they can make a significant contribution to the gene pool by engaging in reproduction.

The struggle for survival takes various forms, all of which involve pain and death. There may be competition with other members of the species for the available food supply. For the weaker ones this can mean disease or starvation. At the same time, the act of consuming food is almost always at the expense of other forms of life. So the possibility of falling victim to the predators that prey upon the species is a constant threat to those less skillful in avoiding them. When it comes to breeding, courtship rites and battles between the males assure that only the more potent have access to the females.

Pain and death, then, are essential to the process of evolution, indeed to the continuance of life. For if all the members of a species survived, they would speedily crowd each other off the face of the earth. On the other hand, none would survive without the stimulation of the impulses that trigger the search for food, the desire to reproduce, and the urge to escape danger. Most of the time these feelings find satisfaction and thereby preserve the individual and the species. Only when frustrated do they become painful. That intensifies the effort until it is either successful or ends in death. But I see no reason to deny that the enjoyment each creature has in the span of its life outweighs the pain and dying it has to experience.

The truth is that pain and pleasure form a continuous scale. The enjoyable sound of a musical note becomes strident as it gets louder until it is actually painful. A good appetite that helps us to relish food turns gradually into hunger and ultimately into starvation. Pain is the overintensification or frustration of a desirable feeling. Sensitivity to pain grows as the capacity for feeling increases. Probably only those with highly developed central nervous systems are aware of it at all. The rest simply react to it instinctively.

So we must not exaggerate the amount of pain endured in the natural world. Conflicts for precedence and domination are usually terminated in the surrender, not the death, of the loser. For those who fall victims to predators the end is usually swift. That is overlooked by those who sentimentalize over their household pets and domestic animals. They forget that the protection provided often increases or prolongs the pain. It would indeed be cruel to let a horse with a broken leg die a natural death instead of shooting it, because in the paddock it would take a long time to die. But in the state of nature a crippled horse would be finished off and eaten in about the time it takes to fetch the revolver.

The sentimentalists also tend to interpret the pains of their pets in human terms. They fail to make the distinction between pain and suffering. Suffering requires the capacity for self-conscious reflection. It is not caused by just the pain itself. When an animal feels pain it reacts in protest and tries to escape it. But it is surprising how quickly it quiets down as soon as the immediate cause of the pain is removed. It has no anxiety as to its future consequences. A castrated calf does not bemoan its impotence. No animal can anticipate and fear the possibility of dying.

Human beings, on the other hand, are concerned as to how long the pain will last, how much worse it may get, whether it will return, what its consequences will be — not just the physical results, but its implications for other areas of life. All these anxieties and fears are what turn pain into suffering. Supreme among them is the recognition which we try so hard to avoid, but which hovers constantly over us, that all our earthly pleasures, hopes, and relationships will eventually terminate in death. For those who can reflect, who can recall the past and anticipate the future, pain can be agonizing. They can suffer remorse, resentment, frustration, and alienation. But they can also know the ecstasy of discovering truth, perceiving beauty, and enjoying love.

The distinction between pain and suffering can also be seen in the amount of pain that can be tolerated under special circumstances. Intense tortures have been endured in stubborn silence by those who believed they were suffering for a worthy cause. Others have accepted long and painful illnesses with a courage and even cheerfulness that amazes us. We ourselves know that when something we want to accomplish makes it necessary we can bear a degree of pain that under other circumstances we would avoid.[9]

If the distinction is valid, it may be questioned whether infants suffer from their natural and unavoidable pains. Again the sentimentalists will object. But the truth is that much of a baby's pain is essential to the development of a human person. Infants learn to distinguish between themselves and their environment by encountering resistance. All resistance is painful, as they clearly indicate when their desires are frustrated or unheeded. Yet without such experiences they could never achieve self-consciousness, maturity, and fulfillment.

Let me emphasize again that at this point I am considering only natural violence and the pain and death that result from it. The injury caused by deliberate human acts in another matter which will be dealt with later. The two must be distinguished because in our paradigm God has given men and women genuine power to become themselves and by their actions to affect each other and God himself. Therefore God or the universe is not to be held accountable for the evil that mankind accomplishes.

This distinction is conveniently overlooked by those who deny that creation can be the work of a good and loving God because of the evil it contains. The argument is sound only insofar as the evil can be attributed solely to natural forces. Yet Ivan Karamazov, for example, repudiates the architect of the universe because of the sufferings of small children. But the vivid and moving examples he gives are all instances of human cruelty.

It is not only by its deliberate acts that human sin increases the pain and suffering of the world. Its accumulated consequences often turn a natural event into a disaster. A tidal wave that swept over an uninhabited island in the Indian Ocean would not be considered evil. The one which hit Calcutta and destroyed the lives and livelihood of thousands of men and women was a major tragedy. But what was responsible for the crowding together of all those people in poverty and misery? Not the forces of nature but human greed and other corporate sins.

Natural violence considered in and of itself produces far less pain than is often attributed to it. It is an integral part of the functioning of this planet that has evolved life and human beings. God cannot intervene to stop or divert a tidal wave without disrupting those natural laws which enable man to cope intelligently with his environment. The integrity that permits the universe and each of its components to become itself is the basis of that self-determination that allows human beings to give themselves freely in love. God cannot intrude into and manipulate the universe without destroying that integrity.

Two questions remain. Is this the best of all possible worlds? We cannot know. But can we conceive a better one? A universe without discord, created directly by divine fiat, seems to us so naïve a concept as to be downright silly. A universe which God manipulated to satisfy his favorites would be intolerable. A universe in which God arbitrarily interfered with natural law could not provide an environment for intelligent self-determined creatures. After all, the world we know has produced us, and gives us the opportunity to learn the art of love.

But is it worth the price? We may feel it is too high when we ourselves are suffering, or still more when we are helplessly watching someone we love suffer, especially if the suffering seems meaningless. Be it noted, however, that if there is no creative mind behind the universe, then all pain, all suffering, indeed all life itself, is meaningless. If, on the contrary, we believe that there is a creator, we must also believe that he considers it worth the price to bring forth creatures capable of knowing him by faith and enjoying him in love. And in the Judeo-Christian tradition we also believe that God himself shares the suffering with us. To that revelation we now turn.

Chapter 3 / **COVENANT**

It would be better if we called the two divisions of the Bible the Old and New Covenants. Testament, if it does not suggest God's last will and testament, implying his death, is likely to be associated with the word testimony. That focuses attention primarily on the revelation of God's nature through somewhat improbable stories and of his will through commandments and laws. It encourages us to look on the Bible as a source for theology and morality rather than the story of God's dealings with mankind.[1]

Revealed theology, in terms of which we must now test our paradigm, is more a matter of history than of doctrine. It rests on God's mighty acts. These take the form of a series of covenants which emphasize God's initiative and choice. For a covenant is not a contract negotiated by two equal parties. It is a relationship offered by God to be accepted and entered into by man. In it God promises; man lays hold on its benefits by making the prescribed response. It is an expression of love for those to whom God offers it, and of trust in his faithfulness by those who accept it.

The first covenant is that of creation, by which Adam and Eve are given dominion over the rest of nature in order that they may be responsible for its care and development, and may offer it, as its priests, in loving obedience to God. The second is the renewal of that covenant with Noah and his family when creation begins anew after the purification of the flood. As these covenants deal mainly with the nature of human sin, they will be considered in more detail in the next chapter when that subject is analyzed.

Here however, we should note three points of contact with our modern concept of the natural world. The obvious discrepancy in the time scheme of creation, with the resulting difference between God's direct and hidden relationship to it, should not blind us to important similarities. In the later of the two accounts (Gen. 1), the order of creation is strikingly like that of evolution—plants, fishes, birds, animals, man. The sequence of increasing complexity and sensitivity was noted early in human thought.

Another interesting passage is Genesis 4:17ff, where the building of the first city is attributed to Cain, the fratricide, and the origin of herdsmen, musicians, and metalworkers to the sons of Lamech, who was characterized by his demand for ruthless and extravagant revenge. This agrees with my suggestion that the human species was already familiar with sin before civilization began.

Most interesting of all is God's promise to Noah that "as long as earth lasts, sowing and reaping, cold and heat, summer and winter, day and night, shall cease no more" (Gen. 8:22). Here is the dependability of natural law which, however, rests on the promise of God, not on the automatic functioning of nature. Through it God guides and develops creation with that unobtrusiveness that permits him to remain the hidden God. Jesus based the perfection of God on this concept when he pointed out that our heavenly Father "causes his sun to rise on bad men as well as good, and his rain to fall on honest and dishonest men alike" (Mt. 5:45).

I cite these instances not because evolution needs the support of scripture, or scripture the support of science, but as illustrations, even in the opening chapters of Genesis, of the realism of the Bible's account of the universe. The authors of these chapters had to use the mythical material available to them. But they intended it to be the history of God's relationships with creation, not just a fanciful tale. And their perceptions of natural law and mankind's physical and cultural origins were not entirely erroneous.

The first two covenants were made with the whole human race. Beginning with the covenant with Abraham, the relationship is with a particular people. God chose Abraham, his descendants through Isaac and Jacob (renamed Israel), and the groups that claim to be their legitimate successors. Thereby arises the scandal of particularity. If God reveals himself through history, it cannot be avoided.

In order to accumulate and pass on a living tradition of revelation, its recipients have to be a distinct and homogeneous group with a continuing integrity. Separation from their neighbors must be clearcut and internal cohesion strong. Furthermore, they must treasure their past as containing specific occasions when God manifested his love for them in unmistakable ways. They are his people and he is their God. He is jealous for their undivided allegiance; they look to him alone as the source of life and favor.

All this is implicit in a covenant. It has, therefore, a built-in rejection of other traditions of revelation. Indeed, it insists there can be no such thing. Some of us today are inclined to be put off by this limited and parochial attitude and by the arrogant claim to be the one true expression of the only revelation of God. We are aware of other great religions that have flourished for centuries and produced outstanding fruit in the realms of thought, art, and spirituality. In the field of morality their achievements are sometimes felt to be inferior to the religions springing from the Old Testament tradition—Judaism, Islam, and Christianity—but these have been better at formulating ethical precepts and laws than at keeping them.

Today we want to recognize the other religious traditions as genuine revelations of God. Each has its own internal integrity which is grounded in, preserved by, and handed on through, its own particular history. In ways quite different from those experienced by the Israelites, other traditions reflect God's choice and love for the peoples who received them, although they may not express the relationship in terms of election and personal love. We, who have the opportunity for a sympathetic contact with them, should study them with reverence for their inherent values and be ready to learn from them.

In so doing, however, we must never disregard the particularity of each tradition, which is the manifestation in it of God's love. Personal love can never be love in general. It is directed toward individuals and specific groups. The Israelites were right in believing they were God's chosen people, the objects of his love in a unique way which he had for them exclusively. Their experience of his love was theirs and theirs alone. Their mistake was to conclude that God has no other manifestations of love—love taking a different form and eliciting a different response—for other peoples and nations. God has, and for each of them it is as particular, as exclusive, and as demanding, as it is for the Israelites and their successors.

For this reason each tradition can be approached only from within. If, as a result of the dialogue that is going on today, the various great religions begin to grow together, it will be because each is able to appropriate and incorporate into itself elements it derives from others.

Individual conversions may occur and be helpful in interpreting one tradition to another. But mass conversions that would absorb one religion into another are to be avoided. So also is an amalgamation on the basis of the least common denominator or of an eclectic conglomeration.

The tradition within which I am writing is Christianity. Although we may glance from time to time at other traditions, the main line of thought will be the revelation that culminated in Jesus the Christ. But like Judaism and Islam, it has its roots in the Old Testament. An exploration of that is necessary to see how compatible it and my paradigm are with each other.

Consuming Fire

The Israelites did not originate in Palestine. They settled there in the second half of the second millennium B.C., probably for the most part migrating from the vicinity of Haran. Originally they were seminomadic clans. It is my conviction that some time deep in their past the area in which they pastured their flocks centered in an active volcano. Its eruptions were for them the special manifestation of their God.

In the Bible the description of God's presence on the holy mountain, Sinai or Horeb, perfectly fits a volcano. The Sinai of the exodus was not a volcano. I believe, however, that the memory of the earlier experience was transferred to it. We are told that: "the mountain of Sinai was entirely wrapped in smoke, because Yahweh had descended on it in the form of fire. Like smoke from a furnace the smoke went up, and the whole mountain shook violently" (Ex. 19:18). "Through the clouds burst hailstones and coals of fire" (Ps. 18:13) —flaming fragments thrown up by the eruption. Other manifestations associated with the theophany were thunder and lightning and an earthquake—the mountains "skipped like rams" (Ps. 114:6).

Even more telling is the pillar of cloud by day and the pillar of fire by night. This is an apt description of the plume of smoke that issues continuously from the mouth of an active volcano, which at night is lighted from below to look like a column of flame. The Israelites at one point restricted their wanderings to the area from which they could see this phenomenon. When the volcano became more active, they gathered to worship the God who came down to them. But the continuous wisp of smoke, which fits an active volcano and nothing else, is to my mind conclusive evidence for this thesis.

A curious objection has been raised to it, however. Psalm 97:5 includes in the theophany: "The mountains melt like wax at the presence of the Lord." That detail is supposed to be incompatible with a volcanic eruption and therefore shows that the description is just poetic fancy, a stringing together of images to indicate God's almighty power. But what better simile could there be than the wax of a guttering candle for the lava flowing down the side of a volcano?

Perhaps this volcano was in the area north of Haran. Genesis tells us, however, that Abraham's father moved there with his family from Ur. So it may be that the Israelites originated in Arabia and worked their way from east to west around the edge of the fertile crescent which stretches from the Euphrates to the northeast corner of Egypt. In that case the mountain where they first knew God would have been in Arabia.

The primitive association of God with the fire on the mount was not restricted to the wilderness experience. It continues as the diapason that undergirds the spirituality of the Bible. Thus, in the contest with the priests of Baal at Carmel, Elijah proposes that the true God shall be "the God who answers with fire" (1 Kg. 18:24). Jesus picks up the same theme, "I have come to bring fire to the earth, and how I wish it were blazing already!" (Lk. 12:49). The author of Hebrews calls us "to worship God in the way that he finds acceptable, in reverence and fear. For our God is a consuming fire" (12:28f; cf. Dt. 4:24).

The two other great natural symbols of God in the Old Testament are water and wind. Both can do much damage, in a flood or tidal wave, in a hurricane or thunderstorm. Even if the original holy mountain was not a volcano, the use of imagery commensurate with it shows that the Israelites identified the manifestation of God with the violence of nature. God produced, controlled, and used its destructive forces. They could not therefore be considered evil.

Instead, they were a source of awe and reverence, displaying the numinous majesty and otherness of God. Such a theophany was both terrifying and fascinating. Because it was the way God came to them, it showed his interest in them, but he was in no sense a tame and useful deity. He was the living God. The Hebrew word for "living" was used as the root of the word for wild animals, never for domesticated. God is essentially untamable.

By the same token, the natural elements of fire, water, and air are to be handled with reverence and respect. They are essential to human existence. But they must be kept under control and properly used. They are manifestations of God's loving care, but like all love they can be dangerous if selfishly exploited. God and his benefits are not to be trifled with. Again, as the author of Hebrews says, "It is a dreadful thing to fall into the hands of the living God" (10:31).

"I form the light and create the dark. I make good fortune and create calamity. It is I, Yahweh, who do all this" (Is. 45:7). The line of thought leads directly from the God who manifests himself in violence to the God who creates. Only a God who is powerful enough and independent enough to destroy the universe without undermining the basis of his own existence, only such a God could create.

The nature deities, the Baalim, were dependent on the land which they fertilized and on its inhabitants. They increased in importance as their people grew in numbers and expanded their territory. But the God of the Israelites tossed the mountains about like playthings. He manifested himself supremely, not in fructifying nature but in devastating it. The violent and destructive forces, the irrational aspects of the universe, are the creation of God.

Once more we must recognize that he creates out of absolutely nothing. I keep stressing this because it is one point on which I disagree with most process theologians. Whitehead held that the universe originated out of chaos when God began to introduce form into inchoate matter. Whitehead was essentially a Platonist and never escaped from the Apollonian concept that God is rational form. Hence the Dionysian, the irrational, must be opposed to him from the beginning. It is the raw material with which he has to work, the source of the defects and evil in his creation.

This is another instance of the God of the gaps — the original gap between chaos and order. The gap has been pushed so far back that the process theologians can get away with it, unless the cosmologists establish that order has always characterized the universe. The God of the Israelites and the God of our paradigm needs no such gap to start functioning. If there was a state of chaos, he created it also. From the beginning he is the author of the irrational as well as the rational. There is no greater need today than to recognize the value and divine origin of the Dionysian side of reality. It is by no means meaningless. Without it God would not be God and man cannot be man.[2]

The independence of the God of natural violence also kept him from being wedded to the land. If, as I believe, his first manifestation was through a volcano, it was a particular mountain. But his presence in a full theophany was sporadic. He came in an eruption and then went away again, leaving only the plume of smoke to remind his people where to expect him when he chose to return. His relationship was with them as his people, not with the land as his territory.

Furthermore, his people were nomads. At first he kept them in the vicinity until they got to know him and to reverence and respect both his almighty power and the personal concern he had for them. But when the time came, he could send them on their wanderings. Because his presence was associated with the violence of nature, he had other means by which he could accompany them.

God of the Fathers

During the dry season when the wilderness steppes had insufficient fodder and water for their flocks and herds, seminomads like the Israelites moved into the cultivated areas after the harvest had been gathered, and grazed their livestock on the stubble. They were therefore in contact with a more settled civilization and tended to long for it. Besides the increase of their cattle and families, these nomads also desired fertile land. In the covenant God made with Abraham, and again with Isaac and Jacob, those were the two benefits he promised.

The land, however, was not to be in the neighborhood of Haran. They had to journey to the west. Historically this was part of the Aramean migrations that took place between 1500 and 1200 B.C. Probably their cause was the pressure of people moving into the fertile crescent from the north. The unwarlike, pastoral Israelites were not prepared to defend the arrangement by which they were permitted to graze their flocks and herds in the vicinity of Haran.

They continued around the crescent until some of them found not only seasonal pasture but unoccupied territory in the mountainous parts of Palestine into which they moved and settled. It was a peaceful penetration, on the whole, tolerated by the Canaanite cities on the plain, either because they had no interest in the mountain areas, or, as some think, because some of the tribes, such as Asher, Zebulun, Issachar, and possibly Dan, were willing to pay for the privilege by providing indentured labor.

God had fulfilled his promise of land and increase. For their part, they continued to worship him. They set up shrines at which they could gather from time to time to renew the covenant. Perhaps each tribe had its own center for more frequent use, but the kindred tribes kept up their contact with each other by gathering periodically at a central shrine. At one time this was Shechem. Later it was apparently moved to Bethel, and possibly then to Gilgal. Just before the establishment of the kingdom it was at Shiloh. The ark, the sacred cult object, probably the throne on which God was thought to be seated when he had made himself present, was kept at the central shrine.

This God was the God of their fathers. In the northern and central parts of Palestine the father seems mainly to have been Jacob, re-named Israel. Abraham and Isaac are more shadowy figures, associated chiefly with the south. But God is called the God of Abraham (Gen. 28:13; 31:42,53) and the Kinsman of Isaac (Gen. 31:42,53), as well as the Mighty One of Jacob, the Stone of Israel (Gen. 49:24). That emphasized that he was the God of the family, the clan, the tribe, not of the locality.

At this stage, it should be noted, the Israelites did not call God Yahweh. That is explicitly stated in Exodus 6:2f. Although this passage is from the late priestly document, it seems to have preserved an accurate recollection. "I am Yahweh. To Abraham and Isaac and Jacob I appeared as El Shaddai; I did not make myself known to them by my name Yahweh." The original God of the fathers was called by other names or, as in the case of the God with whom Jacob wrestled (Gen. 32:30), refused to give any name at all. The name El Shaddai, the God of the mountain, reflects the concept of the cosmic mountain, reaching from earth to heaven and down to the fiery depths of hell. It was the commonest name for the God of the fathers, and may be another indication of his original association with an active volcano.

First and foremost he was the God of the covenant. He had begun to fulfill his promises to the fathers by settling the Israelites in the land. But their hold on it was tenuous. It was essential that God continue to give them increase and protection. The covenant had to be renewed periodically at the central shrine, when God's part in it would be recalled. Then the tribes through their official representatives would recommit themselves to it and instructions as to how the people were to carry out their obligations would be given.

Out of that developed the commandments and the primitive codes. I am convinced that this occurred among the tribes in central and northern Palestine independently of, and indeed long before, the exodus experience. Scholars have noted that the passage on Sinai (Ex. 19–Num. 10) is the latest addition to the wilderness narrative. In Deuteronomy 26:5ff we have an early summary of the exodus which ends: "Yahweh brought us out of Egypt with a mighty hand and outstretched arm, with great terror, and with signs and wonders. He brought us here and gave us this land, a land where milk and honey flow." The omission of any reference to the giving of the commandments on Sinai is conspicuous.

The truth is that the covenant held the Israelites together from the start. The codification of its obligations may well have begun before they entered Palestine. The similarities between the early covenant precepts and the codes of Eshnunna, of Hammurabi, and of Ur-nammu are striking. Those codes were known in the Mesopotamian area but not, so far as has been discovered, by the local Canaanite population. The association of the third code with Ur, where Abraham is also said to have lived, is suggestive. There is a good chance that the Israelites derived their codes from these sources and brought the rudiments of them with them to Palestine.

The renewal of the covenant not only kept the Israelites faithful to El Shaddai, it also preserved the bond between the tribes. Scattered as they were throughout the mountainous regions where communication was difficult, and subject to occasional attack or persecution by their stronger Canaanite neighbors, it was essential that the clans band together from time to time to defend themselves.

An instance of this is recorded in an early poem, the Song of Deborah (Jg. 5). Verses 13–18 list and commend the tribes that responded to Deborah's appeal and rebuke those that did not. Since in verse 4 God is said to have come from Seir (Edom), that is, from the area of Sinai, the episode is usually dated after the exodus experience had been incorporated into the tradition of the northern tribes. This may be so. But that verse could have been edited to fit that later tradition.

The poem is clearly very ancient. The reference in verse 15 to Reuben, "where . . . men hold their long debate," is a slight hint in favor of an earlier date. The tribe of Reuben seems to have broken up and nearly disappeared before the final settlement of the other tribes. In any case, the need for the clans to gather to defend themselves under desperate circumstances must have been a recurring situation from the beginning.

The most significant item in the Deborah episode is the part God played in it. The Canaanites under Sisera were determined to wipe out the Israelites. The combined forces of the tribes that mustered was small and poorly armed. In particular they lacked the dreaded war chariots that Sisera had. The chances of the Israelites' survival seemed slim indeed.

But just as the battle was about to be joined, a thunderstorm came from the direction of their holy mountain. God who manifested himself in the violence of nature was coming to their aid. The storm broke when the Canaanites were crossing the dry wadi of the Kishon, which in a matter of moments became a raging torrent. The chariot wheels stuck in the mud; the horses panicked at the lightning. The Israelites, inspired by their God's coming to their rescue fell upon and slaughtered their enemies.

What has all this to do with the paradigm we are considering? Let us start with the thunderstorm. The Israelites saw in it a direct intervention on their behalf by God. What was the difference between that thunderstorm and all other thunderstorms? Surely the answer is none. The meteorological conditions that produced it were exactly the same as have caused countless other storms in that area. It conformed wholly to the regular functioning of nature. I do not believe that God manufactured it specially or controlled its direction or timing to bring it to that spot at that moment. It was a fortuitous natural event. That it proved useful to the Israelites was pure coincidence.

But isn't that too good to be true? Such a convenient coincidence. When one remembers the tenuous situation the Israelites were in for at least a century or two, and the number of times they were in desperate straits, is it really surprising that in one or two instances natural occurrences turned out to be beneficial? It should also be noted that history is full of fortuitous coincidences. If Harold the Saxon had not been killed by an arrow shot at random, William might not have become the conqueror of England. Storms sank more ships of the Spanish Armada than the English did. Coincidence is no obstacle to history.

Miracle is. History is the account of natural and social events. Their causes all lie within those fields, whether they are deliberately planned or purely accidental. But if God has manipulated either the natural or human components by his direct action, the event becomes supernatural. It may have happened, but it is not history. If, as the Judeo-Christian tradition affirms as its first principle, God manifests himself primarily through history, it must be real history, produced by natural or social cause and effect or by coincidence, and not by divine intrusions. In terms of our paradigm, the mighty acts of God, who is constantly and consistently in control of creation, cannot be exceptions to the rules but rather their supreme expression.

What, then, made the thunderstorm an act of God? Simply the fact that it was so recognized by Deborah and the Israelites. They were human beings with the power to resist the divine inspiration. Therefore with them the Spirit and the Logos could be the more persuasive through the initiating aim and the lure of the potential. The Israelites were receptive to that inspiration and so they recognized the hand of God. If they had not, if they like their enemies had been frightened by the storm, they would not have won the battle. Instead, they saw God at work in it. Their insight made the difference.

That inspiration was not a fortuitous event. It rested on their lifelong conviction that God was in covenant relation with them, that they were his people. This went back through all the experiences of the renewal of the covenant, through all the times of danger in which their forefathers had survived, through the wanderings that had brought them to the fertile land, and all the way back to the inspiration that had recognized their God as he manifested himself in the violence of nature. It was through the processes of nature and history that God had revealed himself, not by miraculously disrupting them.

Exodus

The Israelites saw in the exodus from Egypt the supreme instance of their election by God. "I am Yahweh your God who brought you out of the land of Egypt" (Ex. 20:1). The story was told again and again with ever-increasing elaborations. The editors and the redactors of the Hexateuch, the first six books of the Bible, wove these oral traditions into a more or less plausible continuous narrative of great complexity. To this was added a recasting of the whole in Deuteronomy, and the story of the conquest of Palestine in Joshua. Finally the priestly document was incorporated which added further details to the already overburdened narrative, and inserted a whole book of ceremonial and other laws.

The end result is a magnificent achievement, but under it the original exodus is almost totally obscured. Even disregarding inconsistencies and contradictions, we cannot take the Hexateuch as history. It is mostly interpretation of the exodus event, with the pre-exodus experiences we have already considered added, and also an enormous mass of subsequent experiences and insights.

If it is true revelation of the God of history, however, I contend that at its heart there must have been an actual event. Is it possible so much as to suggest what that might have been? Can we imagine an ordinary occurrence in terms of natural and social processes that could serve as the basis for the inspired interpretation? I want to attempt such a reconstruction which, if you wish, is pure fancy on my part, but which is not without some support in contemporary scholarship.

Tribes kindred to the Israelites who settled in northern and central Palestine were also to be found in the Negeb, the wilderness south of Judea. In particular, they centered around a shrine at Kadesh. Connected with that shrine was a God called Yahweh, who was associated with Mount Sinai. The first reinterpretation that took place there was the recognition by a spiritual leader, Moses, that the Yahweh of Kadesh was "the God of Abraham, the God of Isaac, the God of Jacob" (Ex. 3:14f). Yahweh was identified with the God of the fathers. The name Yahweh gives himself in his epiphany to Moses, "I am who I am," or "I will be what I will be," or however it should be translated, emphasizes that he is the one who acts and is about to act.

One of the Israelite tribes, or part of one, was admitted into Egypt to find fodder. Soon the men were impressed to work on some building project. This would have been especially galling to a nomad. The group took the opportunity one night to escape to the desert. We need not think them a particularly large number. When the overseer discovered their departure he got some soldiers and pursued them.

The Israelites had already reached the far side of a shallow estuary. It is possible to reconstruct out of the biblical narrative a primitive account of the event in which the Israelites traveled around the edge of the estuary and never crossed it. The pursuers also went around the estuary and caught up with the fugitives. But since night was falling, they did not attack at once.[3]

During the night a storm with winds of hurricane force came upon them. The Israelites recognized in it their God who manifested himself in natural violence. The Egyptians, on the other hand, were terrified and fled at the earliest light of dawn. A hurricane can blow the water out of a shallow estuary, like water blown out of a saucer, as those who lived north of Lake Okeechobee in Florida learned to their distress some years ago. So the Egyptians, finding the sea floor exposed, in their frantic flight dashed across it. But when the wind let up the water drained back rapidly into the estuary and the Egyptians were drowned.

The Israelites carried the news of their deliverance to Kadesh, where Moses showed that it proved Yahweh to be their God, who cared for them and upheld them. In the enthusiasm of that experience the Israelites set out for the east bank of the Dead Sea, defeated the Amorites and Moabites, and entered Palestine by crossing the Jordan at Jericho.

The book of Joshua claims to record the conquest of the whole land, but an examination of its contents reveals that chapters 2–9 deal only with the territory of Benjamin. It is, therefore, chiefly an account of that tribe's entry into the land. This probably represents most of what happened at that time. A couple of detached episodes are added in chapters 10 and 11. They may indicate that some of the Israelites already in Palestine were inspired by the success of the newcomers to attack and capture some Canaanite cities.

But the significant episode is recorded in Joshua 24. At Shechem Joshua assembled the tribes and identified Yahweh, the God of Sinai, with the God of the fathers, whom the northern tribes had been worshiping under other names, and whose signal victory over the Egyptians they had not acknowledged. It is noteworthy that in the summary of Yahweh's redemptive acts (24:2–13) there is again no mention of the giving of the law at Sinai. The people agreed, "We too will serve Yahweh, for he is our God" (24:18). In this way the two traditions from the north and the south were fused. Sinai took on the characteristics of the holy mountain of El Shaddai — the thunder and lightning and, I believe, the volcanic eruptions.

The covenant with its developed codes of obligations was also transferred to Sinai. A subtle difference in the attitude toward the codes resulted. In the past they had been read at the local shrines where the tribes gathered to renew the covenant. They were merely explanations of its obligations given by the official teachers at the shrines. They did not have the force of law and were not associated with the awe-inspiring theophanies of the holy mount.

But when both the mount and the codes were transferred to Sinai they were brought together. Moses was held to have received the commandments directly from God in the course of a theophany of full magnitude. This gave the code much higher authority, which was to be the basis of an increasing moralism and eventually of legalism in the Israelite tradition.

Kingdom

So long as the tribal form of government prevailed in Israel, the response to a time of crisis was that described in the Song of Deborah. An inspired leader called the tribes together to protect themselves against the enemy. Those most affected responded, and perhaps some of the others. But more remote clans, like Dan, Asher, and Gilead, remained at home; so also did Reuben because of internal problems. The system worked fairly well as long as the enemy was the little Canaanite city states that were usually engaged in bickering among themselves.

But about the same time as the Israelites were settling into the mountain regions, the Philistines were invading the coastal plain. They established five cities that fully cooperated with each other. When they set out to expand their territory, Israel was faced with a more formidable enemy. Samuel the prophet assembled the tribes for battle, but the Philistines defeated them near Shiloh. In the next battle the ark, which the Israelites had brought into their camp to strengthen them, was captured by the Philistines.

Although the ark was returned and the lost territory temporarily recovered, it became clear that the Israelites needed a stronger and more permanent central authority. So the people demanded a king. The Old Testament reflects two attitudes toward this. One portrays Samuel resisting the idea and warning the people about the tyranny they will suffer. But they insist, and God tells Samuel to comply with their demands, reassuring him, "It is not you they have rejected; they have rejected me from ruling over them" (I Sam. 8:7). The setting up of the kingdom was seen as an abandonment of the old tribal covenant relationship with Yahweh, as indeed it was.

In other stories, however, Samuel showed no reluctance in anointing Saul as the first king, and at the beginning of his reign gave him his full support. This tradition recognized that God was making another covenant with Israel which was centered in the king as his representative on earth. "I myself have set my king upon my holy hill of Zion," says Yahweh in Psalm 2:6f. "You are my son; this day have I begotten you."

But the covenant was not to be established with Saul. He was a transitional figure. A third account of how he became king shows him to have been a charismatic leader like those of the tribal period. When Saul learned of the cruelty the Ammonites intended to inflict on the inhabitants of Jabesh-Gilead, the spirit of God seized him and he assembled Israel to raise the siege of the city (1 Sam. 11). But after he had done so, because of the Philistine threat Saul built up a more permanent army and acted more and more like a king. Unfortunately his unstable character and his conflict with David, who was destined to succeed him, ultimately brought his initial successes to total defeat.

So the covenant was established with David of the southern tribe of Judah. Samuel is portrayed as rejecting Saul and anointing David in his stead. David's career began as a leader in Saul's court, of whose popularity Saul became jealous. When David had to flee for his life, his skill as a guerrilla fighter prevented Saul from capturing and eliminating him.

After Saul's death David won the allegiance of the northern tribes, checked the inroads of the Philistines, captured Jerusalem, a surviving Canaanite city, and made it his capital. This, like his other maneuvers, was a shrewd move because the place had no tribal associations. On the other hand, David brought the ark to Jerusalem, dancing before it in the spirit of the Lord, thereby identifying himself with the old covenant shrines and their charismatic leaders.

It was apropos of that and of David's desire to install the ark in a temple that the prophet Nathan spoke in the name of Yahweh, forbidding David to build the temple but assuring him, "Your house and your sovereignty will always stand secure before me and your throne be established forever" (2 Sam. 7:16). On earth this was fulfilled by Solomon, who succeeded his father David, built the temple, and extended the kingdom so that it became the dominant power in the area.

This glory was not to last. Solomon's son offended the northern tribes and they set up an independent kingdom which was called Israel. At first its capital was Shechem, the ancient center of the tribal confederation, but it was subsequently moved to Samaria, a city newly built for the purpose. Only two tribes remained faithful to the house of David—Judah, from which the southern kingdom took its name, and Benjamin.

The northern kingdom had no settled line of succession. Jeroboam, its founder, was a charismatic leader, and from time to time a usurper would arise, murder the reigning king, and set up a new dynasty. Inevitably the country had its ups and downs, being in almost continuous conflict with Syria, which had its capital in Damascus. In the end, both Syria and Israel fell victims to Assyria, their capitals were destroyed, and their people taken into exile.

The southern kingdom, on the other hand, remained faithful to the Davidic dynasty throughout its existence. It was much the weaker state but it managed to survive the expansion of the Assyrian Empire, only to fall victim to the Babylonians. In 597 Jerusalem was captured and its leading citizens deported. Ten years later it was again captured. It was then destroyed and more of its people were taken to Babylon.

Faith in the covenant with David did not die with the fall of Jerusalem. Unlike the exiles from the northern kingdom, who were absorbed by the population among whom they were settled, those from Judah were held together in the hope that its promise would be honored. When Cyrus, the Persian, conquered Babylon and allowed the uprooted peoples to return to their homelands, there were some Israelites willing to go back to Jerusalem. Their civil ruler was Zerubbabel of the house of David. He disappears from history shortly after the return and no other descendant of David has ever reigned in Jerusalem.

After the exile the Israelites never succeeded in establishing an independent kingdom, except for a brief period under the Maccabees. Yet the conviction that God would fulfill his promises to David persisted. The result was the expectation of a messiah who somehow, somewhere, whether on earth or in heaven, would establish the Israelites as the kingdom of God. Some Jews today still look forward to this consummation. For Christians those concepts formed the basis for recognizing Jesus as the Christ and harbinger of the kingdom.

As the Israelites were enabled to see God's self-revelation in the violence of nature, his guidance and care in the wanderings to and settlement in Palestine, his protecting love in the storms that overthrew Sisera and the Egyptians, so in the history of the kingdom they were led to recognize the hand of God. In the former instances we are dealing with prehistory. The founding of the kingdom, its division and fall, on the other hand, have been recorded in trustworthy documents. Nothing could be more secular than the eyewitness report of David's reign in 2 Samuel. We have entered the realm of history.

Nor are we dependent for our information on the Bible alone. References to affairs in Palestine are to be found in the archeological and literary remains of Egypt and the fertile crescent. This is real history, ordinary history. What happened to the Israelites closely paralleled the experiences of their neighbors. The capture of Israel and the fall of Samaria was fundamentally the same as the capture of Syria and the fall of Damascus.

More significantly so was the capture of Judah and the fall of Jerusalem, even though its acceptance as the will of God enabled those Israelites to survive in exile. As an external event it was no different from the others. Why then was it in a special sense an act of God? Again, because it was so interpreted. This time we know the persons who made the interpretation and something of what they said. So to their contribution we now turn.

The Prophets

The early prophets, such as Elijah and Elisha, were chiefly concerned with the struggle against Baal. When the Israelites entered Palestine and began to learn the art of agriculture, as part of the technique they were told to sacrifice to the local Baal who alone could fertilize their crops. Their loyalty to the God of their fathers, and his association with the violence of nature, kept them from entirely accepting the Baalim. But they either included sacrifices to them on the side or began to treat Yahweh as if he were their Baal.

It was against this that Elijah witnessed in the contest at Carmel by his vindication of the desert God who answered by fire. Subsequently Jehu revolted against the reigning house of Omri, which had even introduced foreign gods into the worship of the court. In bloody massacres Jehu wiped out the priests and adherents of Baal. When Jehu's great-grandson, Jeroboam II, came to the throne, the problem was not the local Baalim but world politics.

The northern kingdom was enjoying a period of prosperity. But injustice, corruption, and luxury were rife. The rulers were more concerned with their foreign policy than with the service of Yahweh. Sacrifices were still being offered with regularity and splendor at Bethel, but to Amos, the first of the literary prophets, they were hypocritical formalities because of the faithlessness of the worshipers. His message, and that of all the later prophets, is beautifully summed up in Amos 3:1, where Yahweh says, "You alone, of all the families of the earth, have I acknowledged, therefore it is for all your sins that I mean to punish you."

God's love for Israel is a responsibility as well as a privilege. Because he is their God and they are his people, they should behave in a manner appropriate to him. When they do not, God must punish them, not for revenge or retaliation, but to open their eyes to their sins and call them to repentance. If they will not heed even that, God has to reject them.

Through Hosea, who followed Amos and saw the threatened destruction coming ever closer to an unheeding Israel, God expressed the pain of his rejected love. "When Israel was a child I loved him, and I called my son out of Egypt. But the more I called to them, the further they went from me. . . . Ephraim, how could I part with you? Israel, how could I give you up?" (11:1f,8). Yet in the end Yahweh must cry, "Because of their wicked deeds I will drive them out of my house; I will love them no longer" (9:15).

The northern kingdom did not heed these prophets and fell to Assyria. But the prophets' message was preserved in Judah. About the same time Micah, a countryman, was fulminating against the sins of Jerusalem, and in 742 Isaiah was called to his long ministry in the city itself. We must not think that these men were misanthropes who liked to look on the darkest side of things and enjoyed denouncing their fellows. It was with great reluctance that they accepted their vocation.

The official lections of the church often obscure this in Isaiah's call by ending the reading at 6:8, "Here I am, send me." But God continues, "Go, and say to this people, 'Hear and hear again, but do not understand; see and see again, but do not perceive.' Make the heart of this people gross, its ears dull; shut its eyes, so that it will not see with its eyes, hear with its ears, understand with its heart, and be converted and healed." Small wonder that Isaiah, commissioned for such a dismal and futile task, exclaims, "Until when, Lord?" But the answer is relentless, "Until towns have been laid waste and deserted, houses left untenanted, countryside made desolate, and Yahweh drives the people out."

The point of this apparently hopeless message is that the old covenants have been rejected by the people. They have been broken beyond repair. There is no longer any hope in them. This does not, however, mean that Yahweh has abandoned his people. He plans something new and better for those who will repent and trust in him. But they must wait on him and not try to save themselves by military alliances and the like.

The teachings of this first group of prophets were codified in Deuteronomy. The Lord gave one last opportunity, "I set before you life or death, blessing or curse. Choose life, then, so that you and your descendants may live, in the love of Yahweh your God, obeying his voice, clinging to him" (30:19). The king Josiah renewed the covenant and put the deuteronomic reforms into practice. But involvement in power politics was too much for him and he was killed in battle against the Egyptians. The remaining kings were vassals of either Egypt or Babylon until the leading people were taken into exile.

During those final years another group of prophets was raised up, chief among them being Jeremiah and Ezekiel. They insisted that Judah's sin justified God's wrath and punishment. Jeremiah urged the people in Jerusalem to surrender to Babylon and accept its dominion. Ezekiel, who was taken into exile with the first group, told his fellow sufferers to accept the situation and remain faithful to Yahweh. Both prophets looked forward to a new and more glorious covenant. That concept was most fully developed by Deutero-Isaiah, a prophet of the exile, who saw in Cyrus' policy the occasion for the second exodus that would bring the Israelites back in triumph to the Holy Land.

It used to be thought that the eschatological passages that promised Yahweh's renewed favor were later additions to the prophets' message. Today, however, some are maintaining that all the prophets balanced their assertion that the old covenants had been made void by the people's unfaithfulness, with the assurance that God was about to do still mightier acts to establish a new covenant. There would be a new exodus, a new Moses, a new law written on the hearts of the people, a new and messianic king of the house of David.

In this way history, even its calamitous and tragic events, was interpreted as the work of God. Thus understood, the Israelites could accept it and remain faithful, though the hopes of the prophets were not realized. The return was a meager affair. Haggai and Zechariah did get a small temple built, which was a disappointment to those who remembered its predecessor. Nehemiah restored the city walls. Ezra reestablished the covenant of Sinai as a strict and elaborate legal code, which was incorporated in the final redaction of the Hexateuch. Those books were read every Sabbath in the synagogues and studied, interpreted, and further elaborated in the rabbinical tradition. All this was a holding operation. But the hope refused to die. Somehow, sometime, the Messiah would come and restore the kingdom to Israel.

There was still another aspect of a prophet's vocation which must be noted. Not only did they accept their call with reluctance and protest. The carrying out of their mission was also fraught with suffering for them. They were feared and hated for their prediction of doom, and were often persecuted for it. That the work of a prophet involved suffering vicariously on behalf of the people was recognized in

Deuteronomy 3:24ff., where Moses takes upon himself God's wrath at their disobedience and is not allowed to enter the promised land.

Jeremiah was the suffering prophet *par excellence*, both in his grief at and resistance to his vocation, which he carried out at the cost of intense interior struggle, and in the persecution he endured at the hands of the rulers in Jerusalem. Ezekiel illustrated this same principle in acting out his message in ways that must have been quite painful, such as lying on his left side for a hundred and ninety days to take on himself "the sin of the house of Israel." Then he was to lie on his right side to "bear the sin of the house of Judah for forty days. . . . I have laid bonds on you, and you must not turn over until the period of your seclusion is finished" (Ezek. 4:4ff).

The supreme expression of this concept in the Old Testament is the suffering servant described by Deutero-Isaiah. He forms a fitting climax to the hope that the second exodus will have its second Moses who will suffer more and accomplish more, not only for Israel but for all the peoples of the earth as well. This insight into the way, and the only way, history can be brought to its consummation in loving union with God was pregnant with significance for the future.

The prophets saw history in all its aspects, favorable and unfavorable, as a continuous and consistent act of God. Their insight has been upheld by the course of history itself. Because the Israelites have believed that God has chosen them, and demonstrated that election over and over again in their experiences of both protection and punishment, they have remained a people through all the vicissitudes of the centuries. Is not that faith justified?

It took faith, often heroic faith. God's hand is no more obviously visible in historical events than it is in the natural universe. To both science and history God, if he exists, is the hidden God who guides unobtrusively and persuades only those occasions of becoming that respond to his lure. His existence can be denied in both areas. But on the other hand, belief in him is not inconsistent with the established facts of science and history, and it does give them the significance for which we long and without which life is futile and absurd—a meaningless, purposeless journey into death. So both nature and history can be the call to faith.

What faith? Faith that God took the risk of creating man, the risk of sin and evil and suffering. Faith that God knows what he is doing. Faith that he can still cope with the situation. Faith that he is working out his purpose and will bring mankind in the end into loving union with him. Faith that it is all worth the risk and worth the price.

T

TAU

THE CALL TO LOVE

Chapter 4 / SIN

When God was believed to have created all things in the universe by fiat, with their natural capacities just as they are today, the origin of sin was hard to explain. Everything as it came from the hand of God had to be good. How then did mankind become evil, and from the very start? That man and woman had sinned is only part of the answer. For how could they who were perfectly good feel temptation or have any inclination to yield to it? How did sin get started and why is it so pervasive?

These philosophical and psychological questions were not of much interest to Jews or Jewish-Christians. So we find little in the Bible that attempts to answer them, least of all in the story of Eden. But in the Greek-speaking world they had to be faced. The traditional Christian doctrine of the fall was developed to deal with the problem. It took two forms: one, associated with Irenaeus, may be called original sin; the other, expounded by Augustine, original guilt. Both attributed the beginning of sin to Adam and Eve in their yielding to the temptation of the serpent. They differ as to the state of man before the fall, the grievousness of the sin, and its resultant consequences.[1]

The Irenaean doctrine is more primitive and has prevailed in the eastern church. It pictures mankind before the fall in a state of innocence that rested on moral ignorance. Taking advantage of her naïveté, the devil deceived Eve into thinking that no harm would follow from eating the forbidden fruit. Rather, she would be closer to God because she would become more like him. If God had really forbidden it, the only reason could be that he was jealous and wanted to keep mankind from its highest good. If he was truly loving, he would want them to eat the fruit. Eve's yielding to these rationalizations and

Adam's complicity in it opened their eyes to the nature and consequences of sin, and so to the moral imperative, but only at the price
of having already violated it.

The initial sin in this view was not an act of arrogance that sought
independence from God. It was the result of weakness; Adam and
Eve were dupes of the devil. Can it really be called sin at all? If they
were incapable of moral discernment, how could they have recognized the temptation as wrong? Was not, in fact, the experience a
good thing? Through it they became aware of the necessity to make
self-determined choices between self-serving and self-giving. They
matured into consciously moral and potentially loving persons. Was
it not a "fall upward," a "happy fault," as an ancient hymn calls it?[2]

In that case, why was it punished? They had to lose their naïve innocence, of course. The divine image in them was somewhat impaired. But why were they expelled from the garden into a world
where labor would be difficult, pleasures few, and suffering great?
Why were they deprived of the fruit of the tree of life? Still worse, why
were these punishments inflicted on their descendants who had not
even committed their "happy fault?"

As an explanation, the doctrine of original sin is illogical and un-
satisfactory. It also fails to exonerate God. Would a loving creator
allow his creatures to be enticed into a sin that they had neither the
insight to perceive nor the maturity to resist, then inflict on them its
ill effects and pass them on to their children? By playing down the
seriousness of the offence, the doctrine of original sin makes its consequences the arbitrary and unjust imposition of a jealous God.

The Augustinian doctrine of original guilt is both more logical and
more horrendous. Man and woman were created perfect, immortal,
and with the wisdom needed to recognize their obligation to obey
God's command in regard to the fruit of the forbidden tree. But Eve
allowed herself to be argued into believing that God's jealousy was
preventing her from achieving her full potentiality and becoming like
God. Her sin was insatiable pride, "vaulting ambition which
o'erleaps itself,"[3] and Adam acquiesced in it.

The result was the expulsion from Eden, subjection to death, and
the total loss of the divine image. Because Adam and Eve were the
founders of the human race, all men were in some sense in Adam and
shared his sin and its guilt. Mankind's integrity and the possibility of
fulfilling its vocation in this world were destroyed. Since the arrogant
revolt of the creature against its creator was an infinite offense, all

human beings are deservedly condemned to hell unless gratuitously saved by God. A few are predestined to be redeemed by Christ; the rest are damned.

This doctrine became official in the west. According to it, even infants who die without baptism are lost because of the guilt they inherit through their parents. Since physical generation is the vehicle of human corruption, the tendency is to look on sexual intercourse as inherently evil. It is the extreme expression of concupiscence, the illicit and uncontrollable desires that have plagued man since the fall. The Reformation carried this doctrine to its logical conclusion. All men and women are totally depraved because they share in Adam's guilt.

It will be seen at once that, far from absolving God from complicity in human sin, the doctrine of original guilt turns him into an ogre. As the reformers recognized, he had to allow Adam and Eve enough inclination to sin in order for them to yield to the temptation, so that those whom he had predestined to damnation might commit the sin for which they could "justly" be condemned. Even less than the doctrine of original sin, does original guilt solve the problem of reconciling the fact of human sin with mankind's creation by a good and loving God.

The truth is that the problem cannot be solved in terms of the Eden myth of the forbidden tree. That was not the issue the author of Genesis had in mind; indeed, it would never have occurred to him. As an Israelite who believed that God manifests himself supremely in the violent and destructive forces of nature, he felt no difficulty in attributing human weakness, — "the heart-ache, and the thousand natural shocks that flesh is heir to,"[4] — to the creative will of God. Genesis is concerned not with the origin of sin but with its nature and consequences.

Self-reliance

The second account of creation, which begins at Genesis 2:5, is the introduction to the narrative of the forbidden tree. In that account man is not portrayed as having any exceptional wisdom, virtue, or power. He was created first because there could be no plants before there was someone "to till the soil." When Yahweh had planted the garden, man was put there "to cultivate and take care of it." Clearly man was expected to work before he had eaten the forbidden fruit.

When God formed the animals and birds, "these he brought to the man to see what he would call them." That statement is rich in significance. It recognizes the importance of language, which gives man the opportunity to form concepts of things and so to be able to think about them when they are not the objects of direct perception. Conscious memory, anticipation, planning, and choice, as well as communication, all depend on the use of language. It gives man control over the universe, animate and inanimate.

In Hebrew thought the name represents the nature of a thing as it is known. Genesis portrays man as not just learning the names of living things but deciding them. "Each one was to bear the name the man would give it." Man to that extent determined its nature, as in fact he has done by cultivation, domestication, and breeding. So both agriculture and animal husbandry are included in the work man was created to perform.

Then God saw man needed a helpmate and created woman, with whom he was to be united in love, expressed on the physical level through the uninhibited use of sex. "Both of them were naked, the man and his wife, but they felt no shame in front of each other." All this suggests that man and woman were to have a share in the ordering and functioning of the universe, both through their pastoral and agricultural activities and through procreation.

To fulfill their vocation they had to remain surrendered to God's will. All had been given by God; all was to be received and used in trusting faith. In the garden the symbol of their obedience was to refrain from eating the fruit of the tree of the knowledge of good and evil. What specifically the author of Genesis intended by that knowledge we shall consider later. For the present it is enough to see the issue in terms of dependence on God.

C. S. Lewis recognized and expressed that aspect clearly in his recounting of the story in *Perelandra*.[5] The scene is on Venus. The man and the woman live on floating islands of vegetation. There is also solid land and during the day they may explore it. At night, however, they must return to a floating island. They are not to have a fixed abode, but leave it to God to determine where they will be when they awake the next morning. They are not to take full control of their lives.

In Eden the serpent appeared. We are so accustomed to identifying him with Satan that we read all kinds of ideas into the Genesis narrative that are not there. When he first appeared, he was not a snake. His punishment for tempting Adam and Eve was to become one. The implication is that in the beginning he had legs. He was the cleverest, the most intelligent of all the animals. I believe he represents man's natural inheritance raised to its highest capacity.

The temptation, then, was for man to use his inherent powers, which he attributes to his own ingenuity, to serve himself. By them he may satisfy his longing for anything and everything that is "pleasing to the eye" and "desirable for the knowledge that it could give" to increase man's dominion over the universe. This, he argued, is what God put him here for, to serve as God's deputy.[6] The more like God he is, therefore, the better. Man is quite prepared to take over the responsibility for himself and work with God as an equal partner. The result was the disruption of his relationship with God.

Genesis depicts this with delightful simplicity. God comes to take his usual evening stroll in the garden. But Adam and Eve do not rush up to greet him. As a result of their self-assertion they have become painfully aware of themselves. They recognize their nakedness. Because they have rejected the love of God, the source of their own capacity to love, the physical organs for the expression of their mutual love are turned for them into a source of shame.

The natural function of sex becomes inhibited and can no longer be accepted and used openly. It must be hidden. Indeed, they themselves must hide from God whom they recognized they had rejected by their overweening ambition. They believed they could get along on their own without him; now they found themselves afraid to face him.

But God's love is unchanged. He sought and called them out. Adam tried to explain the situation on the basis of the consequences of his act—the fear and shame that he felt. He wanted to pass them off as inevitable results of his creaturely status of which he had just become aware. God would have none of it. He at once asked them about the sin, the real cause of their alienation.

Then a further disruption occurred. Adam tried to shift the blame to Eve. It was her fault. She ate first and gave the fruit to him. Ecclesiasticus 25:24, in its diatribe against wicked women, asserts, "Sin began with a woman, and thanks to her we all must die." Male chauvinism has been a recurring feature of the Judeo-Christian tradition. Only recently has the church begun to make tentative efforts to free women from the distrust and subordination this episode has imposed upon them.

Adam did not stop at blaming Eve. She was the woman God had

given him. It was really God's fault for having put man in a situation in which he could not be expected to have done other than he did. Nor was Eve slow in shifting the blame—to the serpent. Again, the implication is that, because God allowed the serpent to tempt her, it was God's fault.

God did not bother to argue the matter. He simply pointed out the consequences they had brought upon themselves. Man, attempting to control nature by his own efforts and for his own purposes, will find it intractable. The more he learns how to exploit it, the more it will strike back at him, until now our technology threatens to exhaust our environment or pollute it to the point where it can no longer sustain life. The tensions over sex in the Judeo-Christian tradition have increased the pain of childbirth and kept women in subjugation to men.

Did the author of Genesis consider death to be a consequence of sin? The first explicit scriptural references to his narrative so interpreted it. Ecclesiasticus 25:24 has already been quoted. Wisdom 2:23f says, "God did make man imperishable.... It was the devil's envy that brought death into the world." On the other hand, Ecclesiasticus 40:8f says, "For all creatures, from men to animals...there is death." In that passage death is recognized as natural.

In general, Genesis assumes the inevitability of death. That humankind is created male and female and bidden, "Be fruitful, multiply, and fill the earth"(1:28), implies it. So does Genesis 3:20, where Eve is called "the mother of all those who live." Death is natural because "God fashioned man of dust from the soil" (*adam* from *adamah*). So God says, "To dust you shall return." In fact, God states that man's burdens will last only "until you return to the soil." Death is the end of his hardships, not a punishment for sin.

Still man is expelled from the Garden of Eden to keep him from eating of the tree of life. This could mean that, although man was created mortal, he could have become immortal if he had not sinned. Certainly sin has made a difference in our attitude toward death. Insofar as we concentrate our interests, enjoyments, and ambitions on the things of this world, death is our ultimate frustration. The existential humanists recognize this. For that reason they see existence as essentially hostile and absurd. If death is the absolute end, they are right.

Other than the loss of the possibility of immortality, no change in human nature resulted from sin according to Genesis. The decreed punishments affected only mankind's outward circumstances. The serpent was debased; man and woman were not. For them there was no inheritable impairment, let alone guilt. Abel, begotten after the expulsion from Eden, is portrayed as a good man. Although Cain, his brother, committed murder, it is not implied that he had inherited a bias toward evil. "Enoch walked with God" (5:24). "Noah was a good man" (6:9). Even in the much later wisdom literature Job is "a sound and honest man who fears God and shuns evil" (Job 1:8).

Taken as it stands, the account in Genesis does not attempt to explain the origin of sin, of human weakness to temptation, or of death. The act in the garden is the first sin in the sense that it is sin number one, since man had just come into existence. It is not the source of subsequent sins. They perforce follow it, but are not caused by it. What the author is concerned to teach is that sin is man's own deliberate fault. It results in an increase of his hardships and sufferings until death releases him from his misery. His disobedience alienates him from God, and therefore from himself, from society, and from nature.

Arrogance

One reason why Genesis 3 has been misinterpreted in regard to the origin and consequences of sin is because it has been taken in isolation. Actually, Genesis 2:5–12:3, insofar as it comes from the author usually designated as the Yahwist, is a continuous account of the nature of sin. The episodes in which sins are committed are not related in a causal sequence, but indicate the increasing evil of man's actions and give various grounds for it. In the context of creation and of man's vocation to be the coworker with God in the universe, man's sin is symbolized by eating the forbidden fruit of the knowledge of good and evil.

It has been recognized for some time that the Hebrew words for good and evil really mean beneficial and harmful. The knowledge is therefore fundamentally not moral but practical. It sees reality as things, things that can be used, things that can be manipulated, things that can be exploited. They become objects of knowledge. They can be dissected, defined, evaluated solely in terms of their usefulness to us. They are treated as inanimate, dead. The living mystery of a subject-to-subject relationship even with inorganic nature, which is the basis of a small child's wonder in the presence of all aspects of reality, is lost. Eating the forbidden fruit has indeed brought death. In our selfish grasping we have died to the life of the world.[7]

The knowledge of good and evil disrupts creation. Instead of accepting the natural world and humbly conforming to it, man judges it on the basis of his selfish desires and aversions. In choosing what he considers good, he raises it into an absolute. He worships it as an idol. In rejecting what he calls evil, he tries to control, exploit, or destroy nature in order to eliminate what is distasteful.

This selfishness is rationalized by depicting creation as deliberately hostile. In Eden the serpent attributes to God as the author of nature the determination to keep man from achieving his potential. The devil "is a liar and the father of lies" (Jn. 8:44). If we recognize the serpent as representing man's own cunning, we can see how, in the interest of our self-indulgence, we deceive ourselves and falsify and distort the natural world.[8]

The Yahwist saw this expressed in the applied science of the more advanced civilizations of his day. Thus Abel, the shepherd, who offers a sacrifice from the flock, is accepted by Yahweh, who rejects the oblation of the fruit of the ground presented by Cain, the farmer. Here is reflected the conflict between the pastoral way of life that characterized the Israelites in their seminomad period and the settled life in the land of Palestine, which brought them into contact with the sacrifices to Baal and other magical practices. The Yahwist, like the Rechabites of a later generation (Jer. 35:1ff), considered the latter a corruption of the pure religion of the desert. He was not entirely wrong.

To the descendants of Cain, as we have noted, are attributed the arts and sciences of civilization. That line of thought reaches its climax in the story of Babel (Gen. 11:1ff). Here the villain is not agriculture as such but the development of city life, which the accumulation of excess goods produced by advances in technology made possible. Man arrogantly proposes, "Let us build ourselves a town and a tower with its top reaching heaven. Let us make a name for ourselves."

In addition to being a climax of culture, the venture had political overtones as well. It was a united project of all the peoples of the earth, whose stronghold would be permanently safe because they would have no enemies. Within the city they were already one in language and culture. Self-sufficiency, prosperity, security would be theirs. They would reach heaven with the intent not of storming it but of equaling it. In the end, alas, internal dissension shattered the dream.

For the Yahwist the confusion was directly caused by God because of insatiable human pride. "This is but the start of their undertakings! There will be nothing too hard for them to do." All through history man's arrogance in attempting too much has brought one civilization after another to ruin. Yet we need not agree with the Yahwist that all human insights into the functioning of creation and all the applications of them in culture and technology are worthless, still less wholly evil. Presumably, God intended that man should have knowledge or he would not have put the tree in the garden, that is, he would not have evolved man's capacity for it and enabled him to attain it.

The knowledge that mankind has slowly and laboriously acquired over the centuries has its value. Though corrupted by sin, it cannot be discarded for a new beginning. We cannot start the process of learning all over again on a reverent rather than a selfish basis. There is no going back. The angel with the flaming sword prevents our return to Eden. Nevertheless there is hope. In Eden God promised the woman that her offspring will crush the head of the serpent (Gen. 3:15). The living God can still lead us on to life.

The question is whether we are in contact any longer with the living God. Is he not dead because we have killed him? How? By treating him also as an object of knowledge, a thing out there that can be analyzed, feared, hated, placated, or denied. We cannot have a living relationship with him because we do not approach him as a subject to whom we can surrender in love. God has become a thing which we can define.[9]

The word define comes from the word finis, end. So definition is always the determination of the ends, the limits, of what is under consideration. For practical purposes this is often useful. It cuts things down to a size that we can comprehend and control. Herein is the basis of the achievements of applied science. But God refuses to be cut down to size by science, philosophy, or theology. The attempt to do so is idolatry, the setting up of a man-made image in the place of God. We do not become like God; he is reduced to the likeness of us. And the purpose of this blasphemy is to bring God under our control, if not by manipulating him, at least by limiting his demands upon us and our obligations to him. Thus we move from theology to morality.

Definitions in morals are the device for reducing to manageable proportions the vocation to love. After all, we do not feel up to living for others. We must take care of ourselves and our own first. So we work out very carefully who is our neighbor and how much we are required to give in each degree of relationship. We meticulously calculate the limits of what is sin so that we are free to do anything short of it. We set the bounds of our duties so that we need not go beyond them.

All this is solidified in a code of laws, customs, and permissible actions, with ample provision for exceptions in our own favor. When such mores are generally accepted, life can become simple. One knows just where one stands and can be as selfish as one likes within the prescribed limits. One of the factors that distresses many of our contemporaries is the loss of an agreed system of moral standards. Unfortunately they have been broken down not by a more demanding call to love but by self-indulgent licentiousness.

We do seem to be going through a period of major change and confusion. The presuppositions of what for centuries has been the accepted way of life are being questioned. Is another Babel falling? If so, let us note that for the Yahwist Babel was not the end. In Genesis 12:1ff God makes a new covenant with Abraham, who was called not just to be the father of the chosen race, but was told, "All the tribes of the earth shall bless themselves by you." If today is the end of an era, it is also the beginning of another.

The call of the God who acts is always toward the future. Salvation and fulfillment lie ahead. The way may be thorny, the work hard, the suffering the more painful because we cannot see its meaning or purpose. We must walk by faith, but we must always be pressing forward. Eschatology, the hope for an ultimate consummation by God and in God, is of the essence of both Judaism and Christianity.

The Root of Sin

The selfish acquisition of the knowledge of good and evil is only one root of sin for the Yahwist. Another is Cain's anger at not finding his offering as a tiller of the soil acceptable to God. Still another is the strange episode in Genesis 6:2ff: "The sons of God, looking at the daughters of men, saw they were pleasing, so they married as many as they chose." It is not easy to grasp what the Yahwist understood by this episode, but the corruption that followed led to the purging of creation by the flood. Some of the popular Jewish literature of the centuries just before the coming of Christ first turned to this episode when they tried to account for the origin of sin. Only later was it attributed to Adam and Eve in the garden.

A couple of passages associated with the flood provided another line of thought. Genesis 6:5 reads, "Yahweh saw that the wickedness of man was great on the earth, and that the thoughts in his heart fashioned nothing but wickedness all day long." In Genesis 8:21 Yahweh promises, "Never again will I curse the earth because of man, because his heart contrives evil from his infancy." From these verses, and others such as Psalm 51:5 and Jeremiah 17:9, the rabbis developed the concept that men and women receive an evil inclination as part of their nature. Those who hold the Christian doctrine of original sin derive this inherent evil from the fall. But the rabbis were not hampered by that doctrine and could include the inclination in God's creation of each individual soul.

This evil inclination was usually balanced in rabbinical thought by the giving of the law, or by a good inclination, or by both. Because of that balance, men and women are free to resist the inclination or not as they choose. It does not excuse their evil-doing. "Do not say, 'The Lord was responsible for my sinning.' . . . He himself made man in the beginning, and then left him free to make his own decisions. If you wish, you can keep the commandments, to behave faithfully is within your power" (Ecclus. 15:11,14f).

James 4:5 recognizes the evil inclination but attributes our ability to overcome it to grace, not to nature. "Do you suppose that scripture has no meaning when it says that the spirit which God implanted in man turns toward envious desires? And yet the grace he gives is stronger." The idea that God gives evil inclinations is so abhorrent to traditional Christianity that only *The New English Bible* has the courage so to translate the verse. Other official versions go through contortions to avoid it.

Because the rabbis had to believe that human nature was originally created directly by God they attributed the inclination to him. Because it leads man to seek what is detrimental to his well-being they called it evil. We, who think in terms of evolution, can avoid both of these allegations. The point was expressed by Canon Wilson in his address to the Church Congress in 1896:

To the evolutionist sin is not an innovation, but is the survival or misuse of habits and tendencies that were incidental to an earlier stage of development, whether of the individual or the race, and were not originally sinful, but were actually useful. Their sinfulness lies in their anachronism, in their resistance to the evolutionary and divine force that makes for moral development and righteousness.[10]

To call animals selfish is an anthropomorphism. They operate in terms of the instincts for self-preservation and reproduction, and if it is appropriate to the species, the herd instinct. These are programmed reactions not deliberate choices of self-indulgence. If the instincts come into conflict, the stronger under the circumstances prevails. Ostriches have developed long legs to allow them to escape danger by running away. But a female of the species will, trembling with fear, advance threateningly toward an intruder to protect her young.

The first hominids operated like any animal through these instincts. Their reactions were not controlled by reflection and conscious determination. The specific evolution of the hominids was to be the development of just these capacities. Physically it involved the increase of the size and complexity of the brain, together with a more erect posture and better coordination between the senses and motor activity. In terms of consciousness it presumably took the form of increasing perception of the distinction between the individual and his surroundings. As Genesis so rightly saw, the development of language must have been an important factor. The naming of things was one of the first acts of man as man.

To become a person is the responsibility of each human being. At birth an infant is hardly different from an animal so far as any conscious action goes. Its search for and taking of nourishment are automatic natural acts. It does not distinguish between itself and its environment. That does not mean, however, that it has no experiences. The eviction from the security and sustenance of the womb is a traumatic shock. It is expelled from Eden to which there is no return.

The infant is precipitated into an uncongenial world where it has to make its own way. It feels hunger and is not sure of finding nourishment. It suffers bodily discomforts and does not know when they will be cared for. Anxiety and fear recur every time its wants are experienced and, if they are not satisfied quickly, resentment and anger are aroused. Here is the taproot of a basic element in human experience, the uncertainty of life. According to the paradigm I am suggesting, birth is a constantly repeated experience. The Spirit, the womb of love, impels us into each occasion of becoming, where we have to cope with a somewhat unresponsive or hostile environment.

If we survive as infants, it is by learning to handle that environment. We discover that certain actions bring help, if not immediately, at least eventually. We come to recognize the source of these benefits as those persons from whom we receive affection and love. Yet they do not always accede to our desires. Some of our actions are approved and rewarded; others are ignored or punished. The latter may increase our resentment and anger, but gradually we learn to comply.

By such experiences the ego is developed. It is essential to self-consciousness and the possibility of deliberate choice. The human person not only must distinguish between self and environment, but must also separate the conscious from the unconscious. Were all the sensations and impulses that come to us through the unconscious allowed to become conscious, the mind would be overwhelmed by an unmanageable confusion. Be it remembered, however, that the ego, like the self, exists only in the sequence of its subjective aims in their conscious and unconscious aspects. On both levels the ego is forming itself in terms of its characteristic way of coping with the given data of experience. But because the ego exists only in this fluid process, it can move infinitesimally from becoming to becoming either toward or away from its highest potential.

The impulses that the ego is striving to satisfy in its formative stage originate in the animal needs for self-preservation. They are inevitably self-centered, although at first they cannot be called selfish. But when they are perceived to be in conflict with the demands of the persons on whom the infant depends for the gratification of its desires, the necessity for choice begins to arise. It can restrain its natural desires to comply with the will of another. This is the germ of the capacity to love. Or it can insist on the indulgence of mere animal wants. To the extent it is allowed to get them satisfied in that way, the anachronism of continuing on a subhuman level is fostered, and with it the choice of selfishness which becomes sin.

Insofar as the infant conforms to the demands of those who minister to him, he adopts patterns and eventually standards of behavior. The latter are interiorized as what Freud called the superego, which serves as the ego's conscience. This also is a necessary development. If the ego had no established principles on which to base its decisions and attempted actions, the necessity of devising them for each occasion would make judgment impossible. To the degree that the interiorized standards are the expression of love, the ego is prompted by them to constructive fulfillment. The difficulty is that, as has been traditionally recognized, conscience can be erroneous.

The persons who minister to the infant are themselves to some extent selfish. The standards by which they operate are derived mostly from the accepted mores of the society to which they belong. That society has legitimized much selfishness. As there has never been a perfect human society, the standards of even a person who responded lovingly in all his conscious choices would still tolerate and possibly approve selfish actions.

The nongratification of natural desires in order to conform to environmental pressures leads to the repudiation of parts of the self. Much of this occurs below the level of consciousness and results in repressions. The rejected impulses do not disappear, however. When they are prevented by the superego and ego from having direct expression, they continue to function indirectly. If a means of sublimation is found, they can still contribute to the fulfillment of the personality. But when they are completely repressed they circumvent the ego in eccentric and often detrimental behavior patterns.

The necessary division between the ego and the unconscious then becomes the frustration and perversion of what are essentially good aspects of our inherited nature. Insofar as the rejection of them becomes conscious, they are labeled by the superego as bad. The most innocent expression of them is considered sin and becomes a source of guilt. The unconscious repression is thereby consciously reinforced. Whole areas of the personalilty are considered inherently evil. They are rejected and feared.

An ideal concept of the self is constructed out of the mutilated remains in conformity with the inadequate, if not actually evil, mores of the society that we learn to accept. When we form and promote this false self unconsciously or unwittingly, we do not sin. But when we get a glimpse of our real potential, yet still cling to the false self and act in terms of it, we are sinning. We deepen the hold of the false self upon us. We often inflict suffering on others as we use them as things for our own gratification. We confirm and establish, for others as well as for ourselves, the selfish mores and erroneous conscience to which the false self is conforming.

By repudiating areas of our real personality, we are also cutting ourselves off from the Holy Spirit who, as our paradigm illustrates, initiates the whole subjective aim, unconscious as well as conscious, in every occasion of becoming. The Spirit, therefore, is rejected along with the depths of our real self. The false and superficial self we construct in its place impedes our response to realilty. The Logos takes it into consideration in determining the proffered lure, but seeks to nudge it a bit toward the fulfillment of the real self. Devotion to the ideal self as we have devised it for ourselves tempts us to reject the lure. When we do, we are strengthened in our selfishness.

Our ideal self is both unreal and unrealizable. There is much to be said for the Hindu concept that it and the world it tries to live in are *maya* — illusion. It is a mistake, however, to absolutize the concept, to say that the ego is entirely illusory. That is the same kind of mistake as to say it is totally depraved. Inadequate and perverted as they may be, the ego and superego are the necessary constituents of our conscious self-determination, through which alone the Logos and the Spirit can bring forth our true selves.

By the same token, the inclination toward self that we inherit from both our physical antecedents and from our environment is not original sin, still less original guilt. It is not even a tendency toward evil, for we are created to be selves. The inclination can be developed in the wrong direction if we inappropriately continue to indulge our natural desires, or suppress and repudiate them in conformity with the misguided mores of our social milieu. It can produce a false self and enslave us to it.

But it can be, and is meant to be, the raw material out of which, by cooperation with the mercy and grace of God, we can actualize our genuine selves. By surrendering, by losing, by dying to the false self we can learn the art of love. That is the process of growth to which the Logos lures us an infinitesimal step at a time, for which the Spirit gives us the power to respond. In that way we become persons, capable of a person-to-person relationship with God, who is love and who makes himself most readily available to us through person-to-person relationships with our fellow human beings.[11]

The Pauline Concept

In the light of theology, anthropology, and psychology, I believe the traditional Christian doctrine of the fall and original sin or guilt should be discarded. We can do so without unfaithfulness to the canonical Old Testament and Apocrypha, because they neither explicitly expound that doctrine nor interpret the Eden myth in those terms. When we turn to the New Testament, it is surprising to discover that references to the fall can be found only in two places, both in letters of Paul.

The first can be eliminated at once. 1 Corinthians 15:21f reads: "Death came through one man and in the same way the resurrection of the dead has come through one man. Just as all men die in Adam, so all men will be brought to life in Christ." This goes no further than Ecclesiasticus 25:24 and Wisdom 2:23f quoted above, which see death as a consequence of Adam's sin. Since in Genesis 3, death follows only because man is denied access to the tree of life and not because he became mortal, Paul need not have believed human nature to have been corrupted by the fall when he used Adam to personify all who die, in contrast to Christ in whom all can find life.

So Romans 5:12ff becomes the crucial passage. Paul starts from the same interpretation of Genesis 3, namely, that all men suffer death because of Adam's sin. But because he is here considering Christ's redemption of man from sin rather than from death, he puts the emphasis on the former. "Sin entered the world through one man, and through sin death, and thus death has spread through the whole human race because everyone has sinned." Due to the shift in emphasis, the last clause replaces "all men die" of 1 Corinthians 15:21, but the fundamental thought was initially the same.[12]

Two further points must be noted. First, Paul says that sin "entered the world" through Adam. This implies that Adam did not invent sin. He found it. Mythically it is represented by the serpent. As I have noted, there is no grounds for identifying the serpent with Satan, still less for postulating a previous angelic fall to account for sin. Whatever the Yahwist intended, we today can see the serpent as representing the survival of instinctive impulses that we gratify by the use of our intellect to exploit nature and to indulge ourselves. We argue that God has given us this universe to enjoy, and he helps those who help themselves to it.

The serpent symbolizes the inclination of man's self-conscious self-determination to gratify his subhuman instincts at the expense of higher values. It is my belief that the ability to recognize value emerges so gradually, both for the human race and for each individual, that the habit of rejecting it has developed before fully conscious choices that are rightly called sin can be made. Thus in a sense sin is potentially present, waiting to enter the world, before it is committed.

The second point is to note that the sentence is left incomplete until verses 15-17. The analogy Paul started to make was to contrast sin and death through Adam with redemption and eternal life in Christ. Why did he break off at verse 12? Because he had been insisting throughout the letter that sin was based on the law, and he suddenly remembered that the law was not given until Moses. Unfortunately he forgot what he had said in Romans 2:14f, "Pagans who never heard of the law but are led by reason to do what the law commands, may not actually 'possess' the law, but they can be said to 'be' the law. They can point to the substance of the law engraved on their hearts." Access to the law through natural reason should have been sufficient to justify keeping from the tree of life those sinners who had not received the law through Moses.

Note that it is only because Paul is thinking of death as a punishment for lawbreaking, not as a corruption inherited from Adam, that the question why "death reigned over all from Adam to Moses" comes up. Paul does not answer the question. He simply returns to his original analogy, "Adam prefigured the one to come." He wants to emphasize that all men and women, Jews and gentiles alike, are one in sin. Insofar as he gives a reason for this unity, it is because all have sinned, not because they have inherited Adam's sin or guilt. The confusion and disjointedness of Romans 5:12ff, which is generally recognized, results in my opinion from Paul's unwillingness to adopt the concept of original sin that is so frequently attributed to him.

In verse 15 he gets back to his subject: all human sin, typified by Adam, is outweighed by the redemption that is available in Christ. Because Paul wants to contrast "one man's fall" with the "grace coming through the one man, Jesus Christ," and because he likes the legal analogy of a "verdict of condemnation" versus a "verdict of acquittal," he does say that "death reigned over everyone as the consequence of one man's fall." That could mean inherited guilt as well as universal death. Perhaps it would be more logical if it did. But Paul did not say so.

To me his failure to be specific is the significant factor. He seems averse to following out the implications of his one-to-one analogy. He may well be saying no more than he did in 1 Corinthians—that Adam deprived mankind of eternal life, which Christ bestows more abundantly. I find support for this in the account of sin that he gives in Romans 7:9ff. "Once, when there was no law, I was alive; but when

the commandment came, sin came to life and I died: the commandment was meant to lead me to life but it turned out to mean death for
me, because sin took advantage of the commandment to mislead me,
and so sin, through that commandment, killed me."

What impresses me is the way Paul's description of his own experience parallels that of Eden. Adam and Eve were living with God.
But the serpent "took advantage of the commandment" not to eat the
forbidden fruit to mislead them into rejecting God. Sin thereby
"entered the world." So when Paul was old enough to learn the law
against coveting, "it was this commandment that sin took advantage
of to produce all kinds of covetousness in me" (Rom. 7:8). Does not
this suggest that the evil inclination, symbolized by the serpent, is
already present in Paul, awaiting the opportunity to entice him into
sinful choices?

If Romans 5:12ff had not been written, I am convinced that
everyone would have attributed to Paul, the pupil of the rabbi
Gamaliel, the rabbinical concept of an evil inclination bestowed by
God at birth. Is a single passage, which by its confusions shows that
Paul himself was uncertain about its logical implications, enough to
prove he held instead the theory that mankind has inherited "a verdict of condemnation" from Adam? If not, then there is no passage in
the New Testament that teaches original sin.

Jesus may have had the evil inclination in mind when he said, "It is
from within, from men's hearts, that evil intentions emerge" (Mk.
7:21). In Matthew 12:35 both a good and an evil inclination may be
indicated. "A good man draws good things from his store of goodness; a bad man draws bad things from his store of badness." The
word translated "draws" is *ekballei*, which means "throws or casts
out." That suggests a permitted eruption of an impulse rather than a
deliberately achieved effect.

Perhaps the most telling indication of the good and evil inclinations inherent in human nature is the parable of the darnel or tares
(Mt. 13:24ff), if we discard the allegorical interpretation added by
the church (13:36ff). The latter explains why there are good and bad
people in the congregation. Its implication that some are created
good by God and others are sown by the evil one is unfortunate, to say
the least. When we look at the parable without that interpretation, it
seems to deal with the individual person, in whom there is the divinely given capacity for good and the inclination to evil, which Jesus attributes to the work of the devil. In this life, both impulses must be

tolerated lest in uprooting—or as we should say today repress-
ing—the evil we destroy the integrity of our personalities.

Paul also personifies the impulse to sin and portrays himself enslaved to it. "Instead of doing the good things I want to do, I carry out
the sinful things I do not want. When I act against my will, then, it is
not my true self doing it, but sin which lives in me" (Rom. 7:19f). It is
possession by an evil spirit. Jesus similarly attributed evil impulses to
demons in the parable of the unclean spirit (Mt. 12:43ff; cf. Lk.
11:24ff), and in his warning to Peter that "Satan...has got his wish
to sift you all like wheat" (Lk. 22:31).

The ancient world was full of devils who were considered the
source not only of temptation but of mental and physical diseases as
well. Ephesians 6:12 calls us to battle them. "For it is not against
human enemies that we have to struggle, but against the sovereignties and the powers who originate the darkness in this world, the spiritual army of evil in the heavens." Jesus considered his success in
casting out devils to indicate "that the kingdom of God has overtaken
you" (Lk. 11:20). Are these outgrown mythical symbols or do they
have significance in our modern world?

Sovereignties and Powers

To discard the traditional doctrine of the fall and original sin need
not result in a failure to take sin seriously. Quite the contrary. It
removes the possibility of blaming the origin of sin on a supernatural
power external to humankind. Instead, it can find the first impulse
toward sin in the survival of the instincts which in animals are not evil
but beneficial. In man, however, they must be controlled by
deliberate self-determination when they are perceived to be in conflict with the higher values of personality of which men and women
are capable.

The natural impulses are to be adjusted to serve the higher good.
They are neither to be suppressed nor inordinately indulged. To do
either consciously is sin. It disrupts and frustrates the real self,
creating in its stead a false and illusory ego. It often inflicts suffering
on our fellows. Worst of all, it establishes sovereignties within ourselves and powers in our society that impel us to evil-doing even when
we want to resist them. We are, individually and corporately, the victims of demons. But they are not fallen angels. They are the creations
of accumulated human sin.

These demons have been around since the dawn of human existence, skillfully adapting themselves to changes in culture and mores. The recent history of the exploitation of others by the self-indulgent use of sex is an example. In the nineteenth century sex was officially tabu, a subject to be avoided in polite conversation and, theoretically, in practice, except within the confines of matrimony. In fact it was indulged in as much as ever but on the basis of a double standard. Respectable women were given no license in the matter, which resulted in much frustration. Men, on the other hand, could indulge themselves, provided their affairs were kept hidden. Yet though socially tolerated, they were morally condemned and sometimes generated guilt feelings that were a burden.

The repression or abuse of sex resulted in so much mental disturbance that, when psychiatry began to probe the human personality, it was at first inclined to blame sex for all the ills of mankind. So the pendulum swung to the opposite extreme. The tabu on talking about sex disappeared. Frankness on the subject reached a new height in the 1960s when male and female nudity became common on the stage. Moral restrictions on sex were widely repudiated. Whether this resulted in more sexual activity I do not pretend to know, but it has been no more satisfying in its blatant than in its clandestine form. Both tabu and open devotion to sex make it a sacred idol and pervert it from its true function as the physical expression of mutually committed love.

Other demons that harass the individual are the lust for security, dominance, possessions, status, and the like. These inordinate desires entice the ego into the pursuit of false and ephemeral ideals, to the detriment of the development of the true self. They are also used by the corporate demons to strengthen their stranglehold on society. The exploitation of them is especially characteristic of the most pernicious of our modern devils, technocracy, which it is worth our while to analyze in some detail.

Millions of dollars are spent on advertising to stimulate our desire not only for things necessary and beneficial, but for worthless gadgets as well. Crazes are fostered for which vast amounts of equipment are required. Conspicuous consumption is encouraged so that the latest models become status symbols. Far from being more efficient machines, they tend to differ mostly in decor and accessories. If we resist that inducement to keep on buying, built-in obsolescence forces us to replace them shortly after their warranty expires, or to spend as much on repairs to keep them operating. To make this possible a huge credit system has been devised for deferred payment. One of the ironies today is that you have no credit unless you are enormously in debt.

All this is necessary not only to employ those engaged by the advertising and credit agencies, but those who work in the manufacturing and allied industries as well. Our economy demands a constant and ever increasing flow of goods from factory to consumer. Things must not last too long or the wheels of industry will slow down. That, in turn, would cause layoffs and those who lost their jobs would have less to spend on purchases. The market would shrink still further.

That vicious circle must be avoided at all costs. So the public is cajoled, lured, tempted, browbeaten, implored to buy. It does not matter how much damage we may be doing to the environment. It does not matter how rapidly we may be exhausting the available resources. Our throw-away culture may be smothering itself in its accumulated trash. The products may be injurious to health — and may so advertise themselves, which in the case of cigarettes has increased their sales. The items may be utterly without value or use. It does not matter. The carousel must keep turning, so buy, buy, buy.

It is doubtful whether the process could be halted or modified, even if someone so desired. For who can control it?[13] The legal owners of the corporations have no say as to policy, as the futile efforts to influence it through stockholders' meetings have demonstrated. Perhaps a few minor externals may be altered to improve public relations, but the essentials of the system are impervious to change.

The decision-makers, insofar as decisions can be made, are the managerial executives. They form a vast interlocking and self-perpetuating bureaucracy. Their primary interest is to keep the process going and growing. Continuity, stability, conformity are the ideals of those at the top, and they see to it that their successors think as they do. Since that is the sole criterion for promotion, the chances of change are nil.

The managers are not interested in the welfare of their workers beyond what is necessary to keep things operating. Organized labor is itself a bureaucracy designed to gear in with the rest of management. In the big battles over renewal of contracts, even when they involve strikes, the union officials would not insist on anything that would upset the established relationships.

The management is not concerned to improve efficiency or the quality of the product. The former might decrease the number of employees, and thus the size of the enterprise and its bureaucracy. The latter might make the products last longer and reduce sales. Competition is no stimulus to improvement because, although illegal collusion is avoided, no major çorporation would lower its prices or improve its product in a way that would give it a real advantage over its competitors. The rivalry that is played up by the advertisements is always in terms of conspicuous externals that make the new model an observable status symbol.

Finally the managers, not being owners, are not overconcerned about dividends. More important is to show a profit, most of which can be plowed back into the company to increase its size and importance. Because of all this, the anonymous corporation runs itself. The management is committed by its nature to letting it function in its own way. No nation can effectively control or regulate its really big companies for they operate on an international scale. They, in fact, dictate to an important extent the conditions in the countries they exploit.

In the United States and many other countries the defense department is one of the biggest consumers and therefore a supporter of rampant technocracy. Together with the other major corporations, its influence on the government is supreme. It can demand and get substantially increased defense appropriations every year. An important factor in justifying the increase is the fiction of a life-and-death struggle between communism and capitalism. Actually, they are slightly different ways in which technocracy organizes its exploitation.

The independence of the juggernaut corporations that technocracy has spawned allows them to function like mindless, impersonal persons. No human being really desires the evils they perpetrate and perpetuate. But no human individual or group can alter the situation. Neither the owners, the managers, the workers, nor the consumers can be held responsible, yet the evil thrives. It is not so much that man has become alienated from society as that society has become alienated from man. In technocracy an independent power of global malevolence has been created.[14]

Demons are made by man out of things good in themselves. Technology can be of great benefit to mankind when human sin does not corrupt it into exploitive technocracy. The viciousness of sin is its destruction and perversion of the good. So pervasive is the hold of our demons upon us that we cannot in our own strength entirely resist them. But to the extent we can, failure to do so further enslaves ourselves and our society. Conscious and deliberate subservience to the powers of evil, even though we refuse to recognize them as such but call them our rights, interests, or legitimate pleasures, is sin against God, mankind, and ourselves.

The injury we inflict on ourselves provokes God's compassion and the Logos lures us from the illusions the demons encourage toward the realization of our true selves. But God's attitude toward the suffering that our sins, individual and corporate, inflict upon others can only be described as wrath. We have been embarrassed by that biblical concept because of our fear of anthropomorphism and because of our insistence that God cannot experience passion. We have preferred a deity of calm transcendence and detached aloofness. It is this concept of the creator, indifferent for example to the cruelty that tortures little children, that causes the Ivan Karamazovs to hand in their tickets to the universe. Thank God, the concept is false.

The real universe is created by a God of love who is outraged at man's inhumanity to man and his spoliation of the universe. He tolerates it because he respects the integrity of human self-determination. But against the evil that we do, and especially against the sovereignties and powers that the accumulation of our sins produce and perpetuate, his wrath is implacable. He is determined to defeat and destroy them. He has acted to overcome them in the only way in which he could engage them in personal combat. He has entered the society that has both created them and is tyrannized by them, in order to redeem it from within. How he accomplished that will be our next concern.

Chapter 5 / **INCARNATION**

Christianity is grounded in the incarnation. It believes that God became man in Jesus the Christ. Reduced to its simplest terms, that means Jesus was truly God, truly man, and truly one person.[1] The problem is to give full value to all three terms at the same time.

At first it was difficult for the church to recognize Jesus as God. The disciples had known him as an itinerant teacher with great power to heal, but with nothing to suggest that he was more than human. As a result of the resurrection experience, they came to realize Jesus was the Messiah who had come humbly as a man to inaugurate the kingdom of God through his teaching and exorcisms, his death and rising again. He would soon return in glory to consummate the kingdom over which he would reign. He was "Lord and Christ" (Acts 2:36).

So even if the authors of the New Testament did not explicitly call Jesus God, they used titles which were bound to be so interpreted by the gentile Christians of the second generation. The problem then became to maintain the integrity of Jesus' humanity. As the professor of theology under whom I studied used to say, "Once you call Jesus God, it's hard to call him anything else."[2] Christian devotion assumes that his divinity would be immediately perceptible. Pious persons frequently say, "If Jesus walked into the room, I should fall on my knees before him." They forget that he would seem to them, as he did to the apostles, a quite ordinary man.

Instead, his manhood tends to be deified. It is felt that God's humanity must be of a special kind, a supermanhood, that should not be subject to the limitations of human nature, or even to some of its normal functions. But in that case Jesus would not be truly man. If divine power operated directly in any aspect of Jesus' humanity, if a divine prerogative overrode his human weakness, if divine wisdom intruded supernatural insights into his human mind, if the divine will determined any of his choices, then God had not assumed a real human nature.

The issue is the difference between an incarnation and a theophany. The latter means God takes some material form to reveal himself or to perform some action. In classical mythology the gods often appeared as men or women. No one for a moment considered that they had become human. They were merely acting a part temporarily for their own purposes. They were manifesting themselves through a human facade, not living a human life. The only real actor was the god.

In an incarnation there must be a full human actor. Even if God used a complete human nature with all its limitations and integrity as an object through which to express himself, that would still be a theophany. He would be acting as if he were a man; he would not be a man. In the latter there must be a human subject becoming itself through the succession of subjective aims. And God's relationship must be subject-to-subject, not subject-to-object.

But on the other hand, an incarnation cannot be simply a love relationship, even if it be raised to the highest intensity, between God and an independent human person. Jesus, in a sense different from all other men and women, must have been the human experience of the Logos, of God the Son, who was intimately and personally involved in it without impairing its human integrity. This is possible in terms of our concept of God which portrays him as both acting in human history and responding to it. The Logos is continually adapting the unchanging divine purpose to the circumstances of the creatures which they to some extent determine for themselves. He is in a constant subject-to-subject relationship with them. A God who is affected by and adjusts to all creatures can also be affected by and live through a particular human experience which he has made his own.

So I hope our paradigm can suggest how God and man in Jesus experienced a single human life. I shall come back to this at the end of the chapter. First, because of the age-long tendency of Christianity to deify Jesus' humanity, it is necessary to establish the integrity of his manhood. We must see what it meant for him to be truly man before we can go on to recognize him as truly God. By this line of approach we shall be following the sequence of the church's original experience of him. Jesus was first known as a man.

Truly Man

Today the theological emphasis has shifted to the humanity of Jesus.[3] Paradoxically, this has coincided with the abandonment by most scholars of the "quest for the historical Jesus," at least in the sense that they admit it is not possible to reconstruct his life from the gospels. Those accounts are not biographies in the modern sense but are collections of detached episodes. Insofar as these are based on the actual words and actions of Jesus, they have been colored by the church's experience of him as the risen Christ. In the process of transmission they have been further adapted and arranged so as to throw light on the problems of a local congregation in the various stages of the church's development from the original Jewish-Christians in Palestine, through the Greek-speaking Jewish-Christians throughout the empire, to the largely gentile church of the second century.[4]

Once this has been recognized, however, the influence of the resurrection and the special local concerns can be detected and discounted. In this way we can sometimes get behind the subsequent interpretation to the original act or teaching of Jesus. Each episode must be considered in itself and only a few can by their internal evidence be placed in a temporal sequence. Yet by careful analysis of them genuine historical material can be recovered. It is not as much as we should like, not enough to write a full biography. But we do get glimpses of Jesus during his ministry in Galilee and his final days in Jerusalem. They are sufficient to give an indication of his character, his message, and the impact he had on his contemporaries.

Because Jesus in his life on earth was first and foremost a man, I believe that one criterion for interpreting his acts, words, and character must be whether a truly human person could have thought and acted in that way. I recognize the danger of judging as consonant with human nature only what I can imagine myself thinking or doing. The same criterion might lead me to deny the exceptional attitudes and actions of many outstanding saints or sinners. Yet if we take Jesus' humanity seriously, we must apply some such test to the gospel records. This is especially important to counteract their tendency to glorify the events of Jesus' earthly life that resulted from their recognizing him as the risen Christ and the Son of God.

He must have been genetically a descendant of the human race and a man of the society, culture, and religion into which he was born and in which he was raised. He had to have all the limitations, not only of humanity in general, but also of the time, place, and world view in which he lived and expressed himself. The presuppositions of his thought included ignorance and misinterpretations of the past, misunderstandings of the present, and uncertainty as to the future.

Physically Jesus was a Palestinian Jew. There is not the slightest justification historically for portraying him as blond, blue-eyed, with a classical Greek physique. He was a hard-working Galilean peasant, with little education or culture even by his contemporary standards. His body was subject to all the usual ills. Since he knew poverty and hence undernourishment, he presumably was sick from time to time.

He had all the natural functions, including sex. As to how that was expressed in his life we have no information whatever. But as it was most unusual for a Jew to reach the age of about thirty without being married, a good guess, and it is only a guess, is that Jesus had had and had lost a wife before beginning his public ministry. Be that as it may, it is important not to think of him as having some kind of glorified body or a charmed human life.

Like any human infant, Jesus had to become a person. He started with the self-preserving natural impulses. By trial and error he had to learn which self-seeking actions were permissible and which had to be curbed. The criteria by which this was determined were the mores of his society and the standards of those who ministered to him. Both included selfishness and sin, corporate and individual. So Jesus' ego had the inherent self-centeredness that is inevitable in any human being and his superego was the interiorization of principles which were far from perfect. His was a normal human nature with all the inclinations toward self-indulgence and self-assertion. As Hebrews 4:15 puts it, he was "tempted in every way that we are."

This was necessary not only for the genuineness of his humanity, but also for the salvation he was to effect. The early fathers recognized that what Jesus did not assume he could not redeem. If God became man in a human nature that had been perfected in advance, he did not become one of us. He did not experience our condition; he did not feel our temptations; he did not refrain from committing our sins. In terms of the doctrine of original sin, he must have taken our fallen nature.[5] Today we can say that he had the usual tendencies toward selfishness that are inherent in the process of becoming a self and that are interiorized from the society to which a person learns to conform.

We must, I think, go further. He learned to love by first acting selfishly and thereby discovering its conflict with love. In other words, like Adam and Eve, and like every human being, he learned the evil of sin by sinning. He had the natural impulses and the desire to satisfy them. He felt frustrated and angry when he could not. To portray Jesus as curbing these perfectly from the start, with no lapses into their indulgence, is to dehumanize him into a stained-glass window saint. What has been said of sentimental ecclesiastical art is also true of much theology. We picture Jesus as neither God nor man.

This follows from our false concept of sin. We have trivialized it. We fault ourselves for minor breaches of the moral and spiritual rules we have made for ourselves or derived from the ideal of respectibility upheld by our society. We castigate ourselves for natural reactions, like flashes of anger, which surely are better expressed than subverted into lasting resentments. Like all Pharisees, we are busily "straining out gnats and swallowing camels" (Mt. 23:24). So we feel Jesus must have accomplished the ideal for which we strive, and have avoided all the lapses that are inevitable in a genuine human nature.

What then becomes of the assertion that he was "without sin"? The answer is twofold. First, when he came to see that a self-regarding action was a violation of love, that it injured another human being, he ceased indulging it. When he found an attitude he had derived from his culture to be in conflict with the call to love, he abandoned and denounced it. Insofar as he could discern the will of God — and in important decisions I believe he was so open to the Spirit that he could discern it — he chose to love. In that way "he learnt to obey through suffering," i.e., through self-restraint (Heb. 5:8).

His encounter with the Syrophoenician woman illustrates how Jesus could learn (Mk. 7:24ff).[6] That gentile asked him to heal her daughter. Jesus replied, "The children should be fed first, because it is not fair to take the children's food and throw it to the house-dogs." Even the word "house-dogs" cannot disguise the contempt and racism of that remark. Jesus was a Jew and shared their prejudice against the gentiles as part of the culture he had absorbed. Notice his statement, "It is not fair." He felt morally required to concentrate his efforts and his gifts on his fellow Jews. As he says in Matthew 15:24: "I was sent only to the lost sheep of the house of Israel." It was both his duty and his vocation to reject that gentile.

But she replied, "Ah yes, sir, but the house-dogs under the table can eat the children's scraps." Faced with such humility, persistence, and faith, Jesus became aware that the gentiles were also human beings who were loved by God and sought his love. They as well as the Jews were capable of responding to the kingdom that was already manifesting itself on earth. From them the demons could be cast out. Through that woman Jesus got a deeper insight into the outreach of God's love. He accepted it and acted upon it. Thus he continued to grow in maturity.

Second, Jesus' sinlessness was therefore an achievement not a gift. If he had been made perfect before he was born, his faithfulness and love would not have been a significant victory for humanity as we know it. It was because he conquered his human weaknesses and prejudices and the selfishness of his society by his self-determined preference of love that he was the second Adam who "to the fight and to the rescue came."[7] We are not redeemed by God's acting on our behalf in a concocted human nature. We are reunited to God because he became one of us in all our failings and overcame them by his human love which, at tremendous cost, was faithful even to death. In that lay his sinlessness.

Birth

Before we turn to the events of Jesus' ministry, we must consider the birth stories prefixed to the first and third gospels. There seem to be two stages of their development. The first is the assertion that Jesus was a descendant of David and was born in Bethlehem, in fulfillment of the prophecy of Micah 5:2. Both gospels provide genealogies of Joseph, which differ widely in details but trace his descent from David.

Matthew implies that Joseph and Mary were living in Bethlehem until after Jesus' birth, when Herod's attempt to kill the child forced them to flee to Egypt. On their return they decided it was safer to live in Galilee and so went to Nazareth, thereby justifying the description Nazarene, which seems to have been associated with Jesus from an early date. Luke places the home of Joseph and Mary in Nazareth. He gets them to Bethlehem for Jesus' birth by recalling a census, which actually took place several years later. For it he says everyone had to go to the place of his ancestral origin, a most unlikely procedure for which there is no historical precedent.

It was probably the Palestinian Jewish-Christians who were concerned to show that Jesus was the son of David and fulfilled the prophecies. So this was presumably the earlier stratum of the birth narratives. It should be noted, however, that in Mark 12:35ff Jesus is portrayed as denying that the Messiah was to be the son of David. That could be a still earlier form of apologetic for the fact that Jesus was born in Galilee, after the church had recognized him as the Christ.

John 7:41f is sometimes cited as indicating that the fourth evangelist did not think Jesus was descended from David or born in Bethlehem. I consider this more likely to be dramatic irony on his part, based on familiarity with at least the earlier stratum of the birth stories. It is the Jews who ask how Jesus could be the Messiah when he comes from Galilee instead of Bethlehem. John expects his readers to see in this an unwitting confirmation of Christ's status because Christians know the tradition that he was in fact born in the city of David. Paul explicitly refers to this tradition in Romans 1:3 when he says that Jesus "was a descendant of David."

Since the Davidic descent is traced through Joseph, the earlier form of the tradition presumably considered him to be Jesus' father. It is possible to claim that Jesus' descent could have been traced even through a foster father, but physical paternity would naturally be assumed unless stated to the contrary. Furthermore, there are indications of a tradition that Joseph was really the father of Jesus. Mark 6:3, in a significant number of instances to give grounds for thinking it may have been the original text, asks concerning Jesus, "Is not this the son of the carpenter and Mary?"[8]

John 6:42 quotes the Jews as exclaiming, "Surely this is Jesus son of Joseph. We know his father and mother." Here it is not likely to be dramatic irony, since the issue is not whether Jesus has fulfilled a messianic requirement, but how a local boy whom they know so well can make such exaggerated spiritual claims.

These positive indications are reinforced by the negative evidence that neither Mark nor John give any indication that Jesus was born of a virgin, nor do any other New Testament books except the first and third gospels. In their birth stories the assertion of the virgin birth has been superimposed on the earlier material. It probably comes from the Greek-speaking church since in Matthew 1:23 it rests on the fulfillment of the prophecy which is quoted as, "The virgin will conceive and give birth to a son and they will call him Emmanuel." The quotation is from the Septuagint, the Greek version of the Old Testament. In the original Hebrew of Isaiah 7:14 the word translated virgin was simply "a young woman."

The reference to Emmanuel and the next verse in Isaiah both show that the passage had been given messianic interpretation. That the Greek version could be taken to imply a miraculous conception was quite understandable, especially in a gentile environment where divine conception of children without a human father was a common myth. But although I think the idea arose in the Greek-speaking church, I question that it was derived from the pagan sources.

The Lucan birth stories indicate what seems to me to be the more likely source of the concept. In Luke 1 the conception of Jesus is carefully paralleled to that of John the Baptist. The miraculous elements in the latter's birth combine those of Isaac, Samson, and Samuel. "Elizabeth was barren and [she and Zechariah] were both getting on in years" (1:7). The Baptist's conception is as marvelous as those of the great Old Testament heroes. But a constant contention of the early church, required by the controversy and rivalry with John's disciples, was that Jesus was in all matters superior to him. What could be greater than conception by a barren woman past bearing? Obviously, conception by a virgin without a human father. And there was Isaiah 7:14f in the Greek translation of the Bible predicting just that of the Messiah.

In the early church the virgin birth of Christ was an easily credible miracle and a help in refuting the disciples of the Baptist. Today, if it is taken to have been a physical fact, it is not acceptable either biologically or theologically. We know too much of genetics to believe that Jesus could have been conceived without a human father. If Mary had become virginally pregnant, her child would have been genetically identical to her, reproducing her exactly. Jesus would then have been a woman. As far as I know, not even the most ardent feminists claim that. There must have been a male sperm in the conception. It must either have come from a human father or have been miraculously created by God for the purpose.

The second alternative raises the theological problem. The concept that God is constantly and consistently guiding the universe by acting through it, not by miraculously intruding into it, precludes the notion that he provided a male sperm out of nothing. But supposing he did. What would be the consequences for Jesus' human nature? One half of his genetic inheritance would have been derived not from mankind but from God. He would have been a semidivine being, half god, half man, not God incarnate in a real man descended genetically from the human race.

Jesus could be truly man only if he had a human father and mother. I believe that the theology of Chalcedon interpreted in the light of modern knowledge forces us to deny the physical possibility of the virgin birth despite its assertion in the gospel stories. In the last century evolution by natural selection forced intelligent Christians to abandon the historicity of the creation myth in Genesis. Today our knowledge of genetics demands a like repudiation of the historicity of the myth of the virginal conception of Christ.

The creeds do not have to be rewritten, however. The myth gives vivid expression to several theological truths, provided we keep in mind its mythical character. First, it indicates that through the action of the Holy Spirit the Logos was in a unique way related to the human nature of Jesus. At the end of this chapter I shall try to state that in terms of the paradigm I have been advocating.

Luke's story of the annunciation portrays Mary's acceptance of her vocation to be the mother of the Messiah (1:26ff). She probably did not think of it in those terms. But she was willing to accept the responsibility of raising a son to serve the Lord. She could do that because she herself was surrendered to his will. "I am the handmaid of the Lord," was not just her reply to the angel. It characterized her whole life. Her responsiveness underlines the significant truth that, when God became man, he did not thrust himself upon the human race. Mary's willingness to bear a son and give him to his vocation whatever it might be was the welcome that God needed.

Matthew's stories emphasize the truth that in Jesus the covenant with David was fulfilled, not only in the sense of realizing the Jewish hopes, but also in the form of reaching out to the gentiles. The visit of the magi gives dramatic form to the point made in the Book of Ruth. As David's great-grandmother was a Moabitess, so representatives of the gentiles come bearing gifts to worship the son of David in his cradle. When we recognize the origin and purpose of the birth stories in the church's developing understanding of the significance of Christ, we can the more fully accept and appreciate them.[9]

Vocation

The Baptist preached a baptism of repentance in preparation for the coming judgment in which the sons of Israel would be winnowed like wheat, the evil ones being destroyed in fire, and the good being led into the ultimate promised land. Baptism was an appropriate symbol of their acknowledgement that their guilt had made those who had

Abraham for their father (Mt. 3:9) no better than the gentiles. Up till then only converts to Judaism had been required to be baptized.

The repeated assertion that John did his baptizing on the far side of the Jordan (Mk. 1:4; Jn. 1:28; 3:26) leads me to think that part of the symbolism was that the penitents were to enter the kingdom by passing through that river, and that the mighty one who would lead them would be the second Joshua. As Jesus is the Greek form of that name, it was easy for the church to believe that the Baptist had recognized and designated Jesus to be the Messiah. In this way the relationship between the mission of the Baptist and the Christ could be given vivid legendary expression. Again, the account was spiritually true even though it did not happen just that way in historical fact.

Jesus was baptized by John, though unrecognized by him. The church would hardly have invented so embarrassing a story out of whole cloth. Its efforts to avoid the implication that John as the baptizer was superior to Jesus who accepted his baptism indicate the difficulty the church felt in the episode. But it was a genuine recollection of what had happened and in the end, as in so many other instances, the church found a way to make capital out of it. Jesus' messiahship had been recognized and hailed at the beginning of his ministry; indeed, according to Luke, while he was still in the womb (1:44).

Jesus was able penitently to accept John's baptism because he was aware of the selfishness which he had expressed in the process of becoming a self, and of some of the sins of his people in which he had to acquiesce because he lived among them. Since he had not been supernaturally endowed with a perfect nature, he could honestly admit his need for forgiveness. No explanation of why he accepted an "unnecessary" baptism of repentance needs to be devised.

The experience was for him the recognition of his call to begin a public ministry. At first he probably conceived it to be the support and continuance of the Baptist's preaching. Matthew 3:2 and 4:17 report that Jesus began to proclaim his message in the same words as John, "Repent, for the kingdom of heaven is close at hand." But before Jesus started on his mission he probably did retire into the wilderness prayerfully to consider the implications of his call. As a result, he came to see his vocation to be somewhat different in character from that of his predecessor.

Some commentators are doubtful about the authenticity of the account of Jesus' temptations. The highly formalized story, with the neatly applied scriptural quotations, has a homiletic ring. The recorded temptations are more likely to have been those of the early church—to use spiritual power for material ends, to depend on signs and wonders to reassure itself and win converts, and to compromise with worldy powers, especially in times of persecution.

Jesus may have felt similar temptations, but we could know of them only if he had told his disciples of his spiritual struggle. In the rest of the gospel there is no sign of Jesus' interest in his own spiritual experiences. If this is authentic, it is the only instance of autobiography. It becomes the more unlikely that it is when we notice that the presupposition of all the temptations is that Jesus considered himself to be the Messiah.

Whether Jesus ever thought of himself as the Christ is still a matter of lively debate. I personally have reached the conclusion that he did not in the sense of the superhuman Son of Man that Daniel 7:13f predicted would come "on the clouds of heaven." Nor did he consider himself a political Messiah who would lead a revolt against the Roman Empire. It is possible that Jesus applied the title to himself in the sense of a human agent who was to proclaim the imminence of the kingdom. But the difficulty of discriminating between that and the other two more popular forms of the concept make it unlikely that he used or accepted it.

Whether or not he thought of himself as the Christ, he surely did not view his vocation as the carrying out of a predetermined plan of salvation. He did not foresee that he would preach the coming of the kingdom for a year or so, ministering to those in need, and then go to Jerusalem to suffer and die. We have so overemphasized his divinity at the expense of his humanity that we think of God coming to carry out a prearranged program of which Jesus was fully aware from the start of his ministry or earlier.

In fact, the New Testament pushes the anticipation of the passion back to his infancy. In Luke 2:22ff Simeon recognizes Jesus as the savior and prophesies to his mother, "A sword will pierce your own soul too." A well-known picture of the holy family in Egypt portrays Jesus toddling toward his mother with arms outstretched so that his shadow forms a cross. Most people today would not put his awareness of his fate that early because it would be unnatural for a small child to have such knowledge of his future.

It is my contention that it is equally unnatural for Jesus to have had it as a grown man. Determining the future is a constant temptation to us. It is the way we try to control our destiny. So important is that to us that we feel there is something wrong with a teenager if he does not have a clear plan for the rest of his life. Schools provide vocational guidance to help him with his problem.

If I were to make a guess as to the nature of Jesus' temptations in the wilderness, among them I should include the desire to know what God intended him to be and how this was to be accomplished. If his temptations included the suggestion that he might be the Son of God in any unique or superhuman sense, his humility rejected it at once. Likewise, if he was tempted to worry about what suffering his vocation might entail, he left that for God to determine and reveal when the time came. His answer was the same as he commends to us, "Do not worry about tomorrow: tomorrow will take care of itself. Each day has enough trouble of its own" (Mt. 6:34).

In saying this, I do not mean to deny that Jesus constantly experienced a most intimate union with God. He called him Abba, the diminutive by which children expressed their affection to their fathers. Joachim Jeremias has found no instance in Jewish prayers of the use of that title in addressing God.[10] Apparently it originated with Jesus. But although it shows how close he felt to his heavenly Father, it does not indicate that he considered the relationship unique to himself. For he taught and expected his disciples to use the same form of address in their prayers.

Because Jesus was living a human life, he was not following a prearranged script. Neither he, nor for that matter God himself, could know in advance with exactly what circumstances he would be faced in the future. Self-determination means that we go from one occasion of becoming to another, influenced by past decisions but not fully determined by them. We must therefore live moment by moment, day by day. What our situation will be a week hence depends on thousands of becomings we and others will achieve between now and then. We cannot arrange them or plan them in advance. Jesus had to live his life in the same way. His also was the prayer of John Henry Newman:

> Keep thou my feet; I do not ask to see
> The distant scene; one step enough for me.

The suggestion that God himself did not know how Jesus' life was to be worked out in detail is shocking to us. For so long we have thought of God as an absolute, all-powerful manipulator of creation, running everything on a preordained plan, that we feel sure he sent Jesus to preach for a while, then to be arrested and condemned, to die and to rise again on the third day. But that is precisely the concept of God that is incredible if God is love. Instead, he gives creation its integrity to become itself. That is true to some slight degree of inanimate nature; it becomes self-conscious choice in mankind, and supremely in Jesus.

In the wilderness Jesus did ponder his vocation. He became convinced his ministry was to have a different quality from the Baptist's. Jesus was not an ascetic from the desert. As the son of Galilean peasants, he had grown up in close association with the soil and its people. He knew their needs and their longings, their weaknesses and their strengths, their sins and their virtues. He felt an overwhelming love for them and a deep kinship with them. He was not called to denounce their misdeeds in the aloof and judgmental thunderings of the Baptist. Rather, he was to move among the people, identifying with them, reaching out to them with the healing love of God.

He then set out to realize his vocation step by step. The gospels reflect the episodic character of his ministry. In many stories and sayings he is dealing with a specific situation or answering a particular question. Others that have lost their occasion in the process of transmission are better understood if they are not treated as general pronouncements. When the individual passages are examined in themselves, apart from the evangelist's framework, they give the impression that Jesus had neither a clearly developed system of thought nor a settled plan of action. As in his confrontation with the Syrophoenician woman, he had to discern God's will as he went along and improvise his response.

Ministry

For the Baptist the advent of the kingdom meant imminent judgment; for Jesus it was imminent hope. John believed the kingdom might be inaugurated at any moment by an outburst of God's wrath against the unrepentant; Jesus saw the kingdom already at work in the manifestation of God's healing and reconciling love. John issued a call to repentance in order to be saved; Jesus demanded a change of heart in order to become loving.

When Jesus expected the kingdom to come is hard to determine, not only because his concept has been overlaid by the various adjustments which the church made to the delay of the parousia, but also because Jesus himself during the course of his ministry may have had to change his ideas as to when it would occur. If the words, "You will not have gone the round of the towns of Israel before the Son of Man comes" (Mt. 10:23), reflect something Jesus said, he apparently expected the kingdom to come while he was ministering in Galilee. When that hope was disappointed, he went to Jerusalem. Details of the passion narrative suggest that he expected it to come before his death.

Distinction must be made between the final consummation—the coming of the kingdom at the end of time—and its inauguration which Jesus seems to have believed was occurring through his ministry. His miracles were evidence that it was breaking in. "If it is through the Spirit of God that I cast devils out, then know that the kingdom of God has overtaken you" (Mt. 12:28). This refers to the cures of physical as well as mental disorders, since many sicknesses were attributed to possession by evil spirits. Thus the man's son whom the disciples could not heal while Jesus was on the mount of the transfiguration is said to have had a spirit of dumbness, but the description of the symptoms points to epilepsy (Mk. 9:17f).

The sickness that results from demoniac possession is in turn connected with sin in Mark 2:1ff. It seems probable that 2:10f is a comment inserted by Mark to attribute authority as the Son of Man to Jesus. When these verses are deleted, the point of the episode becomes the equation of "your sins are forgiven" with "get up and walk." To forgive is to heal and to heal is to cast out demons. By inspiring penitence and faith Jesus was able to rescue people from their slavery to physical, mental, and spiritual evil.

The evidence of the kingdom did not lie in the uniqueness of Jesus' miracles. He himself argued the exact opposite when he defended himself, "If it is through Beelzebul that I cast out devils, through whom do your own experts cast them out?" (Mt. 12:27). Jesus also rebuked John for stopping "a man casting out devils" in Jesus' name because he was not one of the disciples (Lk. 9:49f). Successful exorcisms were bound to be frequent in a society that had to attribute most of its ills to demons. Jesus rejoiced in his miracles only because they validated his message. The penitence and faith that made his healings possible were the response he was seeking. The outreach of the kingdom had penetrated another heart.

It is not possible to review in detail Jesus' teaching about the kingdom of God. I can touch on only a few points. First, there is the statement: "Unlike the scribes, he taught them with authority" (Mk. 1:22).That comment expresses a truth about Jesus, even granting that he did not think of himself as the messianic Son of Man. For he does seem frequently to have introduced his teaching with the clause, "I tell you." In fact, he may have spoken in the first person more often than appears in the gospels, if either the evangelists or the tradition they were using substituted Son of Man for the personal pronoun.

In the sermon on the mount Jesus is portrayed as explicitly contrasting his teaching with that of the law. That Jesus was the new Moses giving a new law from a new Sinai was presumably a concept devised by Matthew. Yet it enshrines a truth. Jesus does seem to have claimed authority to reveal God's will in his own name. His method of teaching differed both from the scribes, who based their pronouncements not on their own insights but on the law which they were merely interpreting, and from the ancient prophets, who consistently prefaced their oracles with, "It is Yahweh who speaks."

Jesus deliberately challenged the accepted standards. He refused to make the law, carefully interpreted and applied to each situation, the criterion for determining exactly the will of God. He saw this as an undue limitation of the call to love. A good example was the concept of *corban* (Mk. 7:11ff). If a person did not want to give his parents something they needed, he could shirk his duty by declaring the thing *corban*, that is, dedicated to God. The point Jesus made again and again is that there is no limit to the duty to love both God and man, and that the two obligations are simply two aspects of the same love.

The parable was a characteristic form of Jesus' teaching. It must not be confused with allegory, which uses symbolic figures to enact a moral or supernatural drama. A parable, on the other hand, is a story of everyday life used to illustrate a particular point. The characters are themselves, not symbols of someone or something else. The details of the story are designed to give it realistic vividness. They do not necessarily have spiritual significance in themselves nor are they to be taken as having Jesus' endorsement. To argue that the parable of the laborers in the vineyard (Mt. 20:1ff) teaches the principle of equal wages for all is as mistaken as to maintain that Jesus approved of dishonest stewards who cheated their employers (Lk. 16:1ff).

But the parables are not merely bland tales illustrating moral platitudes. Smart has correctly called attention to the prophetic parables of the Old Testament.[11] The technique was to get the hearer to judge a situation in which he was not involved and, when he had condemned a certain action, to show how he had done the same. An example is Nathan's story about the rich man who took the poor man's lamb, by which David was led unwittingly to condemn himself for taking Bathsheba and killing her husband Uriah (2 Sam. 12:1ff).

So Jesus used the parable of the two debtors to induce his Pharisee host to recognize why he was less loving than the penitent woman with a bad name (Lk. 7:41ff). The story of the good Samaritan (Lk. 10:29ff) makes the lawyer see that his careful defining of one's neighbor is likewise an avoidance of love. If we knew the circumstances in which other parables were originally told, we might detect a similar technique in some of them.

Jesus' call to love is to be expressed primarily in love of neighbor, for as 1 John 4:20 says, "A man who does not love the brother that he can see cannot love God, whom he has never seen." It should be so natural for us to give ourselves unstintingly to our neighbor and to encourage his development of his highest potential that we are unaware of having done so. This is the point of the last judgment (Mt. 25:31ff), which incidentally is an instance when Jesus did use an allegory for his purpose. He is not just saying that the good will be rewarded and the bad punished. His contribution is that both the good and bad will be surprised to learn that it was the Son of Man whom they had been serving or neglecting in the least of his brothers.

In several sayings and parables Jesus affirmed that the last will be first in the kingdom, whereas the first in this world will be last. In the parables of the lost sheep, the lost coin, and the prodigal son, he declared God's forgiving love for those who had wandered astray. In fact, as someone has pointed out, he portrays God as primarily interested in the least, the last, and the lost. Jesus demonstrated this in deed as well as in word to such an extent that he was called a friend of tax brokers and sinners. He attracted them because he convinced them they would find acceptance in God. Contrary to popular opinion, forgiveness precedes and stimulates penitence, not vice versa. An example is Zacchaeus who was converted because—not before—Jesus visited him (Lk. 19:1ff).

How successful was Jesus' mission? At first he may have had a considerable following among the "poor," the devout humble folk to whom no one paid much attention. But the leaders, the learned, and the well-to-do were opposed to him from the start. In view of Herod's fear of insurrection, it is doubtful if Jesus could have attracted large crowds with any frequency without having been arrested. As it was, Herod seems to have been getting uneasy about him (Lk. 13:31ff). He did, however, have a group of disciples, some of whom traveled with him fairly constantly; others, I suspect, intermittently. It is interesting that the group included women, who played a larger role in his movement than one would expect in so male-dominated a society (Lk. 8:1-3).

There is some evidence that Jesus also had Jerusalem disciples. At least he had friends in that vicinity. Mark mentions Simon the leper in Bethany (14:3) and Joseph of Arimathaea (15:43). The arrangements made for getting a donkey to ride into Jerusalem (11:2ff) and for the Passover supper (14:13ff) indicate that Jesus knew persons whom the Galileans did not. Luke adds two disciples who lived in Emmaus (24:13) and Mary and Martha of Bethany (10:38f). John tells of their brother Lazarus (11:1), of Nicodemus (3:1), and of the Beloved Disciple, who had connections in the holy city (18:15).

If Jesus ever had a period of real popularity, I do not believe it could have lasted long. The supposed triumphal entry into Jerusalem cannot be cited as evidence to the contrary. That Jesus got hold of a donkey in order to fulfill the prophecy of Zechariah 9:9 (cf. Mt. 21:4f) is out of character. It presupposes Jesus considered himself to be the Messiah and was deliberately proclaiming it, albeit in its humblest form. Furthermore, in view of the tensions in the city, which had the Romans on the alert, if Jesus' arrival had provoked such a popular welcome, he would have been arrested and executed on the spot.

The humility that episode dramatizes was expressed, I suspect, by Jesus' entry unnoticed and almost unknown. He may, of course, have borrowed a donkey. If so, it was probably because he was tired, or ill, or perhaps had "dashed his foot against a stone." Once the church had recognized him as the Messiah, such motives would no longer be considered appropriate. So the donkey became the fulfillment of Zechariah's prophecy.

If Jesus and his disciples were expecting the kingdom to come soon after their entrance into Jerusalem, that would account for the jubilation associated with the episode. But the excitement would have been theirs, not that of the crowd. The shout, "Blessings on the coming kingdom of our father David!" (Mk. 11:10) is an anticipation of the parousia that need not imply hailing Jesus as the Messiah.

Truly God

In portraying Jesus as an ordinary man, who so considered himself and was so considered by his contemporaries, I do not mean to imply that he did not make a tremendous impression on those who became his disciples. They saw in him a depth of faith and hope and love they had never known in any other person. In his gospel they found the power to repent and believe in the coming of the kingdom. They were prepared (they thought) to commit their lives to him even to death. Their desertion in Gethsemane is testimony to the confidence they had in him. His arrest was a shock that destroyed everything they had come to believe and hope. Their panic at that moment was inevitable, but it did not prevent them from ultimately giving him their lives and their deaths.

So, in affirming that he was fully a man, we also declare that he was a supreme instance of a human being. He was not superhuman or semidivine. This is essential, not just that mankind can claim him for its own, but so that God could become truly incarnate in him.[12]

As we rightly emphasize his humanness, however, we must be careful not to go to the opposite extreme and deny or make impossible the fact that he is also truly God. If we do, let us make no mistake, we destroy the basis of Christian faith and hope. It is not enough that Jesus be a good man—if you will, a perfect man—united to God as is every other man but, because of his responsiveness, fulfilling God's will and manifesting God's love as had no other man. That would be much, but it is not enough. That would be man acting for God, not God living as a man.

Somehow we must find a way of relating the Logos to Jesus without interfering with the normal operation of his human nature. As in all other men and women, his earthly life must have been a series of occasions of becoming in which his subjective aims incorporated data from its past becoming and the surrounding environment in response to the lure of the Logos. In and through the sequence of subjective aims he developed his human self, with the specific characteristics we have noted in this chapter. None of this could have been disturbed or manipulated by a further intrusion of the Logos.

For Jesus, as for all other creatures that have an internal principle of unity, his subjective aims were inaugurated, empowered, and motivated by an initiating aim. That is normally the work of the Holy Spirit. I suggest that in our paradigm we can indicate the special relationship of the incarnation by maintaining that in Jesus the Spirit allowed the Logos to be the initiating aim. The Logos himself took personal responsibility for the series of subjective aims and the human person that developed through them in the life of Jesus. In that instance the Logos not only adjusted the lure of the proffered potential, as he does for every creature; he also shared in initiating the impulse toward it.

I do not mean that the Logos controlled Jesus' subjective aims. The gap between the initiating and subjective aims was there for him as for any human being. He was free to determine for himself as man how he would respond to the initiating impulse, and to what extent he would rise up to his potential. Jesus could resist the former and fall short of the latter. But because the Logos initiated the process he was personally involved in it from the start. He could experience the becomings as his own human life.

For what is needed is not that the Logos could control Jesus' life but that he was committed to it. It was his human experience and he took the full risk inherent in being a man. He moved from one occasion of becoming to the next with no advance knowledge of whether there would be another occasion or of what influences other beings would have upon it. He was at the mercy of all other creatures in his relationships with them. Above all, he was constantly open to the temptation to reject his highest potential in the interest of a more self-satisfying alternative, for Jesus could have chosen the latter, not only in matters of little moment, but in vital issues between love and self-gratification. The Logos was committed to the choice in advance. What a risk for God to take!

Furthermore, Jesus, in his human mind, could not have been aware of his special relationship to the Logos. If the Logos was to experience a truly human life, Jesus could not think of himself as the Logos living it. That would have falsified his humanness. The very purpose of the incarnation required that he consider himself to be no more than a human son of his beloved Abba.

Perhaps this analogy will help. Suppose a penologist felt he ought to experience being a prisoner in order to understand their needs. If he arranged to be locked up, even though the wardens and prisoners did not know who he was, it would not work. He would not be undergoing the frustration and resentment of a man imprisoned against his will with no possibility of release until his sentence was completed. The penologist could not help being aware that he was in prison of his own volition and could get out when he wished. He would know the situation was faked.

But suppose someone who knew of the penologist's desire was able to arrange that he be arrested, tried, and convicted without his knowing that it had been contrived. Then he would find himself in prison on the same terms as his fellow prisoners. Note, however, that the strategem is effective precisely to the extent that the penologist does not suspect his imprisonment to be faked.

The same applies to the incarnation. Only if the man Jesus did not entertain the slightest suspicion that he was in any unique way related to God, or that he was in a superhuman sense his agent, could he be for the Logos an experience of a human life. There could be no fakery in the setup if truly God was to be truly man.

But they must also be truly one in the sense that God was irrevocably committed to that human life for good or ill. God had to run the risk of failing to love in the face of temptations to selfishness. God had to run the risk of compromising with evil when it seemed to demand more than he could muster in the way of resistance. God had to bear the consequences of evil that became more and more virulent in its attack the more it was resisted. God had to accept, endure, and forgive the response of hate that the spiritual leaders of his people increasingly made to his love.

God had to see his hopes for the coming of the kingdom postponed and finally fading into despair. God had to acknowledge the total failure of his mission and see his most faithful followers flee in bewilderment, panic, and defeat. God had to be arrested, condemned as a criminal, exposed to the most shameful as well as the most painful death. And in the end, the crucified God had to suffer desertion by God without understanding why it happened and without expecting to rise on the third day.

All this had to happen in such a way that the Logos could not extricate himself from the situation if anything went wrong. Had Jesus failed in love, God could not have repudiated him and tried again with another human nature. God's own human nature would have failed. I hope my paradigm provides a means of conceiving this. It does not, of course, explain it theologically or psychologically. All I offer is the picture, which I think relates the Logos to a human nature in a way that makes it truly and uniquely his human nature, without making it more or less than human.

Chapter 6 / **REDEMPTION**

In the second gospel the supreme title for Jesus is Son of God. Not only does Mark use it in the opening verse and at the end of the crucifixion (15:39) but also Jesus is so recognized by the demons (3:11; 5:7), in the divine proclamation at the baptism (1:11), and at the transfiguration (9:7). The title had its dangers. Apparently in the community that Mark was addressing the idea that Jesus was the divine man, a superhuman being beyond suffering and other human weaknesses, was already taking hold. To counter that, Mark emphasized the ordeal Jesus had to undergo precisely because he was the Son of God.

This is most clearly expressed in the three predictions of the passion, which may well be Mark's own compositions. The first follows Peter's confession of Jesus as the Christ (8:30ff). The second (9:30f;cf. 9:12) follows the transfiguration, where the Father designates Jesus as his beloved Son after he has been discussing his coming "exodus" through death (Lk. 9:31). The third follows Jesus' promise of reward to those who renounce all for his sake (Mk. 10:29ff) and introduces the passage in which he tells them that true discipleship will involve sharing his cup and baptism of suffering, and his life of service which he will give "as a ransom for many" (10:35ff).

In this, Mark is rightly interpreting Jesus' life and death in the light of the resurrection and in terms of the experience and problems of his church. He gave the essential truth about Jesus a clear and vivid expression which we greatly need and for which we should be profoundly grateful. At the same time, we must recognize that historically Jesus could not have accomplished the very things that Mark has correctly attributed to him if he had spoken, or even thought, in the manner described.

Had the disciples been told in advance that Jesus was destined to be condemned and killed, and that he would rise again on the third day, they would hardly have panicked in terror at his arrest and gone into hiding until, to their obvious surprise, they experienced his resurrection. And Jesus' endurance of suffering and death would not have been authentic had he known that he was merely acting out a preordained plan which involved only an apparent defeat that would be followed at once by vindication and victory.

The church itself did not believe that. The agony in the Garden of Gethsemane and the cry of abandonment on the cross, both of which have their roots in the earliest strata of the tradition — note the Aramaic words in Mark's accounts of them (14:36; 15:34) — are testimony that the Jewish-Christian church in Palestine believed that Jesus faced his arrest and death with genuine fear and bewilderment.

It must be admitted, however, that it is hard to see how the account of the spiritual struggle in Gethsemane can be accurate in its details. The only three possible witnesses were sleeping and Jesus awoke them just before his arrest. He did not have time to tell them of his agonized prayer even if he had been inclined to do so; and the recounting of his personal relationship with his Father was not characteristic of him. Yet the disciples could have been aware of his emotional distress, and I believe it has been rightly interpreted in the story that has come down to us. The account is true in the ultimate sense of that word.

Let us look at the situation in which Jesus found himself. We do not know just why Jesus had come to Jerusalem. The gospels, looking back on what was accomplished by his final visit to the holy city, are convinced that he went there in order to die, and that he deliberately challenged the authorities by his triumphal entry and other actions. I cannot believe that Jesus had such advance knowledge of God's plan of salvation. Alternative motives can only be guessed. The threat of arrest by Herod may have been a factor. The opposition of local leaders in Galilee may have been another. Jesus may have thought that his message would have a better reception by the more learned rabbis and the divinely ordained rulers of Israel.

Or he may have gone to Jerusalem to keep the Passover as usual, except that perhaps this time the kingdom would come in its fullness. If he had first looked for it in Galilee, his disappointment may have led him to conclude that Jerusalem was the place to expect it. If so, he felt obliged to proclaim his gospel one last time in the temple, the spiritual center of God's people, and make the final plea for their repentance. But now in Gethsemane, when he might be arrested any moment, the kingdom still had not arrived. His prayer could have been that it come before his death.

It did not take any supernatural insight into a preordained divine plan for Jesus to fear that he would soon be arrested. The cleansing of the temple probably occurred, though I doubt that Jesus actually led the mob that drove out the merchants and moneychangers. If he had been that conspicuous, he would surely have been arrested at once, by the temple guard if not by the Romans. My guess is that, perhaps in answer to a question about the corruptions of the temple trade—the exorbitant prices for acceptable sacrificial victims and the unfair rates of exchange—Jesus said something like, "Does not scripture say, 'My house will be called a house of prayer for all the peoples'? But you have turned it into a robbers' den" (Mk. 11:17). The crowd could then have taken it up and passed on, "He calls it a robbers' den," and incited more and more indignant agreement, until the mob on its own began to take violent action.

In that case, the authorities would not have known immediately who had been the instigator, and Jesus would not have been seized forthwith. But an investigation would eventually have revealed that he was to some degree responsible. The next step would be to sound him out. The question about the tribute money (Mk. 12:13ff) must have been asked in Jerusalem, for Galilee paid its taxes to Herod. So also the Sadducees could only have questioned him there because they were the temple party (Mk. 12:18ff). But Jesus parried their questions sufficiently to prevent them from getting direct evidence against him and, mindful of the mob action he had already provoked, the authorities were hesitant about arresting him in the temple.

That is where Judas was useful. If, as the tradition affirms, Jesus' death occurred at the time of the Passover, Jerusalem and its environs were full of pilgrims from all over the world. They were sleeping on the housetops, in the streets, and in the fields around the city. There were, of course, no outside lights except such as could be carried by hand. To find a particular person in that crowd by night it was necessary to know just where to look. Only one of Jesus' own party, who knew where he was accustomed to spend the night, could serve as a guide. I see no reason, therefore, to doubt the tradition that one of his disciples betrayed him.

Jesus was aware of Judas' treachery. It is easy to sense when an intimate friend has become an enemy. The gratuitous account of how Jesus arranged for the place to hold the last supper in such a way that only two of his disciples would know where it was and they only when they had been led there by a stranger (Mk. 14:13ff) indicates that Jesus wanted to prevent one of his party from causing the meal to be interrupted with his arrest. But since Judas had subsequently left the group, Jesus was fully expecting that he would be seized when he went to the place where he usually spent the night.

This was a matter of deep concern to him, but not I think because he dreaded the physical pain that might be inflicted on him. He expected to be arrested by the soldiers of the temple guard. Presumably he would eventually be tried before the Sanhedrin. He can hardly have hoped to convince them of the legitimacy of his message. So they would probably take action to stop his preaching, either by flogging him with the "forty stripes save one" or even by stoning him to death as a false prophet. He had no reason, as far as I can see, to anticipate that they would hand him over to the Romans to crucify him. It was not, therefore, the fear of that horrible and shameful death that caused his agony at Gethsemane. I think other grounds can be suggested for it.

Rejection

To begin with, I think Jesus was afraid that he would again be disappointed as to when the kingdom would come. Would it perhaps be delayed until after his death? In that case, "When the Son of Man comes, will he find any faith on earth?" (Lk. 18:8). I believe Jesus distinguished between himself and the heavenly Son of Man who was to come and would welcome those who had responded to Jesus. Notice the pronouns he uses in Luke 12:8: "I tell you, if anyone openly declares himself for *me* in the presence of men, the Son of Man will declare *himself* for him in the presence of God's angels."

The Son of Man will gather into his kingdom those who are prepared to receive it. But who would they be? Had even Jesus' closest disciples understood his message? Were they aware of the urgency of the issue? Had they who were still wrangling about who would take precedence in the kingdom grasped its characteristics enough to recognize and enter it if he were not there to lead them into it? Their sleeping when he asked them to watch with him in that time of crisis was strong evidence to the contrary.

What was the nature of the messianic kingdom that Jesus expected? Here I find Baker's conjecture interesting.[1] He points out that the kingdom of love as described by Jesus seems to presuppose that life will continue on earthly lines, but far more of loving self-sacrifice will be demanded than is currently being achieved. Jesus' moral teaching is not an interim ethic, a mere holding the line until the final judgment and a heavenly kingdom terminate our terrestrial experience.

The Baptist gave a true interim ethic when he instructed those who came to him to carry on as they were. Even the tax brokers and soldiers were to continue in their jobs, but to operate honestly and considerately (Lk. 3:10ff). Paul gives the same kind of advice in 1 Corinthians 7:29ff. One should behave properly, of course, but "those who have to deal with the world should not become engrossed in it. I say this because the world as we know it is passing away."

Jesus' description of the kingdom has a different tone. I do not think this is entirely due to the adaptation of his teaching to the delay of the parousia and to the needs of the church during the possibly long interval before its coming. The evangelists, especially Luke, have so reinterpreted Jesus' gospel. But in its original proclamation there was no time for a long earthly sojourn while awaiting the parousia. "The kingdom of God is near. I tell you solemnly, before this generation has passed away all will have taken place" (Lk. 21:31f).

The this-worldly element in Jesus' teaching cannot, therefore, be ascribed to his legislating for "the church militant here on earth." He may have used this-worldly examples to give a vivid description of the quality of love that characterizes the kingdom. But when he says we are to forgive our brother not seven times but seventy times seven, he is not really anticipating that our present earthly existence will last that long.

Baker's thesis follows a different line. He holds that Jesus' concept was that the parousia would begin with an earthly millennium, the reign of the Messiah on earth for a thousand years with those who were prepared to receive him. Baker says that Jesus feared that none of his disciples had understood his message and that, if he were about to be put to death, he would have accomplished nothing. He could not even accept death as a martyrdom that would enhance his teaching if, in fact, no one understood it. His disciples would conclude that he had been mistaken and any hopes he had aroused would soon be forgotten as unrealized and unrealizable (cf. Lk. 24:19ff).

I should put it slightly differently. Whether Jesus expected an earthly millennium or used this-worldly images to indicate the love that characterized the kingdom, he believed himself called to prepare people to enter it, and felt misgivings that even his closest followers would not be ready to do so unless he were there to guide them. So I suggest his prayer in Gethsemane was that either the parousia come at once or that he be spared long enough to lead his disciples into it.

But with all his agonizing fears for them, he still felt he had to leave the issue in God's hands. He had proclaimed the gospel openly and was prepared to defend it openly. It was his duty to stand by his guns. To save himself by running away would put his own safety above the integrity of his commitment to his proclamation. The prophets' vocation in Israel was to stand firm in the face of inevitable persecution. But at least their message had survived. From what he knew of his disciples he had grave fears that his message would not. It took all the will power he could muster to remain faithful.

He was arrested by the temple guard led by Judas. Some argue that Pilate himself had Jesus seized by his own soldiers, tried and executed him without the Jewish authorities having any part in the proceedings. It is true that the evangelists are all concerned to throw the principal responsibility for Jesus' death on the Jews. Since the communities for whom the evangelists were writing lived in the empire and were under the threat of persecution by it, it is understandable that they should want to portray Pilate as having been misinformed by the Jews, or even forced to accede to their demands in order to keep the peace, despite his recognition that Jesus was innocent. By the same token, the evangelists were saying, the Jews who, especially after A.D. 70, were actively hostile to Christians and frequently caused them to be arrested as insurgents, were accusing them falsely. But that bias of the evangelists can be conceded without going to the opposite extreme and attributing to them the total invention of the Jews' involvement.

The disciples may have known little of what happened to Jesus after his arrest, but some of them were with him when it took place and would have known whether he was seized by Jewish or Roman soldiers. Furthermore, I believe there is a genuine recollection behind the story of Peter's denial. Why should the church have invented it? It is emphasized by all the evangelists and always placed at the high priest's house. It is in character for Peter to have lingered for a while in the background after the others had fled, until he himself was challenged and threated with arrest.

With his departure in heartbroken grief, the Galileans lost contact with the proceedings against Jesus. I am inclined to agree with those who think that soon after they fled they left Jerusalem and headed for home. This would account for the confusion as to what happened to Jesus while he was in the hands of the Jewish authorities.

It is extremely unlikely that a meeting of the Sanhedrin could have been convened. It was forbidden to judge a capital offense at night and, if it was during the Passover time, it would have been difficult, not to say impious, to have assembled many of its members. A good possibility is that the high priest and his immediate advisers decided that it was dangerous to delay until after the Passover ceremonies in order to try Jesus before the Sanhedrin. Instead, they would hand him over to Pilate.

The activities of Jesus and his followers could be interpreted as a threat to the Roman peace. Pilate was sufficiently sensitive to the danger of an uprising that he would need little evidence to convince him that one was threatened. He would have no scruples against putting Jesus to death even on the Passover itself, if that feast had already begun the evening before. Best of all, he would undoubtedly use crucifixion as the form of execution. That, for a Jew, was the ultimate in a shameful death, since public nudity was to be avoided at all costs and the cross would bring Jesus under the curse of the law on those who were hanged on a tree (Dt. 21:23).

The high priest may have summoned the leaders of the parties in the Sanhedrin to his house in order to inform them of the policy he had determined upon and the reasons for it. With their acquiescence the high priest had Jesus taken to Pilate the next morning. He made sure that Pilate appreciated the seriousness of the charge against Jesus and the desirability of his execution without delay, and left him to his fate.

We can discount the evangelists' picture of the Jews shouting for Jesus' death and hounding Pilate to condemn him. Such behavior would hardly have been tolerated at a Roman trial and certainly would not have influenced Pilate if it occurred. The truth is that we have no firsthand evidence of what happened before Pilate. Presumably there were no disciples present, if for no other reason than that the pretorium was out of bounds for devout Jews during the Passover. It should not surprise us, therefore, if the accounts deviate from what is otherwise known of Roman procedure.

So we cannot assess to what extent the famed Roman justice operated in Jesus' case. He was presented to Pilate as an insurrectionist and the cleansing of the temple was probably attributed to him as evidence. The Jews were emphatic in their condemnation of him and, so far as we know, no one defended him against the charge. He may not have tried to defend himself even if he was given the opportunity. But Pilate may have condemned him summarily as an insignificant but potentially dangerous troublemaker who had better be disposed of quickly.

Although I have already questioned the alleged participation of the Jews in the trial, one dramatic episode deserves special attention. It is the demand that Barabbas be released instead of Jesus. Scholars insist that there is not a shred of evidence that Roman governors were expected, let alone required, to release a prisoner on a local feast day. Such a custom is especially unlikely in Judea. For Pilate to be induced to release a prisoner already condemned for insurrection in place of a man only accused of that offense and whom he is supposed to have thought innocent is something we can be sure did not happen.

Where did the story come from? The name Barabbas is an anomaly. It means son of (*bar*) the father (*abba*). Since Abba was uniquely Jesus' appelation of the Father, Barabbas would seem to signify precisely this relationship. I find myself wondering whether the origin of the story is not to be found in an early gnostic attempt to protect Christ as the Son of God from involvement in Jesus' suffering and death. Barabbas, the Son of God the Father, who had been revealing himself in Jesus, is released before the human Jesus is condemned and crucified. If so, someone in the tradition, perhaps Mark himself (15:6ff), has used the story both to dramatize the Jews' guilt and to emphasize the fact that Jesus truly suffered, though undeservedly, the punishment of an insurrectionist and a murderer.

Calvary

Pilate condemned Jesus to death. The scourging was, as Mark rightly implies, the normal preliminary to a crucifixion. Luke's suggestion that Pilate proposed the flogging as a substitute is part of that evangelist's apologia for him. John reflects the same idea when he says that Pilate presented Jesus to the Jews after he had been scourged and mocked, in one final effort to save him (19:1ff).

The mocking is mentioned by all four evangelists, but in Luke it is attributed to Herod, a Jewish puppet ruler, not to the Roman soldiers. Efforts to find precedence for it have not been too successful. Its origin may be an attempt to show how Jesus' enemies misunderstood his messianic role. The title on the cross may have a similar significance. The first three gospels also have Jesus mocked by the servants of the high priest, who assumed that he was claiming to be a clairvoyant.

Criminals were required to carry the crossbar to the place of execution. Jesus, we are told, proved incapable of doing so and Simon of Cyrene was compelled to carry it for him (Mk. 15:21). Mark's naming of Simon's sons has led some to conclude that they were known to a local church that preserved this tradition as their recollection. Its partial corroboration of Jesus' inability to carry his cross leads us to ask why he could not. He was a strong peasant used to hardship. It is true that the scourging was a terrible experience, leaving the back raw and the body quivering with pain. But despite it most criminals were able to struggle to the place of their execution dragging their crossbars. Why not Jesus?

I see his weakness to be due not to physical causes but to the agonizing uncertainty that he experienced in Gethsemane. He still could not believe that his death before the parousia was really God's will, since it meant the utter failure of his mission and might even indicate that he had been totally misguided. His spiritual reluctance expressed itself by making it almost physically impossible for him to go to Calvary.

The mourning women and Jesus' answer to them give an opportunity to predict the destruction of Jerusalem (Lk. 23:27ff). Other details are mentioned because they were seen as fulfillment of Old Testament prophecies. Whether they were invented for that purpose or assumed to have happened because they were customary we have no way of knowing. The offer of drugged wine is based on a known act of charity by the women of the city. We are told Jesus was crucified between two thieves. He "was reckoned among transgressors" (Is. 53:12).[2] The soldiers threw dice for his clothes: "They divide my garments among them; they cast lots for my clothing" (Ps. 22:17). The victim's garments were the perquisite of the soldiers.

The spectators mocked and reviled him. "They stare and gloat over me" (Ps. 22:17; cf. 22:7-8), an easy thing for the bystanders to do because the victim's body was lifted only a short distance off the ground. It would seem that his arms were stretched out along the crossbar and tied tightly to it. A peg driven into the upright served as a saddle. The entire weight of the body therefore fell on the armpits and crotch. The victim was writhing continuously in a vain effort to relieve the agony. Nails were sometimes added to help restrain him. "They pierce my hands and my feet" (Ps. 22:16). The picture of Jesus hanging with calm dignity on the cross ignores and falsifies the real horror of that form of execution.

There were also the swarms of insects and the burning heat of the sun. That Jesus should have called out in thirst is quite possible. "My mouth is dried out like a potsherd; my tongue sticks to the roof of my mouth" (Ps. 22:15). The soldiers' sour wine was at hand in case anyone was moved to moisten his lips. "When I was thirsty, they gave me vinegar to drink" (Ps. 69:23).

The more miraculous items have symbolic meaning. The darkness at noon and the earthquake emphasize the cosmic solemnity of the event. The rending of the temple veil indicates that a new access to God has been opened, one not available under the old covenant. The holy men who rise from the dead anticipate the resurrection of which Christ is the first fruits. The words from the cross reported in John should also be taken as highly symbolic, as are the refraining from breaking Jesus' legs and the piercing of his side with a lance.

It is unlikely that anyone heard and remembered what, if anything, Jesus said when he was dying. But the words recorded in the first three gospels have special significance. Luke 23:34 tells us that Jesus prayed for the forgiveness of those who crucified him. All we know of his character and teaching leads us to believe that this must have been his attitude toward them. It is one of those inspired interpretations by which the real spiritual truth is revealed.

The story of the penitent thief (Lk.23:39ff) gives dramatic expression to important aspects of the reconciliation that was in fact accomplished on Calvary. It was after Jesus prayed for forgiveness of his enemies that the thief found the power to cease reviling him and to repent of his crimes. When he asked Jesus to remember him, he was immediately accepted, forgiven, and assured of eternal joy. Our understanding of the meaning of Christ's redeeming work would be poorer without that beautiful legend.

Mark 15:34 tells us, "Jesus cried out in a loud voice, '*Eloi, Eloi, lama sabachthani?*' which means, 'My God, my God, why have you deserted me?'" Those are the opening words of Ps.22, with which so many details of the crucifixion are associated. Whether Jesus actually said them or not, they are a profound insight into the deepest aspect of Calvary. They point to what I believe must have been Jesus' experience when faced with death.

The fear he had in Gethsemane that he might die before the parousia and that all he had worked for would be lost was proving justified. He felt God had abandoned him and he could not see why, unless his conviction that he was called to proclaim the kingdom had been mistaken. Instead of acting and teaching in God's name, had he been promulgating an error? Instead of the faithful and obedient son of his beloved Abba, had he been a deluded fanatic? God's desertion of him, leaving him to die in agony and despair, shook his faith in his mission, yes, in himself.

Let us be quite clear about this. Jesus was put to death. After he was arrested he had no further choice in the matter. He was condemned, tortured, and executed. He did not give himself to it. He endured it. It was all undeserved, meaningless, irrational. He experienced the existential absurdity of life. He could not see it as a sacrifice, for in the agony and abandonment of Calvary he could no longer discern God's purpose and had no hope of final victory.

Von Rad points out that faithfulness in suffering without a glimpse of its purpose was anticipated in Jeremiah. "It is still Jeremiah's secret how, in the face of growing skepticism about his own affairs, he was yet able to give an almost superhuman obedience to God, and, bearing the immense strain of his calling, was yet able to follow a road which led ultimately to abandonment. Never for a moment did it occur to him that this mediatorial suffering might have a meaning in the sight of God."[3] Unless we are prepared to assert that Jesus' suffering was less than Jeremiah's, we must insist that Calvary was equally incomprehensible to Jesus.

In his bewilderment on the cross, Jesus did endure the fullness of human despair. But if he remained true to himself, he accepted it without retaliation, without resentment, without self-pity. Even when he felt abandoned he still cried to his Father, "My God, my God." It was the ultimate act of faith made in the teeth of utter darkness. Although Luke softens the impact of Calvary by omitting that cry of dereliction, we must believe with him that Jesus faced and entered death with the prayer, "Abba, into your hands I commit my spirit" (23:46).

This is redemption. Jesus stopped evil dead upon the cross. How? By accepting the dark side of human life and society, the alienation that results from human sin, and the futile suffering it causes. This was not making up for sin, not bearing its penalty. This was reconciliation with that which sin had turned into evil, reconciliation in the only way possible, by embracing it. By so doing, man in Jesus became whole again. All the illusory hopes were abandoned, all self-will sacrificed, not to a worthy cause but to an ignoble execution. It was the emptying of self into the abyss of nothingness. In that total loss of self, man found himself, at-oned with himself and atoned with God.

But if all this was borne only by the man Jesus, if God stood by and let him suffer, if God really did abandon him, then God is not love. It is not enough that God intended to vindicate Jesus subsequently, to raise him from the dead, for neither vindication nor resurrection would erase the suffering. It is not enough that God sympathized with the agony of his beloved but merely human son, for sympathy always falls short of the pain itself, especially since God knew the purpose and value of the suffering, as the man Jesus did not.

No. "God in Christ was reconciling the world to himself" (2 Cor. 5:19) only if God himself was hanging on the cross, only if God himself suffered the agony, the disgrace, the destruction of all his hopes; only if God himself felt abandoned by God and in that abandonment distrusted all he had striven to accomplish. Granted that the capacity to love requires that man have the conscious self-determination that made sin possible, and granted that man had to suffer the consequences of sin in order to be redeemed as a responsible person, then only a crucified God, who suffered the consequences responsibly along with man could be a God of redeeming love.[4]

The Christian gospel affirms that God has done just that. God has dared to be a man and as a man has won the victory. On Calvary God and man faced and conquered, endured and forgave, all the divisive and destructive enmity sin can devise. The cross is the quintessence of evil. Jesus, truly God and truly man, embraced it in faith and love, and behold, it was the tree of life.

The Last Supper

I have delayed discussing the last supper until after considering Calvary because, although it comes first in time, it links the cross to what followed it. To see it performing that function, we have to distinguish what the supper meant to Jesus and his disciples from what, after the resurrection, the eucharist has come to mean in the life of the ongoing church.

From the historical viewpoint, the phrase "last supper" has a wrong connotation. It suggests that Jesus planned one final meal with his disciples before his death. The trouble he took to insure that Judas would not know where the meal was to be held indicates that he feared arrest. But he did not know for sure when that would happen and what its consequences would be. We have assumed for so long that he was consciously following a prearranged plan that we accept its implications without question.

Once we recognize that Jesus was as ignorant of the future as is every human being, it becomes clear that what he wanted was an uninterrupted supper with his disciples because he might soon be forcibly separated from them. He was aware that death might possibly, perhaps even probably, follow his arrest, if human events ran their course. But if the agony in the garden truly reflects his thoughts and feelings, he still hoped that God would intervene and prevent it. Therefore Jesus was facing only the threat of death, not its certainty, when he went to supper with his disciples.

When we so understand the situation, I think we have to revise most of our ideas about the meaning and purpose of the supper for those who took part in it. To begin with, we must ask why Jesus went to considerable trouble to hold it on that particular night. The arrangements for the upper room must have been made in advance, probably several days before. If the supper was held solely because Jesus feared his arrest, it is remarkable that it was unwittingly put on the last possible occasion before that event. It seems more likely that there was another reason why the supper had to be on just that night.

The first three gospels give such a reason. It was the Passover meal. We need not review the inconclusive discussion on whether or not it was. Those who maintain that it could not have been an event that took place only once a year because the disciples from the start celebrated it more frequently have a point. Do this "whenever you drink it" does not make sense if the final blessing of the cup was an annual occurrence.

It is more probable that Jesus regularly held solemn religious meals with his disciples. What should be noted, however, is that the two actions Jesus singled out for special emphasis are those which such solemn meals, so far as the Jewish evidence goes, had in common with the Passover supper. So he could have given them a significance on that occasion which he intended them to have at the more frequent fellowship meals.

The accounts we have of the last supper in 1 Corinthians 11:23ff and the gospels are cult narratives that give a basis for the eucharist. But they are rooted in a historical event. If we keep constantly in mind that Jesus was not founding a church and therefore was not consciously instituting a sacrament for its worship and communion, I think we can detect behind the accounts what he did and meant on the original occasion.

Jesus was afraid that he might soon be arrested and would lose contact with his disciples. At the start of the meal he could have said something like, "I may not have another opportunity to dine with you before the coming of the kingdom." In the gospels this has been made more explicitly eschatological, "I tell you solemnly, I shall not drink any more wine until the day I drink the new wine in the kingdom of God" (Mk. 14:25).

The meal itself opened, as did all Jewish meals, with the breaking of bread. The host took a loaf, blessed God for having provided it, broke it, and shared it with all present. It was the action by which the table fellowship was formed with each other and with God. After the action was completed, Jesus probably said something like, "Remember me when you do this."

The meal ended with a cup of blessing. Over it the host thanked God for the wine, the meal, the exodus, the covenant, the holy land. The cup was then passed around the table. After "all drank from it" (Mk. 14:23) Jesus said, "Whenever you do this, remember me." The final cup of blessing was used only at the Passover and at solemn religious meals. So in repeating the command, Jesus was asking them to continue to assemble at such meals in his memory.

Why? Because it was essential that the disciples hold together and keep alive their expectation of the kingdom. They had so poor a grasp on his teaching that his arrest might cause them to conclude that he had been mistaken, to give up hope, and to disband. So he told them to gather from time to time at a solemn meal, such as he had often had with them, in order to bear him and his teaching in mind until the parousia occurred. He was providing for the continuance of their fellowship during the very short interval before the end came.

So understood, the last supper fits naturally into the situation in which Jesus and his followers found themselves on the night of his arrest. It fulfilled a need that Jesus could perceive without any superhuman foresight. It also served a purpose in relation to what God was to accomplish in the events that were to follow.

Luke associates the appearances of the risen Christ with a meal. Acts 10:41 says, "We have eaten and drunk with him after his resurrection from the dead." He made himself known to the disciples at Emmaus by the breaking of bread. When he appeared in the upper room there was food on the table which they could give him to eat. It seems likely that at least some of the resurrection experiences took place at the solemn fellowship meals that Jesus had urged his disciples to continue.

Those meals, therefore, were an essential factor in the perception of the significance of God's action in Jesus the Christ. But they originated in a normal historical event. Jesus kept the Passover with his disciples at a time when he feared arrest. He took the occasion to provide them with a means by which they could keep their fellowship together and remind each other of his gospel concerning the nature and imminence of the kingdom. When the worst had happened, far worse than anything Jesus himself had anticipated, the disciples, after recovering from their original shock, obeyed his command and in their fellowship meals experienced his resurrection.

That, however, was not the end of their significance. How the eucharist as it has been celebrated down the centuries was derived from those meals we shall consider in the next chapter. But in order to justify the development, we need not read back into Jesus' mind concepts and intentions he could not have entertained. God manifests himself through history by giving ordinary events meanings beyond the perception of their participants. In that way the Logos through the Holy Spirit has instituted the eucharist out of the last supper.

Resurrection

In 1 Corinthians 15:3ff, Paul gives the credal statement he received from the tradition, "that Christ died for our sins, in accordance with the scriptures; that he was buried; and that he was raised to life on the third day, in accordance with the scriptures." He probably learned it at Damascus after his conversion. To it he adds a list of witnesses to the resurrection which he may well have got from Peter and James when he visited Jerusalem three years later (Gal. 1:18f): Christ "appeared first to Cephas and secondly to the twelve. Next he appeared to more than five hundred of the brothers at the same time, most of whom are still alive, though some have died; then he appeared to James, and then to all the apostles." To that list Paul adds, "Last of all he appeared to me too."

The first thing to note is that this is a list, not a series of accounts. I fully agree with those who hold that the narratives of the resurrection appearances are a late development.[5] Mark's gospel has none (16:9-20 is a later addition). In Matthew there are two encounters with the risen Christ. In one he redundantly and inconsistently repeats to the women what the angel told them at the grave (28:9f). The other is more of a summary of the resurrection experience than a story (28:16ff). Only in Luke and John are fully developed narratives to be found.

It has also been pointed out that the first five appearances listed by Paul could have occurred in Galilee.[6] The theory is that the disciples fled home from Jerusalem, if not directly from Gethsemane, then right after Jesus' condemnation or crucifixion. Peter (Cephas) at least remained long enough to deny Jesus in the high priest's courtyard. If this thesis is correct, the original resurrection experiences were independent of any knowledge of an empty tomb.

Peter is listed as the first witness. Luke 24:22ff explicitly denies that Christ appeared to the women. But when the disciples returned from Emmaus, they were greeted with, "The Lord has risen and has appeared to Simon" (24:34). There is good reason to think that the resurrection was first revealed to the church through Peter. It is important, therefore, to see if we can discover any hints as to how he came to believe that Christ had been raised up.

Two passages in the gospels may have originally been an attempt to describe Peter's experience. The evangelists who record them have used them for different purposes, so they vary in details. But they have enough in common to make it likely that they are derived from the same tradition.

In Luke 5:4ff, Peter's encounter with Christ is turned into his initial call. The miraculous draft of fishes, however, and the numinous quality of the figure of Jesus are more appropriate to his risen than his earthly life. Peter falls on his knees in worship and cries, "Leave me, Lord; I am a sinful man." That makes more sense after the denial than at Peter's first call to follow Jesus.

In John 21 the miraculous draft of fishes is attributed to the risen Christ. Because this chapter was added to the gospel, probably after the original author was dead, the appearance is designated as Jesus' third. But the decision of the disciples to go fishing, that is, to return to their old life in Galilee, suggests that they thought their following of Jesus had ended. The astonishment they felt at his appearance and their hesitation in recognizing him are hardly appropriate if they had already seen him twice before.

It is likely that this is another version of Peter's initial contact with the risen Christ. His penitence is a prominent feature. He is allowed to reverse his threefold denial by a threefold act of love. On the basis of that he is commissioned as a shepherd of Christ's flock. The author of John 21 has adapted the story to his purpose of explaining that the death of the Beloved Disciple does not invalidate the gospel.

The emphasis on Peter's penitence may well be the clue to his priority in experiencing the resurrection. All the disciples were devastated by their shock and grief at Jesus' condemnation and death. Peter more so than the rest because his denial added weight on his heart. It involved him personally among those who had rejected Jesus. For him the question: How could this disaster have happened? became: How could I have done such a thing? He, unlike the others, approached Calvary as a sinner who had contributed to it. In his struggle with grief, penitence, and despair, he pondered on what had happened in the light of the Old Testament.[7]

Again and again God had called Israel to return to his love. But the prophets who had delivered his message had all been rejected by their contemporaries and suffered at their hands. Jeremiah in particular had been arrested, maltreated, and almost killed. Others were believed to have been scourged, persecuted, slain (Mt. 23:34f). Indeed, the true prophets were distinguished from the false by their rejection and suffering. The bearing of it was somehow part of their vocation. They suffered vicariously on behalf of the people.

Because of his sin, Peter identified himself with those who had rejected God's emissaries. Although Israel had sinned and had to bear the consequences to some extent, those who repented were able to be restored to God's love. The prophets were vindicated by Israel's survival, a survival made possible by the prophets' faithful endurance of suffering and disgrace.

Did not the rejection and suffering of Jesus show that he was a true prophet? Were there not indications in the scriptures that a final messenger would suffer in that way before the coming of the kingdom? Was not Psalm 22 practically a description of the crucifixion? Had not Jesus died in accordance with the scriptures that he might bear and overcome the sins of his people? Would he not be vindicated and be able to express his forgiving love?

Perhaps after a night spent fishing and meditating along these lines Peter reached the point where he could believe that Jesus' death, despite all the appearances to the contrary, was in accord with God's will and that his love had conquered — not been conquered by — the sins that crucified him. Such a faith was the necessary prerequisite to an experience of the risen Christ. For the resurrection confirmed and vindicated that insight of faith that the Spirit inspired; it did not force men and women to believe it by a stunning demonstration. No miracle designed for that purpose would be effective anyway. As Jesus said in the parable of Lazarus, "If they will not listen either to Moses or to the prophets, they will not be convinced even if someone should rise from the dead" (Lk. 16:31).

Paul also had to see in Jesus the fulfillment of the scriptures before he could experience the resurrection. At first he had thought that the cross proved God's total repudiation of Jesus' life and teaching. But the constancy and faith of the Christians he persecuted finally brought him to see that "Christ redeemed us from the curse of the law by being cursed for our sake" (Gal. 3:13). Then he, too, on the road to Damascus saw the risen Christ.[8] As his list indicates, he considered his experience to be in the same class with the others.

According to Luke it was a vision and audition which Paul's companions did not share (Acts 9:7;22:9;26:13f). Paul himself, however, seems to distinguish between his resurrection experience and a vision (2 Cor. 12:1f). Whatever form it took, it was an objective revelation in the sense that it broke in upon him from outside his mind when he had so opened himself to the faith the Spirit initiated in him that he could embrace the Logos. Then he knew that the Jesus he had been persecuting was alive and vindicated — indeed, that he was the Christ.

Peter's recognition of Christ was a feature of the two stories we have considered. It is explicitly confessed in Matthew 16:16ff, which must also be associated with the resurrection, since it was only through that experience that Jesus was seen to be the Messiah. Peter's confession is followed by his establishment as the rock on which the church is to be built. That parallels his call to catch men rather than fish (Lk. 5:10) and to shepherd the flock (Jn. 21:15ff).

Peter proceeded to do this. He assembled the leading Galilean disciples, probably at a solemn fellowship meal. Inspired by his faith, after some struggle with doubt, they too were able to experience the risen Christ. Their designation as "the twelve" suggests that they considered themselves the leaders of the twelve tribes of Israel in an earthly anticipation of the messianic kingdom that was soon to come in its fullness (Mt. 19:28). Meanwhile they were to gather the people into it.

Over five hundred of them withdrew to a retired spot. This must surely have been in Galilee where most of Jesus' ministry had been exercised. Again it was at a solemn meal as is reflected in the feeding of the five thousand. Its miraculous character and the inclusion of fish, an early symbol of Christ, support that conjecture. So also does John's association of it with the eucharist in Chapter 6. The placing of those feedings in the public ministry may also be a recollection that Jesus had such fellowship meals with his followers during his earthly life. When they reassembled at one after his death, as he had commanded, they experienced his resurrection.

Word of these events reached James, the Lord's brother, and possibly others of Jesus' family and friends who had known him before his ministry. It was hard for them to recognize the long-awaited Messiah in a person who had been to them just an ordinary peasant. But the testimony of those who had come to believe caused them to rethink the question. James himself, and perhaps others, found the faith to see the Christ. James is singled out because kinship was of great importance in Jewish culture and, as Jesus' brother, he was destined to become the head of the Jewish-Christian church in Jerusalem.

After his personal encounter with Jesus as the Christ, James joined the earlier leaders for another corporate experience by "all the apostles." Paul's use of that title, together with Matthew's summary in 28:16ff, which may reflect this episode, points to what may have been the introduction of a new factor. The anticipatory messianic fellowship was not simply to wait in Galilee for the imminent consummation of the kingdom. Whatever the danger might be, they were to proclaim it publicly to Israel. So the leaders set out for Jerusalem.

Christ Alive

All four gospels say that the Galilean women visited the tomb and found it empty. The details are contradictory both between the narratives and in the stories themselves. Indeed, the account in Mark 16:1ff bristles with difficulties. Why, for instance, did the women set out to anoint the body of Jesus if they knew that the grave was closed by a stone they could not roll away?

When the women entered the tomb, they saw a yong man in a white robe, "and they were struck with amazement. But he said to them, 'There is no need for alarm. You are looking for Jesus of Nazareth, who was crucified: he has risen, he is not here. See, here is the place where they laid him. But you must go and tell his disciples and Peter, "He is going before you to Galilee; it is there you will see him, just as he told you."' And the women came out and ran away from the tomb because they were frightened out of their wits; and they said nothing to a soul, for they were afraid."

It will be seen at once that the final two sentences contradict each other and that the last is more in keeping with the earlier portrayal of the women. The command to tell the Galilean disciples, specified by the mention of Peter, is not obeyed. It was probably added to the story to point to the appearances in Galilee which were known to have occurred.

The appearance of the angel and the rest of his message may be an earlier addition. The original form of the resurrection proclamation by those who had experienced it was simply that Jesus "was raised to life" (1 Cor. 15:4). When the empty tomb became part of the tradition, the proclamation was given greater authority by putting it into the mouth of an angel. The next step was to attribute it to Christ himself as in Matthew 28:9f. This is also reflected in the appearance to Mary Magdalene (Jn. 20:1,11ff).

So the original kernel of truth behind the legendary development is that one or more Galilean women went to visit the tomb where they thought Jesus had been buried. Even putting the visit on the first day of the week may reflect Christian liturgical practice. The women, to their horror, found the tomb empty. Terror-stricken, they told no one about what they assumed was a robbed grave, until the Galilean disciples returned to Jerusalem with the proclamation that Jesus was risen.

Where had the body gone? If it was removed by human agency, perhaps the most plausible theory can be based on Acts 13:29, which asserts that it was those who crucified Jesus who "took him down from the tree and buried him in a tomb." It is hard to see how that idea could have survived if it was not true, since tradition had turned Joseph of Arimathaea into a disciple who buried Jesus reverently (Mk. 15:42ff). But if Jesus was hurriedly thrust into an available grave to dispose of his body before the Sabbath, it might well have been moved elsewhere for permanent burial before the women visited the original site.

Like all natural explanations, however, that is mere conjecture. We cannot even be sure that the body was removed by human agency. We are becoming increasingly aware today of psychosomatic factors in disease. It would be rash to dogmatize about the interrelationship of mind and body at death and after, and to deny that under exceptional circumstances the body might disintegrate rapidly.[9]

What is important is that we recognize that the empty tomb was not known to the disciples in Galilee when they experienced the resurrection. It is not a necessary prerequisite to belief that Jesus was raised from the dead. In particular, it does not mean that the risen Christ was a resuscitated corpse or that the physical components of his earthly body had to disappear for him to have risen. Because the empty tomb is an unnecessary detail, I am inclined to think the original kernel of the story records a fact, even though we cannot now determine how or why the body disappeared.

Luke and John describe appearances that took place in Jerusalem and its environs. The implication of both Mark and Matthew is that Christ appeared only in Galilee. If we have interpreted Paul's list correctly, all the witnesses he named had their experiences there. The stories in Luke and John are full of vivid detail. All these factors have led some to classify them as legendary developments that are not based on real events.

My conclusion is different. There is evidence that Jesus had Jerusalem disciples who were largely unknown to the Galileans. Why could not they also have had experiences of the risen Christ independently of those in Galilee? Once more, they would not have been based on knowledge of the empty tomb since the women who discovered it told no one about it, especially not people they hardly knew.

Paul's failure to include these appearances in his list can be explained. He probably got his information from Peter and James. They were from Galilee and were interested only in the appearances there. They dominated the church in Jerusalem. But there were Greek-speaking Jews who were converted to Christianity as well. Acts tells us that they had difficulties with the Galileans (6:1ff) and that they returned to their homes throughout the empire after the death of Stephen (8:1). It was through them that the mission to the gentiles developed.

If the memory of the Jerusalem experiences was preserved chiefly by the Greek-speaking Christians, that would account for many of their peculiarities. When the accounts were taken to gentile cities, they lost contact with those who had originally experienced them.

They were open to the elaboration which the pagan love of legends about their heroes and gods would have encouraged.

Two specific elements in the resultant stories can be accounted for by that environment. First was the emphasis on the missionary outreach of the church which characterizes several of them. Matthew 28:16ff makes the same point, as that gospel was also composed for a church outside Palestine. But it was one in which the Jewish-Christian influence was still strong, and therefore the reference is a summary not a story.

Second, there was the need felt in the third and fourth gospels for demonstrating the reality of the resurrection to the gentiles. Their notion of the afterlife was that the soul escapes from the body. If the Hebrew concept of resurrection was to be proclaimed, the physical reality of Jesus' body had to be made clear. So he invites the disciples to touch him, and he eats before them.

The vividness of these accounts causes difficulties for us today. They, even more than the empty tomb, suggest that the risen Christ was a resuscitated corpse. If we recognize them as legendary accretions, what can we say was the nature of the experience of Christ that justifies belief that he was raised from the dead? The answer must be found in the Hebrew perception that the total personality is a unity of body, mind, heart, soul, and whatever other aspects one may designate from time to time for special purposes. If, as some of the Jews came to believe by the time Jesus lived, the person really survives death, it has to be through the resurrection of the whole personality, including the body.

Insofar as those who experienced the risen Christ tried to conceive what he was like, they probably thought in terms of an assumption into heaven such as that of Elijah (2 Kg. 2:11). Note that he and Moses, who was also thought to have been taken directly to heaven, appear at the transfiguration, which may be a reflection of the resurrection experiences (Lk. 9:28ff). What "assumption" meant was that Jesus in the fullness of his being had been raised from the dead and exalted to God's right hand. He manifested himself as both vindicated and alive.

This conviction had nothing in common with the forlorn assertion by a group of discouraged people that the spirit of their defeated and slain leader lives on. Those who say that are fully aware that they mean something different from the disciples' insistence that Jesus had so revealed himself that they knew he was still living and had called them to prepare men and women for his second coming when the kingdom of God would be consummated. They believed that the Spirit he had bestowed on them was not a pale reflection of his spirit. Rather, they had received the Holy Spirit so that they could carry on in his name. They proved the truth of their conviction by acting upon it in a way they could never have devised for themselves.

What then can we today say of the resurrection? In Jesus, God as a man fully responded to the lure of the Logos. In that life, teaching, death, and resurrection, humanity achieved its full potential. Mankind has become united to God and entered upon eternal life. The portion of the universe in which we live has fulfilled its purpose for the first time. Creation made the response of love to its creator. Because of the fullness of Jesus' response, the total subject he had become through his subjective aims in his earthly life was able to survive death and continue to become itself through subjective aims in another world.

But Christ is only the firstfruits on earth as well as in heaven. Creation itself has yet to be culminated in love. This can be done only by overcoming evil and sin by suffering their consequences in redeeming and forgiving love. The way of the cross is still the road to victory. As Jesus called those he met to follow him and led those who responded through the darkness and despair of Calvary to the experience of his resurrection, so Christ calls all who will follow him now that he may express through them his own love. That love is not just perfect human love. God himself is involved. For "it was God who reconciled us to himself through Christ and gave us the work of handing on this reconciliation" (2 Cor. 5:18). That is our call to love.

When our God of all compassion
   came as man to set us free
from the chains of self we fashion,
   shouldering our iniquity,
     struggling onward,
   he ascended Calvary.

Doomed to criminal's execution,
   innocent of sinful strain,
Jesus hung in destitution,
   yielding up his soul in pain,
     God forsaken,
   yet to God restored again.

For his love our hearts consenting
   to pursue love's humble course,
envy, pride and greed repenting,
   purged by suffering, shame and loss,
     in deep darkness
   we embrace his holy cross.

Then that darkness is the glory,
   hidden in our human veil,
of our God's redemptive story
   how by death shall life prevail:
     love triumphant
   which upon the cross we hail.

Ω

OMEGA

THE CALL TO HOPE

Chapter 7 / **MISSION**

God dared to create man. He risked the evil human beings could produce through their sins. God dared to become man. He risked yielding to our temptations and suffered rejection, agony, and death because he persisted in love. God dares to continue his work of redemption through man. It is the ultimate risk. Yet because men and women can be saved only with the cooperation of their conscious, self-determined response, the final victory of his love still has to depend on human freedom. We can forward or frustrate God's work. He has put it into our hands.

There is a medieval legend about the angels at the ascension. After they spoke to the disciples, they caught up with Christ and one of them asked, "Now that you are leaving the earth, how will you carry on your work there?" Jesus replied, "There are Peter and John and Andrew and Bartholomew, and Mary Magdalene and Martha and Joanna and the rest. They will carry on in my name." "But suppose they let you down," the angel persisted, "What other plan do you have?" Jesus answered, "I have no other plan." God still dares to be man.

The primary work of Jesus was to proclaim the kingdom of God by word and deed. The deeds included not only the witness of his example to the character of the kingdom of love, but also the acts of forgiveness and healing that he was able to perform in those who responded to him with penitence and faith. Those acts were signs that the kingdom was already becoming present and active through him. They stimulated the hope that led others to make the response of penitence and faith by which they took their places among those who were eagerly expecting the kingdom of God. So they in turn became witnesses to it and missionaries for it.

We have noted that the basic common feature of the resurrection accounts is the call to witness. Except for what we can infer from the other books of the New Testament, the only record we have of the primitive church is the Acts of the Apostles. The central theme of that book is the missionary outreach of the church. Peter's sermon on Pentecost started the process among the Jews in Jerusalem. Included in their number were Greek-speaking Jews from all over the world. Stephen is portrayed as winning many converts among them.

After Stephen's martyrdom the Greek-speaking Jews scattered to their homelands, taking the gospel with them. Philip converted the Samaritans, who were accepted in the name of the Jerusalem church by Peter and John. Then Peter was led by the Spirit to baptize Cornelius the gentile, and his action was approved by the church at Jerusalem. Meanwhile Paul was converted. At Antioch the mission to the gentiles had begun in earnest. Barnabas, who was sent by the Jerusalem church to supervise the situation there, got Paul to help him.

From Antioch Paul and Barnabas set out on missionary journeys that planted the church in Cyprus, Asia Minor, and Greece. Finally, Paul was taken as a prisoner to Rome and made contact with the church in that city. The structure of Acts is the work of Luke, but the missionary activity of Paul is confirmed by his own letters and the others attributed to him. Such single-minded zeal for mission, however, may not have characterized the primitive church as exclusively as Luke asserts. Even he cannot completely disguise a lack of enthusiasm in Jerusalem for the conversion of the gentiles.

An unfortunate false impression as to the nature of early missionary activity is given by Luke's concentration on the work of two individuals, Peter and Paul. Paul, who with Barnabas was formally commissioned by the church (Acts 13:2f), is portrayed as personally inaugurating and supervising the congregations in the area covered by his mission. This has led in recent centuries to the idea that evangelistic work should be done primarily by specially trained and authorized professionals, and that they should keep the infant churches under strict control for many years. But the concept does not have the precedent it claims in the expansion of the early church, as a careful examination of the New Testament shows.

Paul did supervise, by letters and visits, the churches he founded. Having proclaimed the gospel, he did what he could to see that it was rightly understood and applied. He answered their questions, corrected their errors, and encouraged their development. But he put the running of the church, its organization and outreach, into local hands from the start (Acts 14:23). As he wrote in 1 Corinthians 1:17: "Christ did not send me to baptize, but to preach the good news." The reference is only to baptism because that is the subject Paul is discussing. It represents, however, the preparation and training of converts and the administration of the local congregation. The rapid growth of the churches, even in the places he visited from time to time, was accomplished by the members of the congregations themselves.

We can also see from his letters, or those attributed to him, that churches had been formed in many places where Paul never went. The persons who started them presumably had been converted when they visited cities where the church had already been planted and took the gospel with them when they returned home. We must not let the account of Paul's labors in Acts blind us to the truth that we know the names of the founders of no other local churches.

Christianity was established in Damascus before Paul was converted and in Antioch before Barnabas arrived. We have no idea who took the gospel to Alexandria or Rome. Paul's letter to the latter church shows it to be flourishing before he visited it. Peter may well have been martyred in Rome, but it is not likely that he founded the church there. The "missionaries" in the primitive church were not professionals sent out, supported, and directed by a central organization. They were converts who took the gospel wherever they went.

The church spread in this way for many centuries. Even when we begin to learn the names of the "apostles" to certain places, they are usually the bishops who organized an existing church, or at least found the way prepared for them by Christians already on the scene. For instance, when Augustine was sent to the Anglo-Saxons by Pope Gregory I, he was welcomed by King Ethelbert of Kent because his queen, Bertha, was a practicing Christian. Their daughter married Edwin, king of Northumbria, and took Christianity with her to that kingdom.

Augustine of Canterbury also illustrates another form of missionary outreach in that he was sent to England with a group of fellow monks. The Celtic church converted many areas by that method. The monasteries they established at once began to draw members from the local population and rapidly became indigenous.

After the Reformation a change occurred. Organizations for the furtherance and control of missionary activities were founded—the Sacred Congregation of Propaganda in the Catholic church and many societies in the Anglican, Lutheran, Calvinist, and other Reformation churches. To them must be credited the worldwide propagation of the gospel in the eighteenth and nineteenth centuries. But this method had two serious disadvantages.

First, the new churches were kept culturally, financially, and ecclesiastically dependent on the church that founded them, and their officials for far too long were supplied by it. They remained foreign missions rather than native churches. As Archbishop de Mel once said of his area of the Anglican church, "The British sent us a potted plant; we are now taking the seeds and sowing them in the soil of India." Today that process is spreading in the former mission fields, but it still has a long way to go.

The second disadvantage has been even more disastrous. The restriction of missionary activity to specially trained workers, whether clergy or laity, has given the impression that outreach is the duty of only some Christians. This is as true of domestic missions, when they are recognized as such, as of those in foreign parts. One result is that the established congregations feel their obligation is at most to give some financial support to these ventures. The laity, and even at times the parish clergy, recognize no call to spread the gospel other than the effort to induce a few more socially acceptable people to become members of the local congregation.

Insofar as Christians dispense themselves from outreach to those who need not only the gospel but also the warmth, acceptance, and ministrations of the Christian fellowship, they are rejecting the very purpose of their baptism. We are incorporated into Christ's risen humanity in order that he may continue through us—through all of us—the work for which he suffered, died, and rose again. He wills to express to every man, woman, and child we can reach his self-sacrificial, redemptive love. To fulfill that vocation a special gift of the Holy Spirit is bestowed in baptism.

The Holy Spirit

In Hebrew the word for Spirit, *ruach*, is feminine. I believe we should do well to refer to the Spirit in that gender. The all-masculine concept of deity that has dominated the Judeo-Christian tradition is responsible for the portrait of God as absolute power and dominion. He plans, executes, controls, manipulates, and overrules creation in an exclusively intellectual way. There is no room in him for such feminine attributes as intuition, affection, contingency, the non-rational, and the numinous. It is high time that they be recovered.[1]

In Proverbs 8:22ff. divine creativity is associated with Wisdom, for which the Greek word *sophia* again is feminine. We tend to rationalize wisdom, but it is much deeper than that. A college professor was accustomed to spend his vacations in a cabin where a local woman was hired to cook his meals. Over the years he had found it helpful to consult her about matters that were troubling him, because her advice was always apt. One day he exclaimed, "How is it you are so wise?" "I have to be," she replied, "I never had a chance to get educated." Wisdom is more than book learning and rational concepts. It is rooted in that intuitively perceptive faculty which we associate with the feminine aspect of human nature.

In the Bible, however, Wisdom is a creature. A similar attempt to relate the feminine to God without actually attributing it to him is the symbol of the church as the bride of Christ (Rev. 21). The distinction is made between Christ as God and the church as the human society responsive to him. But just as Jesus' own humanity tends to be deified and become less than human, so the church becomes sacralized and divorced from ordinary human life. As the bride of Christ it is looked upon as already "glorious, with no speck or wrinkle or anything like that, but holy and faultless" (Eph. 5:27). The application of such concepts to the institutional church is the basis of its hankering for infallibility and triumphalism.

A more personal symbol of the church as the feminine cooperating with God was found in the Virgin Mary. Hers was the willingness to bear and nurture him who was called to proclaim the imminent kingdom. She brought him forth to the world. Likewise, through the church Christ comes into the world to proclaim and promote the kingdom of God.

After the resurrection, when Jesus was recognized as the Son of Man, Mary became the mother of the Messiah. Her importance for the church in the latter part of the first century is demonstrated by the assertion of the virgin birth. Then the doctrine of Christ's divinity developed and Mary was called the mother of God. It is noteworthy that Nestorius objected to that title as late as the fifth century on the grounds that it imperiled the true humanity of Christ.

But the church took the opposite course. Mother of God, or the Godbearer, to give a literal translation of the original Greek title, became her official designation. The increasing reverence paid to her and the insistence on her sinless holiness eventuated in the west in the doctrine of her immaculate conception. That has not been officially accepted in the east, but both halves of the church have for centuries maintained that she went directly to heaven at her death. This legend is strikingly similar to those of Greek heroes—Hercules for example——who became gods. It comes close to effecting Mary's deification and so goes a long way toward incorporating the feminine into God. It is interesting that Jung, who was so keen on that point, hailed the official dogma of the assumption of Mary as a great achievement of the Roman Catholic Church when it was promulgated in 1950.[2]

The price of that achievement, however, was high. I believe it makes it harder than ever to recognize the integrity of Jesus' human nature; indeed, it seriously jeopardizes his relationship with mankind. The very source of his humanity has been deified. Insofar as Mary is a symbol of the church, all the objections to its deification also apply. They become the more serious because Mary as a person is easier to conceive as a god.

Until recently, in popular Catholic devotion Mary had to a large extent superseded both Jesus and the church as the bringer of salvation. Jesus tended to become identified with the Father as a wrathful judge who is induced to be merciful by Mary's intercession. Admittedly, these were corruptions, but the way was opened for them by trying to satisfy through Mary the need for the feminine aspect of deity. When not used for that purpose, devotion to Mary is and should remain an important element in Christian spirituality. She symbolizes the church as the human response to God that allows Christ to enter the world. And in her we reverence the role of true motherhood in human society. But both these symbols demand that the integrity of her humanity be strictly preserved.

The deification of man in Jesus and of woman in Mary is not the right answer to our need to include the counterpoise of the sexes in our concept of God. I believe the best solution is to see the Holy Spirit as the feminine principle in the Trinity. In providing the initiating aim of each instance of becoming, she is the womb of creation. Her patience and persistence in urging, but never compelling, each creature toward its highest potential is the divine expression of true motherhood. Her insight into the very depths of God is the supreme exercise of intuition. Her creativity, however, is in response to the Logos, who displays the masculine aspects of rational planning and adjustment. She hears the Word and enables him to become incarnate, not only in Jesus, the Word made flesh, but also in a lesser but genuine way in all reality insofar as it responds to the lure of its potential.

The functioning of both masculinity and femininity in the Godhead is implied in Genesis 1:27: "God created man in the image of himself, in the image of God he created him, male and female he created them." We are justified, therefore, in associating them with the Logos and the Spirit. But this should be counterbalanced by obeying the injunction against making any image of the first person of the Trinity — certainly not an imperious or a sentimental old man. For he represents the transcendent and eternal source of all potentiality who is beyond male and female, personal and impersonal, rational and irrational, being and nonbeing. God is more than a superlative reflection of human nature.

Still we are made in his image and the recognition of the two aspects of sexuality in him helps us better to understand ourselves. Some schools of modern psychology maintain that our creation as male and female means not only the separation of the sexes but also the presence of both elements in every man and woman. This has been obscured for us by the all-masculine concept of deity. In imitation of him men have felt they must establish and prove their manhood by the supression of their feminine side. That then turns into what Jung calls the anima, which expresses itself in irrational moods — anger, sulking, self-pity, depression, and the like. The result is a maimed and divided personality alienated from itself.

On the other hand, the development of the cult of Mary to compensate for the exclusively masculine God has had a detrimental effect on woman's self-image. Although it has been a factor in bettering the position of women in Christian culture, it has concentrated on motherhood as the sole basis of her significance. Women have been encouraged to consider the feminine function of child-bearing to be their principal contribution, to confine themselves to the domestic duties of homemaking, and to avoid the masculine world of affairs. This has suppressed the other side of woman's nature so that it has become in the subconscious a hostile animus. When it goes on a rampage of compulsive and irrational dogmatism it is as hard and frustrating for a man to cope with as the compulsive moodiness of the male anima is for a woman.

We could hardly find a better illustration of how a sound

spirituality must be grounded in a true concept of God. Because we have denied the duality of sex in God we have suppressed it in ourselves. The result has been alienation both within the self and between the sexes. Pious exhortations to love will not overcome the problem. We need a better understanding of ourselves and our interrelationships. We shall the more easily attain to that as, through the Logos and the Spirit, we are led to a deeper knowledge of the God in whose image we are made.

Inspiration

The Logos in luring each occasion toward its highest potential is applying the Father's basic idea to the actual situation. In this way the meaning and purpose of creation is revealed from instant to instant. John is quite correct when he has the Logos say: "I am the way, the truth, and the life" (14:6). In directing each occasion toward the lure of the Logos, the Spirit is guiding into truth. She is enabling that occasion to discern and become what God means it to be.

To the extent that the occasion responds to her prompting and realizes its potential, it achieves God's purpose. Sometimes for human beings that purpose becomes consciously articulated. They see the hand of God at work in nature or history. So the Israelites discerned God in the volcano, the thunderstorm, the hurricane, and in the escape from Egypt, the fall of Jerusalem, the return from exile. Likewise the Christian sees the Logos incarnate in the natural and historical life of Jesus.

It is permissible to call the latter "the myth of God incarnate,"[3] provided three points are kept clearly in mind. First, myth is a story or statement about the relationship of God or the gods to the universe. It may or may not be true. What makes it a myth is that its principle subject is an alleged divine activity. Second, the myth of the incarnation relates God in a unique way to the actual human life of a man. I have tried to sketch that life in the two previous chapters on the basis of an interpretation of the historical facts available. There has had to be much interpretation, but I have taken as my criterion the humanness of that life. Third, the Christian believes that the personal involvement of the Logos in the experience of that human life is true. That myth is a historical fact about God.

The perception of this truth began with the resurrection experience. Although Judaism had never consciously anticipated that the Messiah would be put to death, the disciples were convinced that Jesus' shameful death was in accord with God's will, a necessary element in the divine preparation for the kingdom. They tried to prove it to their fellow Jews by finding the fulfillment of Old Testament statements in the life of Jesus. Psalm 22 and Isaiah 53 were rich sources for this, but other passages were used as well. As Paul asserted in 1 Corinthians 15:3f, both Christ's death and his resurrection were "in accordance with the scriptures."

These interpretations, I firmly believe, were true to the basic significance of Jesus' life and death in the divine purpose of salvation. But though some of the events so interpreted were known to have happened, others were assumed to have occurred, and still others were simply imagined. My contention is that in all this the Holy Spirit was guiding the church to recognize the incarnation. It had its roots in history, but inspiration is seeing the transcendent significance of history.

Through the experience of the resurrection the church was convinced that Jesus was the heavenly Son of Man. But the truth of the incarnation could not be fully expressed in terms of that concept. In Jesus the divine Logos was experiencing a human life. As the gospel moved into the Greek-speaking world, Son of Man became Son of God. That insight was subsequently expounded in the thought world of greek philosophy. Theological statements were formulated that have kept the church on the rails down the centuries. They may need restating today, but the truths they enshrine can be abandoned only at our peril.

The development of this theology did not originate in speculation. It had first been rooted in the gospel story itself. The accounts of healing and exorcism lent themselves to the attestation that Jesus was God incarnate. I believe the cures were accomplished by the penitence and faith that Jesus inspired. That inspiration was not achieved by a superficial intellectual process. It was engendered from the depths of his being. Jesus was "aware that power had gone out from him" (Mk. 5:30). He saw that power as evidence that the kingdom was breaking in through him.

The church came to see it as evidence of his divinity. The miraculous element was stressed, amplified, and heightened. Probably other stories associated with Greek theophanies and mystery cults were transferred to him. He, who for the Jews was the fulfillment of Old Testament prophecies, became for the Greeks to some extent the fulfillment of their myths. Also the desire to know more about the events of Jesus' life, especially his passion, and about the people involved in it led to legendary elaboration.

The restraint of these trends in the gospels is more remarkable than their occurrence. The Spirit kept the church from wandering too far from the historical facts. In describing the resurrection, however, there were no such facts except the subjective experiences themselves, and possibly the empty tomb. Christian imagination had freer play here. But once more, the balance of vividness with restraint is astonishing, despite the inevitable growth of the story with the telling. In this surely we must see the control of the Spirit.

I do not deny that many of these trends got out of hand. In particular, the integrity of Jesus' humanity has been impaired. But it is only in the last two centuries that the detrimental significance of that has been noticed. In earlier times the divine manipulation of creation was assumed to the extent that direct interventions by God were not considered unnatural. Today the physical and behavioral sciences force us to recognize that they would be if they in fact occurred.

Along with these insights, however, the Spirit has inspired a critical and scientific investigation of the Bible that has enabled scholars to detect and assess the process of its development. This has been helpful in isolating the truly human basis for the life of Jesus. The Spirit has also enabled philosophers, theologians, and other Christian thinkers to find concepts by which the fundamental truths of "the myth of God incarnate" can be expressed in terms of contemporary culture and thought.

Because Jesus, when he returned as Messiah to establish his kingdom, would judge men and women on the basis of the precepts he had inculcated during his earthly ministry, the church was eager to preserve the memory of his words and deeds. Since much of his teaching was couched in pithy or poetic sayings or in the vivid imagery of parable, and since the Jews were well trained in memorization, we can be sure that at least some of his words and actions have been accurately recollected and transmitted.

At the same time, it should be recognized that the church was interested in this material for its teaching and preaching value. It was applied to the particular problems that confronted the local congregation. That application might be different from what Jesus had in mind. So some sayings or parables may have been reinterpreted or misinterpreted, and their original significance can no longer be discerned.

When questions arose to which no answer could be found in Jesus' teaching as it was recalled, appropriate Jewish practice might be applied, especially in largely gentile congregations. Christianity won many of its first converts from among those gentiles who had been attracted by Jewish moral monotheism. It was natural for the church to continue to uphold those standards and to attribute them to Jesus.

In time, codes of Christian behavior developed. Since Jesus was eager to free people from the legalism that restricted the call to love, the codification of his moral teaching would seem to be moving in a contrary direction. To some extent it was. Christianity has been plagued with a moral rigidity that has often distorted the gospel. But it must also be remembered that the teaching of the prophets was preserved because it was codified into law. Had the early church not done the same with Jesus' teaching, we would know far less of it.

We must not be surprised that many of Jesus' sayings, parables, and answers to critics have an affinity to the current rabbinical teaching. Jesus was a Jew and expressed himself through that thought world. Even more influenced by it was the Palestinian church that first collected and interpreted his sayings. What impresses me in the collections of rabbinical parallels assembled by Bultmann and others is not the similarity of their structure but the difference of their tone. No doubt I am prejudiced, but I find a more vital call to unlimited love in the reported words of Jesus.

Also, the gospels serve another purpose besides their historical and theological aspects. They give the fundamentals of Christian spirituality. Many years ago I wrote a book in which I took the accounts of the resurrection appearances in their traditional devotional interpretations as the basis for meditations on the spiritual life.[4] I found they illustrated to an amazing degree the relationship both of the church and of the individual soul to God.

I do not believe this is fortuitous. The Spirit guided the church to record in the New Testament, as she had in the Old Testament, the ways of God with mankind. The scriptures reflect the experience of the church, both the old Israel and the new, in its spiritual dimensions. They are for us, in all aspects of our relationship with him, the Word of God.

The Body of Christ

Each of the four evangelists received the traditional material he used through a particular church. It reflected the interests and problems of that local fellowship. In writing his account the evangelist selected and shaped his material to emphasize what he believed the congregation needed to remember if it was to remain true to the gospel. The New Testament was written not only by the church but for the church.

Mark countered the concept of Christ as a semidivine being who could not suffer, by asserting that, precisely because he was the Messiah, the Son of Man had to bring in the kingdom by his passion and death. The agony in the garden and the cry of dereliction on the cross climax Mark's emphasis on the genuineness and extent of Jesus' suffering. Those who would follow Christ must be prepared to share in similar tribulations.

Matthew's gospel reflects two disparate interests. On the one hand, there is the affirmation of Jesus' messiahship from Old Testament prophecies and a legalizing of his teaching as the fulfillment of the law. On the other hand, the gentile mission is prominent, beginning with the visit of the wise men and ending with the command to "make disciples of all the nations" (28:19). Perhaps a Greek-speaking Jewish-Christian church somewhere in Syria might combine those two factors.

Both Luke and John are even more church oriented. Luke sees the ministry and death of Jesus as a past historical action by which salvation was accomplished. Even the life and work of the primitive church is pictured in Acts as another stage of salvation history that is over and done with. The delay of the parousia has demonstrated the need for a continuing church. To meet that need is the aim of Luke's organization and presentation of the traditional material in both his gospel and his account of apostolic times.[5]

For John the parousia has already begun on earth in the new age of the Spirit. His gospel describes the way the Logos inaugurated this through Jesus, who from the beginning knows himself to be the Christ and is so recognized. He came from heaven to do the Father's will and accomplish his work, just as in our paradigm the Logos applies and actualizes the Father's basic idea for creation. So he can be portrayed as saying in a final prayer before the passion, "Father, . . . I have glorified you on earth and finished the work that you gave me to do" (17:4). The freedom and integrity of Jesus' humanity is not John's concern. But since Jesus in all important matters did respond faithfully to the lure and intention of the Logos, a fundamental truth has been recorded for us. Jesus did bring in the new age of the Spirit, of which the outward and visible form is the church.

I have maintained that, due to the limits of Jesus' foresight and his expectation of an imminent parousia, he had no thought of founding a church. But that is just what he did. We have here perhaps the most important reinterpretation of his significance that the Spirit has guided us to perceive. The call to prepare for the kingdom, and the way to do so, are both being continued in the church. The break-in of the kingdom in Jesus' human ministry is present for us in the extension of his humanity through the Christian fellowship. The fullness of the kingdom is yet to come. But to some degree it can presently be experienced.[6]

Probably nothing has done more damage to the Christian gospel than the outright identification of the institutional church with the body of Christ. The fact that the visible church is composed entirely of sinners is ignored. Their sinfulness corrupts in some measure all its official acts. A brief glance at any other branch of the church than the one to which we belong will at once produce a whole catalogue of errors. I hope today we are sufficiently mature to recognize that the other branches can see as many faults in us. For all have "sinned and forfeited God's glory" (Rom. 3:23). To identify any organized group with the body of Christ, from the local congregation on up to the major divisions of the church, is an extremely dangerous blasphemy.

Yet the church as the body of Christ cannot be entirely invisible. If his humanity is to function objectively in contemporary society, it must have more than a spiritual presence in the hearts of the faithful. As the Logos submitted himself to the limitations of a truly human experience in order to bring salvation to the world, so he has to continue that work through the church, the even more limited and sinful extension of that humanity. Our paradigm maintains that both the Logos and the Spirit are constantly adapting the Father's basic concept to the overcoming of human sin. So the failings of the church can be overcome insofar as its separated branches recognize that they are as far from being holy as they are from being one.

The body of Christ can function on earth only if it has an outline and structure. The rite by which one is made a member of it has been from early times the sacrament of baptism. Its significance for the candidate is summarized in Acts 2:38. "Be baptized in the name of Jesus Christ for the forgiveness of your sins, and you will receive the gift of the Holy Spirit." The rite was derived from John's baptism and Jesus' reception of it.

Jesus probably became aware of his call to his public ministry when he was baptized. The gospel accounts, however, are not designed to describe his experience. They are cult legends giving the basis for the Christian sacrament of baptism. Jesus' going down into the water — so much better symbolized for us if we are immersed — is our sharing in his death and resurrection. "When we were baptized we went into the tomb with him and joined him in death, so that as Christ was raised from the dead by the Father's glory, we too might live a new life" (Rom. 6:4).

We die with Christ in order to be reborn in him. The voice from heaven, "You are my son," is appropriate to the baptismal covenant by which we become adopted sons and daughters of our heavenly Father. Of even greater significance is the descent of the Spirit in the form of a dove. For it is at baptism that the Christian is fully empowered by the Holy Spirit.

But Christians cannot claim to have been the only recipients of the Holy Spirit. She supplies the initiating aim of all occasions of becoming. What then is the new relationship established through baptism? In our paradigm I have indicated that the Spirit lets the Logos become the initiating aim of his human nature. For those baptized into him, I believe she allows the corporate expression of his risen humanity to influence the subjective aim of each occasion of experience.

When discussing evil, I suggested that corporate human sins can become independent demonic powers. They have a malignant influence that can be accepted or rejected by the subjective aim. The corporate expression of the risen Christ is a power capable of having a redemptive influence. It can cast the demons out of us and give us healing and wholeness. Jung's archetypes of the collective unconscious might provide an even better analogy. They are the fundamental symbols that undergird the functioning of all human minds. So for Christians the body of Christ makes present the breaking in of the kingdom and supplies the basic symbols of faith, sacraments, and prayer.

The Holy Spirit makes it possible for Christians to be responsive to and live in this corporate humanity. They too can show forth the redeeming love of Christ. As always, the prompting of the Spirit can be rejected, in whole or in part, by the subjective aim. But the opportunity to respond is given. To the degree that we do not hinder our incorporation in Christ, the Spirit is able through us to make the church visibly manifest in the world.

The Eucharist

The church becomes most clearly visible when the fellowship gathers to celebrate the eucharist.[7] Its fundamental characteristic is community. At the last supper Jesus was ensuring that his disciples would continue to meet at sacred meals in order to keep him and his teaching in mind. When they did so after his death, they experienced his resurrection. He made himself known to them in the breaking of bread.

Once the presence of the risen Christ was associated with those meals, they would begin to be considered his appointed means of contact with them. When the vividness of the first resurrection appearances faded, Christians continued to break bread and share the cup of blessing in his memory and were convinced of his presence, even though it was no longer perceived in the same way. Rather, it was at first associated with the assembled fellowship, as I believe we find in Paul's account in 1 Corinthians 11:23ff, which he says he received from the tradition.

Paul reports that after the bread-sharing ceremony, Jesus said, "This is my body for you." (Most scholars agree that the verb "given" or "broken" was added later.) The words were not spoken over the bread. Jesus thanked God for it with the usual Jewish blessing. The words came after the ceremony and referred to the table fellowship that it had formed.

When Paul uses "body of Christ" he always means the corporate aspect of the church. Even in the verses following the account of the supper he speaks repeatedly of "eating this bread," never of eating Christ's body. It is because of the Corinthians' disorders and lack of charity at their common meals, and because of the dissensions dividing their church, that Paul rebukes those who eat and drink "without recognizing the body."

The same corporate reference is found in the words Paul attributes to Jesus after the sharing of the cup of blessing. "This cup is the new covenant in my blood." The emphasis is on the covenant to which the fellowship owed its origin, and on the death on Calvary by which it was established. In the Pauline account, therefore, it is when the congregation assembles in loving fellowship to share in the bread and the cup that Jesus makes himself present and they proclaim his death until he comes in the final parousia.

The next step was the association of Christ's presence with the bread and cup that were shared. It was an inevitable cultic development. If Christ became present through partaking of the bread and cup, he was symbolized by them. The thanked-over (eucharistized) bread became his body objectively present. The use of the blessed-over cup to commemorate the covenant established by his death led to identifying its contents with his blood. That development is reflected in the liturgical alteration which has shaped Mark 14:24 so that "This is my blood, the blood of the covenant" parallels "This is my body."

By that process the fellowship meal became a sacrament. In the fourth gospel the new emphasis is explicit. "If you do not eat the flesh of the Son of Man and drink his blood, you will not have life in you" (Jn. 6:53). But note the verbs. Christ's presence is appropriated by the eating and drinking. The community renews itself in Christ by communion. That paved the way for the eucharist to become a communion sacrifice.

In both Hebrew and Greek practice the peace offering was a particular form of sacrifice. Unlike holocausts and sin offerings, it always ended with a communion meal on the victim of the sacrifice. Its purpose was praise and thanksgiving. So the eucharistic oblation is offered on behalf of creation which can make a grateful response to its creator through mankind — its priest in whom it becomes conscious of itself. At the same time we give thanks for our redemption which the Logos effected by his loving forgiveness that persisted even to his death on Calvary.

The eucharist is a memorial sacrifice like that of the Passover. The Jews did not just recall the exodus, the visit to Sinai, and entrance into the promised land. They relived them each year by reenacting the final meal before leaving Egypt as it is described in the Old Testament. Thereby they were renewed in the covenant of Sinai and recommitted to its observance. So when the Christians reenacted Jesus' final meal with his disciples in thanksgiving for their redemption, they came to see it as their reliving his death and resurrection by which it was accomplished. Thus they were renewed in the new covenant and recommitted to it in him.

This also came to be seen as Christ the priest in his body the church offering his sacrifice to the Father in worship. But in what sense was Calvary a sacrifice? I have insisted that in Jesus' mind his death was the defeat of his hopes and the apparent rejection by the Father of all that he had tried to accomplish. It was a disaster, not a sacrifice pleasing to God. Nevertheless he accepted even that in obedient love, and God received it as man's supreme self-oblation. It redeemed suffering into triumphant love.

We should note that love never sees itself as sacrifice. The moment we start thinking how much we are doing for someone we shift from love to selfishness. In real love our concentration is wholly on the beloved. Rupert Brooke expressed this in his sonnet.

> If I should die, think only this of me:
> That there's some corner of a foreign field
> That is for ever England.[8]

After Brooke died it was said of him that he had made the supreme sacrifice. He did not think of himself in that way. It was his love of England that motivated his fighting and dying for her integrity.

Jesus' ignorance of the function of his death in the process of man's redemption made his faithfulness more, not less, self-sacrificing. So the church rightly views the representation of his obedience in the eucharist as its sacrifice of thanksgiving. By reliving the death and resurrection of Jesus in grateful remembrance the church is renewed as the body of Christ.

The Gifts of the Spirit

Baptism and the eucharist provide the outline of Christ's body. They differentiate its acknowledged members from the rest of the human race. The ordained ministry of the church provides its structure. The need for this was felt quite early. In Ephesians 4:11, an epistle that develops Pauline concepts, we read that the ascended Christ's gift to some "was that they should be apostles; to some, prophets; to some, evangelists; to some, pastors and teachers."

The first three groups are charismatic in the sense that as individuals they have a special grace to proclaim and interpret the gospel. The last group, on the other hand, looks like the local church officials. By the end of the first century, in some areas at least, they had developed into the monarchical episcopate—a single local bishop with presbyters and deacons ordained to advise and assist him.

The ordained ministry, however, was not intended to displace the priesthood of Christ. "We have a great priest set over the household of God" (Heb. 10:21).[9] His priesthood is expressed in the first instance through the whole corporate fellowship of the church, which is "a chosen race, a royal priesthood, a consecrated nation" (1 Pet. 2:9; cf. Rev. 1:6; 5:10; 20:6). The self-perpetuating fellowship of bishops is its traditional organ of unity and continuity. It enables the one church to spread across the continents and down the centuries.

Human nature being what it is, there have been corruptions. Some bishops and other executive officials have lorded it over the church and each other. The whole catalogue of sins has been committed by clergy of all ranks. Worse still, the ordained ministers have tended to look upon themselves as the real and full members of the church, and the laity have been all too prone to cede that position to them.

Nevertheless, if the church is to function as the body of Christ, it must have the structure of an authorized and hierarchical ministry. Far from usurping the priesthood of all believers, it validates it in each local congregation by sacramentally uniting it to the priesthood of Christ. Unfortunately the present divided state of the church obscures that truth and disrupts that unity. We can only pray and work and hope for the day when we shall all be one.

In Romans 12:6ff Paul includes among the gifts of grace in the body of Christ administration and leadership. He also lists almsgiving and works of mercy, as well as prophecy, teaching, and exhortation. The affairs of the local church and its members are thereby covered. The gifts of the Spirit in 1 Corinthians 12:8ff include some of these, but others of a more special nature are added—the gift of healing, the power of miracles, the recognizing of spirits, the gift of tongues and the interpretation of them.

For Paul these charismatic gifts did create problems, as does their recrudescence in the modern church. There is the danger that those who receive them will consider themselves privileged. They may use them for their own gratification or exaltation. Sometimes their enthusiasm becomes oppressive and they make excessive claims for the significance and value of these gifts. Thus faith healers may give the impression that only a lack of faith keeps any sick person from being healed; and those who pray in tongues may seem to question whether those who do not are praying at all. These exaggerations, however, are a small price to pay for the deepened receptivity to the Spirit that is being manifested.

Paul puts the charismatic gifts into perspective when he insists that they, just as much as the more functional ones, are bestowed for the benefit not of their recipients but of the whole church. Their purpose is the upbuilding of the body of Christ. Paul uses that analogy for the church to emphasize the interdependence of all parts of the body on each other and the necessity for each part to make its unique contribution (1 Cor. 12:12ff). Therefore, in the next chapter he expounds the way that is better than any ecstatic gift — the way of love.

That is basic to the spiritual life, which is life in the Spirit of love. The opening of our hearts to her will begin with the ordinary ways of prayer. In meditation we recognize that she is directing our subjective aims toward the Logos and the potential he is proffering to us. We try, quietly yet deliberately, to surrender to her influence (inflowing). Then the Logos can lure us deeper and deeper into the love of God. In liturgical worship we hear the Word speaking through the church. We can offer ourselves as members of Christ's body and be given the grace to live and serve in him.

For our part, we must surrender our self-dependence and security. We cannot be upheld by the Spirit so long as we are standing on our own feet. We can learn to swim only by letting go of the bottom. Prayer is abandonment to the Spirit so that in her we can live and move and have our being.

On this foundation prayer can rise to mystical heights and plumb the depths. "The Spirit too comes to help us in our weakness. For when we cannot choose words in order to pray properly, the Spirit [herself] expresses our plea in a way that could never be put into words" (Rom. 8:26). There is no limit to what the Spirit can effect in us to the extent that we surrender to her. But the purpose is never just the salvation and sanctification of our own souls. Rather it is to love God in our fellows so that we "together make a unity in the work of service, building up the body of Christ" (Eph. 4:12).

The Servant Church

Paul uses the analogy of the body of Christ to depict the interrelationship of the members of the church. In Ephesians 1:22; 4:15; 5:23 and Colossians 1:18; 2:19, the concept is developed by contrasting Jesus as the head with the church as his body. Some today hold that these epistles were written not by Paul himself but by his disciples. They do reflect a church with more internal organization than in the earlier letters.

Christ's function in the church is portrayed as coordinating and uniting its members. He "is the head by whom the whole body is fitted and joined together" (Eph. 4:16). He also "saves the whole body" (Eph. 5:23), which must submit to him. So the emphasis is still on the interdependence of the fellowship. I cannot see that anywhere in the New Testament the further concept of Christ as head using his body the church for his continued activity on earth is ever clearly expressed.

Yet I believe that the analogy can legitimately be extended in this way and that it is through the inspiration of the Holy Spirit that it has been. The idea is implied in the incarnation itself. In Jesus, the Logos expressed himself in an ordinary human life. He fully accepted its limitations. In order to continue so to express himself within the confines of human society, he has united himself to a community that has been able to persist down the centuries and spread around the earth. The church is also his body, despite its ignorance and error, its weakness and sin. Both its individual members and all the communities, local and worldwide, which they form can and do resist his will. So Christ's body the church is far less responsive to the Logos than Jesus' humanity was. But provided we keep that in the forefront of our thought, the analogy is valuable.

Just because the church is potentially an organ through which the Logos can continue his human activity, it must not be deified. The Logos did not override the limitations of Jesus' manhood, nor did he use it to exhibit his glory. Jesus was in life and death an obscure, misunderstood, and ultimately rejected man. When the church is most truly his body it shares the same experience. In its primitive vigor it drew its members from the poor and lowly, and was repeatedly persecuted by the Roman Empire. Down the ages a similar faithfulness has been displayed, not only by the church itself in times and places where it has suffered adversity, but also by groups within it even when, or perhaps especially when, they were repudiated and oppressed by the official church itself.

One of the values of modern historical research is that we have been able to recover a clearer concept of the position actually held by groups that have been condemned as heretical or schismatic. For many we can now see the value of the insights for which they contended and suffered. I am becoming convinced that the church experienced a significant loss every time it condemned a heresy. In the confusion of the time, the condemnation may have been justified to preserve a truth that was more important under the circumstances. But it would have been better if the church could have humbly listened to what the others were saying and tried to understand their contentions so that an integrated consensus was reached. In many instances today we are able to use our perspective to recover rejected insights and provide a needed counterbalance to one-sided "orthodox" doctrines.

The basic temptations of the church are those attributed to Jesus in the wilderness. To turn stones into bread is to use spiritual power for material gain. In its crass form of selling sacraments or church offices this is not common today. Instead, it takes the form of a constant preoccupation with the raising of money. The institutional church devotes a major portion of its energy and skill to devices for that purpose, ranging from every member canvasses to bingo. In a capitalistic economy the church does need money and it should pay its employees adequate wages. Funds would be forthcoming, however, if the church would concentrate on its proper mission in the spirit of poverty.

An example of failure in this regard is what has been called the "edifice" complex. The local congregation feels it must have an enormous plant—a large church, which is used only a few hours a week, a parish house, and if possible an education building. To erect these it amasses a debt and its amortization, along with maintenance and repairs, absorbs most of its resources. All this is flagrant unfaithfulness to Jesus who had "nowhere to lay his head" (Mt. 8:20). One simple room that can be used for worship, meetings, and recreation would greatly reduce expenses and would also express more clearly that the Christian life is all of a piece, not divided into secular and sacred, and that its eucharistic center is a fellowship meal with God and with each other.

The second temptation is to exploit spiritual resources in order to persuade others or to convince ourselves of the value of the Christian life. Far too often the impression is deliberately fostered that, if we go to church regularly, say our prayers, and pay our pledge, God will protect and prosper us. The idea that the righteous will flourish easily turns into the belief that those who flourish must be righteous. This is untrue on two counts. The successful are often those who most selfishly capitalize on the corruptions of modern society. And God has no more intention of wafting Christians gently into heaven than of letting the Christ float gracefully down into the temple court.

On the other hand, the temptation to seek proof of our spiritual health is equally disastrous. The correct performance of a self-selected routine, if that is the approach that appeals to us, or a self-stimulated feeling of spiritual euphoria, is taken as proof that all is well with our relation to God. While it lasts this sense of well-being easily becomes the basis of a holier-than-thou pride. When it fades, as eventually it must, there is danger of concluding that Christianity is worthless after all and abandoning it. The church does its members a grave disservice when it sells itself on the basis of benefits provided.

The most dangerous temptation is for the church to seek control over the kingdoms of the world or to utilize them for its own aggrandizement by engaging in power politics. It means that the institutional church must gear in with the establishment and share its responsibility for the injustices it perpetrates and tolerates. Instead of identifying with the poor and downtrodden, it sides with their oppressors. When groups within the church induce the state to legislate what they consider Christian moral precepts and to enforce them on non-Christians, they are turning the church itself into a force for tyranny.

Insofar as the church yields to these temptations it ceases to be the body of Christ. It is no longer the agency of his outreaching and redeeming love. It has become concerned with its own wealth, its own achievements, its own ascendancy. It exists for itself and its members, not for the people outside it. Its missionary thrust is blunted and it seeks greatness in making its authority felt by lording it over the world. But the injunction, "Anyone who wants to become great among you must be your servant," applies to the corporate fellowship and to ecclesiastical institutions as well as to individual Christians. Since "the Son of Man himself did not come to be served but to serve," the vocation of the body of Christ is to be the servant of the world (Mk. 10:44f).

Finally, we must note that even service can be corrupted by selfishness. It can be used as a means of dominating others, making them do our will "for their own good." Few attitudes do more harm than "smother love," or the benevolence described years ago by a *Reader's Digest* quip: "She is the sort of woman who lives for others. You can tell the others by their hunted expression." Genuine service is not doing things for others but helping them to achieve for themselves their own potential.

Above all, true service is not motivated by a desire for reward in terms of gratitude, compliance, or appreciation. There is no more horrible parody of Jesus' attitude than the familiar hymn:

> O Jesus, thou art pleading,
> In accents meek and low,
> "I died for you, my children,
> And will ye treat me so?"[10]

That demanding stance is spiritual blackmail. When Christian individuals or groups become guilty of it, they dissociate themselves in practice from the body of Christ.

God is love. The way of Christ is the way of love. "Love is always patient and kind; it is never jealous; love is never boastful or conceited; it is never rude or selfish; it does not take offense, and is not resentful" (1 Cor. 13:4f). The Logos still wants to follow that way in man, as man. For this he has formed his church. In the power of the Spirit of love the way can be followed. It must be followed. For the Christian it is the only way to the kingdom of God, the way of hope.

Chapter 8 / **Liberation**

The root meaning of redemption is to buy back. In reference to persons it means to ransom from slavery. The Christian dispensation, accordingly, is redemption from enslavement to sin, evil, and the devil. Jesus accomplished it in his life and death. He resisted temptation so that in all important issues he chose love over a sinful surrender to indulgence or assertiveness. He also forgave the sins of those who rejected and crucified him. On the cross sin comes to a dead end. When it meets Jesus' love there it can go no further, for he endured all the evil that can be afflicted by man and by the devils generated by human sin.

Jesus coped with the cultural limitations and subconscious motivations that shape a genuinely human life. He was the victim of the political, economic, social, and religious evils of his day. He was misunderstood and rejected to the point of despair for the success of his mission. His desertion by God on Calvary undermined his faith in himself. Yet through it all he persisted in obedient love. By that love he broke the chains of sin and evil, and of those aspects of death that are the consequences of evil.

The resurrection proclaimed man's freedom in Christ. Men and women can become members of him to enjoy that freedom. The early church had a ceremony that symbolized this aspect of baptism. The candidates, dressed as slaves, stood facing west and repudiated the devil. Sometimes they spat at him. Then, turning east, they knelt to surrender to Christ.

Those who are sensitive to Nietzsche's rejection of Christianity as a slave religion may feel that such symbolism should be avoided. But can it be? That the Christian "must be slave to all" (Mk. 10:44) is implied in the precepts that characterized Jesus' teaching—to turn the other cheek, to agree with one's adversary quickly, to love one's enemies. "Happy the gentle (lowly, meek): they shall have the earth for their heritage" (Mt. 5:4). These were precisely the elements in Christian teaching that infuriated Nietzsche.

The truth is that enslavement to Christ is emancipation. We all are to some degree slaves of the sovereignties and powers that prey on our society, of our inordinate desires, and of the false ideals of the ego we have made for ourselves. Christ will not allow us to serve two masters. So if we genuinely serve him we shall have to repudiate those idols we have made and worship.

Furthermore, to serve Christ is perfect freedom. His one desire is that we shall achieve our true selves. To this end he makes our future potential constantly available as a present lure. That is the point stressed by the theology of hope. It refuses to see the eschatological consummation either as something to be experienced at the end of time, or as something already realized in the church, still less in a secular utopia. Rather, it is the possibility of taking a step forward toward our own liberation and that of our society, which the Logos is presenting to us in each occasion of becoming. We are called to embrace eternal life here and now and to do all we can to give its characteristics practical expression in our community.[1]

Marx also believed in the eschatological call to create history, or at least to cooperate with its inevitable development. He saw Christianity as a hindrance, a means the bourgeoisie could use to keep the depressed and exploited masses submissive to their lot. It is the opium of the people that teaches them to accept their present hardships as the divinely appointed road to their future glory. So it becomes a bulwark of the status quo.

> God bless the squire and his relations
> and keep us in our proper stations.

It must be admitted that the institutional church has taken that stance in the past and by and large still does.[2]

But Christian hope is not dead. In Latin America, the third-world area that has been traditionally Christian, a theology of liberation has developed. In the past the Catholic church has been completely supportive of the establishment. In exchange for a privileged position it has cooperated in keeping the people in ignorance and impoverishment, reconciling them to their lot by promises of postmortal bliss. Today, taking off from the constitutions of Vatican Council II, but going beyond them, a movement in the church is recovering the eschatological dimension of the gospel.

It sees the role of the servant church as identification with the anguish of the downtrodden and the stimulation of their efforts to redress their wrongs. This does not mean supplying them with a ready-made ideology or strategy. Instead, it aims at helping them perceive and articulate their victimization, discover their integrity and worth as human beings, and find mutual support and encouragement in a community of love. In this work Catholics and Protestants have been able to cooperate with each other and with those Marxists who are not committed to communist totalitarianism.[3]

The keynote of this approach is that theory is developed from practice, not the other way round. The intellectual leadership tries to supply the education and the opportunity for discussion and planning that will develop leaders among the oppressed and enable them to design their own programs for reform. The clergy, including bishops, who have been active in this movement have found themselves in opposition to both the state and the established church. Price of participation has been high—inhibitions, imprisonments, torture, and even death.[4]

A similar movement is black theology. Some of its exponents have been understandably angry and have expressed the gospel in terms of a total rejection of white Christianity, which has been party to black enslavement and oppression for centuries. Their antagonism to the white liberals who thought they were trying to help them came as a great surprise. But it was justified both because the whites demanded positions of leadership on the sometimes unconscious assumption of their superiority, and because it was essential that blacks recover a sense of their own worth which years of enslavement had undermined. They must devise their own plans, make their own mistakes, and realize their own power, if they are to become fully themselves.[5]

Genuine independence is just what the establishment is unwilling to grant. In the United States the Episcopal Church has learned something of its cost. Its efforts to fund organizations that were working for radical reform, without dictating their policies, aroused intense hostility in many of its wealthier members. Church finances deteriorated rapidly, even after the program was largely abandoned. Now that church is faced with a schism, ostensibly in protest over ordaining women to the priesthood. Not only is the enfranchising of women another aspect of the liberation movement, but the schism is drawing much of its support from the major beneficiaries and staunch upholders of the politico-economic status quo. They are opposed to change in any form.

The staple excuse for avoiding Christian impact on the social order is that the function of the church is to convert individuals to God. It should shun politics and economic affairs, and concentrate on saving and sanctifying souls. But spiritual growth is rarely possible among the victims of poverty and discrimination who, because their energies are totally occupied with keeping alive, cannot begin to reach their human potential. Spiritual growth is even less possible among their oppressors. For both groups there can be no liberation that does not begin with the radical removal of the social causes of deprivation at whatever cost such reforms may demand of the establishment.

But there is a "cop out" in the opposite direction as well. Those who, in the name of Christianity, throw themselves into schemes for social reform as a way of avoiding genuine confrontation with themselves and costly personal surrender to Christ are more likely to harm than help the people they think they are serving. When their attempts to "do good" are resented as unwarranted interference and domination, they are offended at what they consider lack of appreciation and gratitude. They either become more strident and abrasive in the advocacy of their pet panaceas, or get discouraged and give up. Not being liberated from the selfishness and evil by which they themselves are enslaved, they are incapable of liberating others.

The truth is that the dichotomy between individual spirituality and the social implications of Christianity is false. Neither can function without the other. For it is Christ who acts through the servant church to redeem the world. He calls men and women into fellowship with him, not just that they may be saved, but that he may go forth in them to express his love to others.

The two aspects, the personal and the social, are so intimately intertwined in spirituality, as in all aspects of human life and growth, that they can neither be separated nor arranged seriatim. It is a mistake to say that one must first be united to Christ before going out to serve him in the world. It is equally erroneous to say that one must seek and find Christ in the suffering brethren before one can know him at all. Both approaches have to be followed simultaneously if one is truly to grow in Christ, though the balance between them will differ from person to person. This should be kept constantly in mind while we, perforce, consider the two aspects in succession.

Enslavement

The Greek word *metanoia* means to change one's mind, one's perception, one's point of view. In reference to sin it is repentance in the full sense of both repudiating it in the past and intending to avoid it in the future. But in a deeper sense it means finding a new meaning in life, a new purpose and the way to pursue it. It means conversion. Such is the impact that Christianity should have on all aspects of our existence. On the personal level it is the liberty that sets us free. For those brought up in a Judeo-Christian environment, with its heavy emphasis on the moral law, a primary hindrance to this freedom is enslavement by a sense of guilt.

Guilt is experienced in two forms. One is pathological. It emanates from the unconscious as a result of the struggles and repressions incidental to the formation of the ego and superego. Psychiatric therapy has had success in helping people to recognize the origin of the alienated aspects of their personalities and not to feel guilty about them. This often produces reintegration of a divided self. It is, however, an amoral adjustment. It cannot deal with the second type of guilt feelings.

These are legitimately generated by a deliberate rejection of a recognized call to love. They are the proper response to sins. To deal with them, the Christian process of reconciliation has been designed. It calls for penitence, the admission that the conscious choice of natural desires or infantile reactions when they conflict with love is an offense, not only against self and neighbor but, above all, against God who is love. It is a refusal to be what God calls us to be and what, with the assistance he supplies, he is trying to let us become. When we repent these choices and actions, when we turn back to God, we find in him immediate acceptance and the opportunity to renew our loving surrender to him.

Unfortunately, in its efforts to stimulate legitimate repentance, traditional Christian spirituality has tended to endorse the notion that our sense of guilt and expressions of penitence are what induce God to forgive. We are encouraged to stimulate feelings of shame and to be as groveling and persistent as possible in the declaration of our sinfulness. We are to think of ourselves as essentially evil, the objects of God's wrath, until our frantic self-abasement persuades him to redeem us.

Such self-centered spirituality is dangerous on several counts. It can make the cross not the center but the end of the Christian life in this world. We are told to imitate Christ by accepting and enduring suffering, but as our deserved punishment, even inflicting it on ourselves by practices of mortification. Self-hatred, self-rejection and self-torture all flourish from this root. We so insist on our sinfulness that we remain in our sins, instead of accepting forgiveness and entering into the risen life. Catholic asceticism has often fallen into these errors.

Protestant spirituality expresses them in terms of total depravity. Every human being is held to be by nature alienated from God and can be rescued solely by God's unmerited (and arbitrary) act. So we ask God to forgive not our sins but our inherent sinfulness that corrupts everything we do. "Forgive us all that is past," "there is no health in us," "forgive what we have been, amend what we are."[6] Once again, by protesting that we are and remain sinners we reconcile ourselves to our sinfulness and dispense ourselves from having to rise to newness of life.

All this can be flattering to our pride. Our asceticism and self-denial are expressions of our own efforts. Self-discipline can easily turn into self-righteousness. On the other hand, by considering ourselves hopelessly sinful, we can excuse ourselves for our faults and from removing the resultant evils. We can develop a sense of complacency at having admitted to God that we are as wicked as he considers us, although we really do not think we are that bad and have no real intention of changing.

To protest against excessive penitence is to invite the charge of not taking sin seriously. Actually it is the other way round. Instead of groveling helplessly in our sinfulness, we are to take responsibility for our sins and the evil they cause. Western spirituality has been so afraid of Pelagianism—the idea that we can save ourselves by our own efforts without Christ—that it has gone to the opposite extreme. It has left the whole process of redemption to God, without any real cooperation on our part. Only God can release us from sin and that will be accomplished mostly after death. In this life we are content to bemoan our sinful state, which for many of us isn't so unpleasant after all, instead of accepting forgiveness and entering by self-sacrificing love into the glorious liberty of the children of God.[7]

From what does this liberty free us? From enslavement to the flesh? Not if by flesh we mean our bodies with their instincts, desires, lusts. The body as the prison house of the soul is a Greek not a Christian concept. When we add to it the exaltation of the reason over the emotions, virtue is pictured as primarily the control of the passions by the mind. Natural impulses are consciously suppressed and our unconscious repressions affirmed. Indeed, the unconscious itself is repudiated as the degrading side of human nature, that which we have in common with animals.

That division of our personality into soul and body is contrary to Hebrew thought. As the Yahwist tells us, "God fashioned man of dust from the soil." A human person is first of all a body. Evolution tells the same tale. A continuous physical process develops from simple primitive cells to increasingly complex organisms. When Adam's body was formed, God "breathed into his nostrils a breath of life, and thus man became a living being" (Gen. 2:7). If we want to use the term soul (*animus*), it is that which animates the body. Human personality functions best when mind and body, reason and emotion, conscious and unconscious are cooperating to the fullest possible extent to form the total self.

The unconscious is by far the larger proportion of our personality. It is the area that first receives the data from the outside world through the senses of the body. It determines what shall be transmitted to the conscious mind. By interrelating the data received and associating it with past experiences it molds the form in which it is presented. It is the essential link of the ego with reality.

Insofar as the unconscious is repressed, however, it cannot present its data directly to the ego. It has to use devious methods in which the natural impulses are distorted and perverted into destructive channels. The ego can neither stop them nor deal with them rationally. Instead, it has to rationalize its surrender to the flesh to which it is enslaved.

How can we be liberated? This enslavement has been caused by our efforts to conform to our environment. We found we had to submit to the requirements and prohibitions of those who ministered to us as children. We unconsciously repressed the forbidden impulses in conformity with the mores they demanded. To the degree that these precepts became conscious it was through their interiorization as the superego. This whole process of adjustment was motivated by the need to become a self that was acceptable to the society in which we found ourselves.

Projecting the proper image is a necessary stage in the survival and development of a person. The question is to what extent it remains the principal objective. As adults, is our chief concern still the impression we are making and whether it wins approval? If so, it is because we are anxious about our acceptability and are willing to adopt the world's standards and expectations at whatever cost to the self. That surrender to social pressure, to what Heidegger calls *das Mann*, is abandonment of the freedom to become an authentic self. It is enslavement by the world.

We can see why the same phenomenon can be called submission to the flesh by Paul, and to the world by John. Whole areas of the personality are forced into disruptive and irrational expression because they have to circumvent their rejection by the ego in its anxiety to make itself acceptable to society. The place where the fetters have to be broken, therefore, is at the point of acceptance. We must begin to feel that we can be, indeed are, appreciated and loved without having to hide the real self behind a false front.

"Christ died for us while we were still sinners" (Rom. 5:8). "I did not come to call the virtuous, but sinners" (Mk. 2:17). "Your sins are forgiven. . . . Your faith has saved you; go in peace" (Lk. 7:48,50). "Think of the love that the Father has lavished on us, by letting us be called God's children; and that is what we are" (1 Jn. 3:1). God loves me enough to die for me and to accept me as I am. So I can accept myself. I need not be ashamed of those natural impulses that society has taught me to reject. I can even understand and accept the distorted forms they have been forced into. In response to Jesus' love I can let them learn to express themselves in a more loving way.

The impact of the gospel is acceptance. We can find this in Jesus the more easily if it is expressed through a community. It is what we should be experiencing in the local Christian fellowship. The church is grievously remiss if even the most disreputable sinners are not made to feel welcome. Jesus' embracing love alone can free us from the pressures that make us reject ourselves. In him we overcome the world and need no longer "obey our unspiritual selves," i.e., the flesh (Rom. 8:12). We can stop projecting our false image and begin to reflect the image of God.

It is in the depths of our real selves that we find the Spirit urging and empowering our response to the potential the Logos offers. "Everyone moved by the Spirit is a son of God. The Spirit you receive is not the spirit of slaves bringing fear into your lives again; it is the spirit of sons, and it makes us cry out, 'Abba, Father'" (Rom. 8:14f). "Fear is driven out by perfect love" (1 Jn. 4:18). "Do not be afraid of those who kill the body but cannot kill the soul" (Mt. 10:28). We need not fear suffering and death because Jesus has conquered them by his love. We need not be anxious before God or before men. In Christ we can be freed from sin and guilt, from the world and the flesh.

Moralism

What of the devil? "Fear him rather who can destroy both body and soul in hell" (Mt. 10:28). We have seen how the accumulation of sin can produce demonic sovereignties and powers that enslave us through the world. The symbolism rightly portrays their independence from the control of any persons or groups. Is there value in the concept of the devil in a more spiritual sense?

The ultimate division perpetrated by the knowledge that distinguishes good and evil is in God himself. The Greeks, from whom we derive the dichotomy between reason and the rest of our nature, expressed this in their concept of deity. The olympian gods were rational, though they sometimes used their reason to rationalize their whims. Over against them were the chthonic powers, the gods of nature and the underworld. Officially repudiated as evil, they were surreptitiously placated by dark and secret rites. Or, interestingly enough, they became the agents of salvation in the mystery cults, through which the irrational side of life was embraced.

The same tendency has infected Christianity. God is often portrayed as wholly good in a sense that removes him from any relationship to those aspects of reality we find unpleasant. Natural disasters, disease, the capacity and urge to sin are considered contraries to God. Such is not the Old Testament concept. The destructive, the frustrating, the irrational, the dark side of reality is as deeply rooted in God as what we humans find acceptable. From Yahweh's point of view both aspects were included in "all that he had made, and indeed it was very good" (Gen. 1:31).[8]

We contradict God. We insist that the irrational is evil. It undermines and destroys the meaningfulness we think we perceive in the universe. It is antagonistic to us, so we reason it must be to God also. Whether we call it the devil or not, evil in all its aspects, including the human capacity to sin, is seen as an opposition in the universe that God cannot control. If its existence is not taken as proof that there is no God at all, it is viewed as an anti-god. The result is two half-gods, one transcendently and sentimentally good, the other naturally and intriguingly evil.

Jesus, on the contrary, believed in the one God of the Old Testament, who allowed the tower at Siloam to fall on those who happened to be beneath it (Lk. 13:4). There was no rational explanation why they died rather than others. In the end, Jesus accepted the irrational himself. In the face of defeat and abandonment on the cross he could only cry, "Why me?" Because he received no answer, because on Calvary God in him suffered and embraced his dark side, the dichotomy human rationality has imposed on God was overcome. The Hebrew concept of reality was affirmed. The mystery cults were fulfilled. The irrational was reinstated and redeemed in that expression of divine and human love which reunited God with himself and with man.

That makes possible man's reunion with himself and with God. For in Christ we can now accept with the same self-sacrificing love the irrational, the dark side of God, the shadow side of ourselves, and the suffering and evil caused by human sin. But it requires our taking our full responsibility for the divisiveness we have perpetrated on the universe, on humanity, and on God by our exploitation of them all — yes, including God. We must repent and return to the God who is beyond good and evil.

The great obstacle is moralism. The established mores are codified into laws, rules, and regulations that are often elaborated to cover the whole of life. The next step is to divinize the entire juridical corpus. A favorite device of moralists is to expound the decalogue in such a way as to include all human behavior. The thunder of Sinai is invoked to enforce the prohibition of even innocent pleasures because their overindulgence would be sinful. We deify our consciences although they unhealthily suppress natural desires and unduly restrict social relationships.

Juridical morality takes much of the joy out of life. We are victims of our Puritan inheritance that holds it sinful to have a good time. This does more than restrict our pleasure. Play is an important antidote to taking things too seriously. The grim determination to do our duty and bear our cross is the attempt to save ourselves by our works. God's gratuitous reconciliation can only be accepted in grateful joy. That can express itself in genuinely creative work, which is much closer to play than it is to drudgery.[9]

Worst of all, a legalistic concept of sin and guilt leads to a juridical doctrine of atonement. Somehow Jesus must make up for our sins in order to persuade or allow the Father to forgive us. From this springs those inherently immoral theories of propitiation, expiation, vicarious suffering, substitutionary punishment, and imputed righteousness. They turn God into a tyrant and deepen rather than heal our alienation from him.[10]

It should further be noted that laws, whether ecclesiastical or civil, are always formulated and promulgated by the establishment to uphold the status quo. They are the bulwark against change which the beneficiaries of the current situation want at all costs to prevent. The church is to be for them a haven of security and a source of complacent comfort. If possible, they persuade the state to legislate in their favor and urge the church to uphold even its unjust laws with the fullness of divine sanction.[11]

Moralism is spiritually evil as well when by defining our duties it restricts our obligation to love. That kind of moralism must be distinguished from true morality. We need moral guidance to help us discern what in the given situation is the most loving thing to do. In the many choices that face us each day we could never get the decisions made if every time we had to start from scratch. That is not necessary because similar circumstances recur with enough frequency that rules can be devised to cover them.

Some of the standards will come from our past experience, but we also need the guidance of traditional mores because we are neither wise nor good enough always to perceive for ourselves the best course. A sound moral code will deal mostly with our relationships with our fellow human beings, and its precepts will principally be negative. Its chief purpose is to keep us from infringing on the rights and integrity of others. The limits it defines should be to our selfishness, not to our love.

For our only positive duty is to love without restraint. Every situation must be judged in that light. The statement is neither a platitude nor an invitation to license when the implications of love are properly understood. Unfortunately, in modern usage the word is extended to include selfish indulgence. Indeed, the phrase "to make love" is an accepted euphemism for sexual intercourse, licit or illicit. Love is also sentimentalized to mean having nice feelings about someone, or doing things for others that please them, no matter how harmful they may be.

The love that is our obligation is *agape* — reverence and respect for the integrity of others and helping them to be their highest selves at whatever cost to us. In the final analysis that, and that alone, is the criterion on which our choice in any situation is to be based, and no laws or regulations to the contrary should be allowed to restrict our freedom to love.[12]

Such love can be found only in God. "We are to love, then, because he loved us first" (1 Jn. 4:19). All Christian spirituality should have as its goal an openness to his love. Prayer is essentially surrender to him. It will include the full acceptance of ourselves because, as I have noted, our deepest contact with the Holy Spirit is through the unconscious, and because only to the extent that we possess ourselves can we give ourselves wholly to God and our neighbor.

The expression of that love is always worship. That will not be restricted to liturgical services, though they are important articulations of it. A Godward rather than self-seeking attitude will characterize our private devotions as well. Worship will also take the form of service as we reach out to others in the love of Christ. When we fail, we are to repent in order to accept forgiveness and go forth again to serve. Penitence, morality, spirituality are all handmaidens of love by which we are freed from the shackles of sin, selfishness, and evil.

Injustice
We grow in love by service and for service. The social implications of Christianity are inseparable from the personal. Because all individuals are shaped by the society in which they live, our concern for them must include a societal dimension. Wherever we look in today's world we see gross injustice, oppression, discrimination, and deprivation. The situation is steadily deteriorating. The rich are getting richer and the poor poorer on both the national and individual levels.

In America it is easy for those of us who are fairly well off to close our eyes to this truth. As Michael Harrington pointed out back in 1962, the fifty million poor in this country are largely invisible. The worst of their hardships is that they live neglected in the slums and economic underworld, incapable of moving into the mainstream of national life. And if we visit the "less developed" countries, we usually go as tourists, staying in places designed for our comfort and pleasure. When we are shown the poorer districts it is as quaint examples of another way of life.[13]

This is a matter to which Christian *agape* cannot be indifferent.

The church has often appeared to be on the side of the oppressors. It has insisted on upholding "law and order" without recognizing that the phrase means supporting the establishment. Law is enforced and order maintained by all kinds of social pressures. This is a form of violence; although, because it is legal, we never give it that name. We restrict the word to attacks on the established order, thereby successfully hiding from ourselves how oppressive it is.

Our prisons are full of the poor, especially those who are victims of racial or economic discrimination. They are there, not because they are more criminally inclined but because they cannot afford good lawyers. Even in democracies the depressed classes are more subject to officially imposed violence than their more affluent countrymen.

When an oppressive government is entrenched, and the more so if there is no real opportunity for electoral change, many claim that it can be unseated only by violence. The techniques for manipulating public opinion and for silencing or eliminating opposition are so effective today that a government willing to apply them ruthlessly would be difficult, if not impossible, to dislodge by peaceful means. Therefore, it is argued, it is permissible for the oppressed to resort to violence to counteract the violence of the government.

As a matter of practical politics, the contention would seem to be justified. It can, of course, be pointed out that two wrongs do not make a right; but to that it can be answered that those who are inescapable victims of dehumanizing oppression are choosing the lesser of two evils when they revolt. In countries where the church has been closely associated with a tyrannical government and with an economic system that has impoverished its inhabitants in the interest of foreign exploitation, leaders who recognize that Jesus was above all the friend and defender of the poor argue that he was a revolutionary and they should be also.

Some maintain that Jesus himself used violence. The episode to which they most frequently point is the driving out of the merchants from the temple with a whip of cords (Jn. 2:15). I have stated why I believe that, although the episode may have been triggered by something Jesus said, he took no active part in the actual expulsion. Nor can the issue be resolved by reviewing the teaching attributed to Jesus, for statements that can be construed as for or against violence tend to balance each other out. The emphasis he put on love, even for one's enemies, however, may tip the scales toward the negative.[14]

I believe there are two good reasons why Jesus did not endorse or advocate violence as a way to redress political wrongs. First, he was expecting the imminent coming of the kingdom in which God would finally overthrow evil. Revolutionary action was unnecessary. Second, it was unwise because any attempt to throw off the Roman yoke could only result in the destruction of the Jews themselves, as in fact happened in A.D. 70. In terms of his expectations and the actual circumstances in which he lived the encouragement of violence would have been foolhardy. But that was a judgment on a particular situation. Because Jesus never made any explicit pronouncement on the subject, I do not believe we are justified in holding that he forbade ever using violence. Each case must be judged on its own terms.

Jesus definitely was a revolutionary. He identified himself with the poor and outcasts. He showed them his love by accepting them and associating with them. The religiously respectable were distressed by his upsetting the established social order. He further outraged them by violating Sabbath and other regulations to perform acts of mercy, and justified them in the name of love. He encouraged the downtrodden to recover their human dignity and wholeness through penitence and faith, and by being as loving as they could under their circumstances.

The upraising of the poor seemed threatening to the political officials. They feared it might lead to an uprising. Jesus was recognized and condemned as an insurrectionist because he loved and encouraged love. Since he refused to acquiesce in the evil of his day, the authorities felt he was resisting them and disturbing the peace. He was a dangerous radical.

Passive resistance is the modern form of the tactics Jesus used. Gandhi and Martin Luther King were successful in applying them. But they carried their civil disobedience to much greater lengths. In India Gandhi's followers would "attack" a salt depot by sitting in front of it. The soldiers would beat them with sticks or even fire on them. The wounded would be carried off and immediately others would take their places. Eventually the soldiers would give up in disgust. But they had something of the British sense of fair play that limited the amount of cruelty they were willing to inflict on unresisting victims.[15]

In America the freedom marchers had the advantage of the communication media. When the nation saw on television how the police let dogs loose to attack the protestors, a wave of moral indignation forced the authorities to accede to their demands. The question is whether passive resistance will work in a country where the government is more relentless in suppressing agitators, using secret police to ferret them out and arresting suspects before they have a chance to organize a public demonstration.

Today when a dictatorship is overthrown it is usually by a revolutionary group, organized outside the country, that captures it by force. Unfortunately the change is then from one dictatorship to another. Governments established by violence are likely to keep themselves in power by violence. Beneficiaries of the old regime may be destroyed, but new beneficiaries take their places and the number of oppressed and impoverished is not appreciably decreased. Revolt, even in the name of liberty, seldom liberates.

Jesus' method proved more successful, at least in the sense that it survived persecution and finally brought the Roman Empire to accept Christianity. It is worth noting how this was accomplished. Jesus attacked the evil of his day, not with violence but with love. He disengaged himself from the established structure, both religious and political, in order to reach out to the persons oppressed by it. It cost him his life, but he had touched enough men and women for his cause to survive. Through the resurrection experience they were reunited and empowered in his love.

They propagated his teaching as far as they understood it, and by the same method. They did not seek power or control in either church or state. Instead, they built up their own community and when it was repudiated and persecuted by the establishment, they bore the suffering without retaliation. They became a disengaged, self-contained society, reaching out in love to all men and women, but especially to the poor and outcasts, and welcoming them into the fellowship when they responded.

In the church, individuals discovered their true humanity and were upheld by mutual support and concern. All was not perfect, of course, as the disputes reflected in the New Testament clearly indicate. But enough of the spirit of Jesus survived to keep the fellowship together and enable it to grow and withstand even the systematic and intense persecutions of the third and fourth centuries. In the end, it triumphed.

But it took a long time, three centuries in fact. It may be asked whether the evils of the present day—the speed at which they are getting worse; the misery and destruction of human values that they impose on rapidly increasing millions of men, women, and children; the threat of exhausting our natural resources and of polluting the environment to the point where it can no longer sustain life — can be tolerated for as long as three hundred years. The modern pace may be too fast for that.

Perhaps, therefore, some violence may be needed to dislodge the oppressors, and even in more democratic societies to call attention to the plight of the invisible poor. But the danger that violence, even liberating violence, will breed violence is so great that successful revolt must do all it can to restrain and abandon its use when it comes into power.

I still maintain that each situation must be judged on its own merits. I do not believe the church has the right to condemn all use of counterviolence as an absolute evil. It must today be on the side of radical reform and to be effective it may have to support movements that do not fully coincide with the highest Christian ideals. In allying with them the church must also retain the right to independent judgment, and it could be a factor in limiting their misuse of power.

At the same time, from what I know of the Latin-American situation, I think the most effective moves in the right direction are those in which the church, or at least some of its members, have sought out the poor and tried to give them the education and support that helps them recognize their human dignity and band together to work for it. In Chile this led to the election of a relatively liberal government, until our corporation interests used an official American agency to finance the establishment of a dictatorship that destroyed the democratic process and sent thousands to prison, exile, or death.

There are no easy solutions. Any Christian who thinks there are is denying the riches of the gospel. One point is clear to me. The Christian cannot identify unreservedly with any proposed theories or programs. There is no Christian blueprint for utopia. On the other hand, he cannot stand aloof. Today there are no innocent bystanders. The Christian must identify with the cause of the oppressed. That does not mean he should join their movements. If his upbringing and situation associate him with the oppressors, his mission is to them — to open their eyes to the injustices that are being perpetrated and to induce them to be less oppressive. That will be a far greater contribution than anything he could accomplish by inauthentically becoming one of the oppressed himself.

Idolatry

Man has been called a tool-making animal. But that capacity is shared at least to some extent with apes and other forms of life. What seems to be more specifically characteristic of humankind is the power to conceptualize. So it may be more accurate to define man as a symbol-making animal. Symbols are essential to our process of thought. They give it a form that can be grasped by the mind and communicated to others. But when the symbol becomes an object that can be manipulated, it becomes an idol.

When concepts and theories, principles and projects are considered absolutes in themselves, still worse when they are extended to cover the whole of reality and offered as the solution of all problems, they are being treated as gods. The truth originally perceived through them is distorted. Instead of liberating, it enslaves. When in its absolute and divinized form it is forcibly applied to a particular society, it becomes a virulent agent of oppression.

Those who are unsympathetic to communism can readily see that process in it. Marx had important insights into the injustices of the capitalistic economics of his day. He rightly recognized that when a man is forced to sell his labor in order to make a living, it becomes a commodity. To that extent a man is turned into a thing, an object to be used rather than a person who works to create. The worker tends to be made part of the production machinery and, like the mechanical parts, the unskilled laborer is interchangeable. This trend has grown since Marx's day by the development of the assembly line, where each worker repeats one simple operation.

Marx also saw that the power to buy and use a man's labor resided in the ownership of capital. He concluded that the solution of the problem lay in the abolition of private property and the destruction of the bourgeois class, which he seems to have expected to collapse because of its own internal corruption and decay. This simply has not happened in the advanced capitalistic countries. Rather, a good proportion of the laborers have been raised into the middle class.

Marx's ideas were put into practice as absolutes not in heavily industrialized countries but in Russia, a land of peasants; and not by the rise of the laborers but by bourgeois theorists who seized control of the government. The dictatorship of a minority has enforced its concept of communism ever since. It is widely recognized that it has become a religion, and I believe a form of idolatry.

Admittedly, it is hard for us to judge fairly, for we have been persuaded for so long to view it as an absolute symbol of evil. It should be remembered that there are keen minds in Europe and elsewhere who find much truth in Marxism and heartily embrace it. More and more people today are recognizing that Marx was one of the great thinkers in his field. Yet I do believe that the absolutization of his ideas, the interpretation of all reality in terms of them, and the attempt to find in them the panacea for all ills have grievously distorted their truth and produced their full share of injustice and oppression.

It is easy for us to see that in communism. We find it difficult to discern the same process in our American way of life. I can hardly do more than list some of our ideological idols. The first is democracy. The birth of the United States of America is unusual in that violence was used by the colonists in separating from England, yet it was not particularly evident in the ensuing government. The reason is probably to be found in the necessity for thirteen independent colonies to federate. Pet ideologies of minorities could not be incorporated into the government, still less enforced.

Yet there were privileges agreed upon, such as states' rights and electoral franchise only for male property owners. The constitution before the bill of rights was added was more interested in property than justice. The question of slavery was tacitly avoided. Slowly the franchise was extended, though not until the twentieth century were votes given to women, and only in the 1960s were blacks in the south permitted to register in significant numbers.

The democratic principle of government by the people through universal suffrage has never been achieved in the United States. Because voters know little about the candidates for office, who are selected by party machinery, elections do not mean much. Interest groups with enough money and power can usually get what they want. The impoverished and disenfranchised, who most need help, have no political clout, so even "poverty programs" rarely benefit them. Racial prejudice is still rife and prevents those trapped in the ghetto slums from getting the education and employment that would enable them to realize more of their human potential. Still we pride ourselves on our great achievement of democracy—the land of the free and the home of the brave—and blind ourselves to the hopeless misery to which many of our citizens are condemned.

The truth is that the United States is as poor an advertisement for democracy as the Soviet Union is for Marxism, as their mutual recriminations constantly assert. The problem is that both ideologies are idols that insist, "There can be no other god but me." So the Soviet Union tries to capture the capitalistic countries for communism and the United States seeks to make the world safe for democracy by supporting governments opposed to communism, even when they are totalitarian dictatorships.

As a result, Russia and the United States view each other with antagonism, suspicion, and fear. Each feels constrained to maintain an immense defense establishment with an astronomical budget. If only a fraction of that appropriation could be diverted to housing and education, both countries could do much to stamp out the conditions that deprive so many of their citizens of the opportunity to become fully human.

Capitalism is another American idol. Like communism and democracy it is not essentially evil. It has made possible the application of scientific discoveries to the improvement of the standard of living. That could be a real boon. But it has spawned technocracy, an all-demanding, all-devouring deity in whose service everyone must constantly be anxious about the morrow, concerned with what to eat, and drink, and wear.

The heart of the problem, as I see it, is that capitalism was born in an economy of scarcity, when there was not enough to go round, so each person had selfishly to grab as much as possible. It has not been able to adjust to the potential economy of abundance that modern technology makes feasible. If throughout the world we could use our know-how to grow nourishing food and to produce the maximum of well-made goods, designed to last, with due economy of natural resources; and if we could devise a means of equitable distribution to the whole human population, most of the physical ills of mankind could be alleviated.

Another ideology is socialism. It rests on the sound assumption that imprisonment in poverty is not the result of the laziness or inherent incompetence of its victims. Rather, it is caused by social pressures which they are not able to control or escape. Hence society must solve the problem. Marx's formula for producing and distributing the necessities of life, "from each according to his ability, to each according to his need," is logically the answer.

In democracies, however, it takes the form of the welfare state. Besides being very expensive, it has other faults. It concentrates attention on material things and at best compensates for the injustices of poverty instead of removing them. As welfare is administered in the United States it destroys self-respect and actually locks its recipients into poverty. Finally, when the welfare state becomes an idol, the panacea for all ills, it seems for many to make life not worth living. In Sweden, where it is most developed, the suicide rate is among the highest in the world.

A few years ago another idol was embraced — the counterculture. Young people became disgusted with capitalistic technocracy and tried to disengage from it. The endeavor, which had been so successful in the primitive church, did not produce the hoped-for "greening of America." They simplified their needs so that they could pay minimum attention to what to eat, drink, or wear, and so escaped from the economic rat race.[16]

They formed groups for mutual support, based on love as they understood it, which perhaps involved more self-expression than self-giving. They sought their values in modern art and oriental cults like Zen. Both the latter, as they understood them, encouraged concentration on the existential experience with no interest in its ultimate significance. This idolizing of meaninglessness, while it allowed them fleetingly to escape from an oppressive sense of duty into a rich immediacy, deprived them of the sense of transcendent purpose that had enabled the primitive church to persevere.

Meaning

So we come back again to the question of meaning. For those of us who believe there is ultimate meaning in the universe, what is its basis and nature? I do not think the question can be answered categorically. All we can hope for is to get it into sharper focus and face up to the alternatives involved.

First, I am convinced it is an all-or-nothing proposition. Either there is an ultimate purpose or there is no real meaning at all. In a machine it is not enough that one part is designed to move another part so that the whole assembly runs smoothly. The machine itself must achieve some purpose. Otherwise there is no significance in the functioning of its parts. So men and women, as factors in the universe, can have real and objective meaning only if the whole is basically meaningful.

Human beings can concoct immediate, and even long-term, goals for themselves, which may keep them happily occupied. But unless there is an ultimate meaning in creation, there is no criteria by which these goals can be evaluated. If A wants to make wealth the objective of his life, B dominance over others, C sexual self-indulgence, and D the integrity of every human person, who can say D is right and A, B, and C are wrong? The claim that humanity takes precedence over every individual, and that one ought to respect the dignity of other human beings, can be answered: "Phooey! The only human I am interested in is myself. Why should I accept your plea for humanity in a universe that cares nothing for humankind, indeed, does not care at all. Since I have to determine meaning and purpose for myself, I have an absolute right to decide what it shall be."

Granting the premise, the conclusion is correct. But such a meaning cannot sustain us when we are faced with ultimates. That is a vital matter. The psychiatrist Viktor Frankl asserts, on the basis of his experience as a Jew in German concentration camps, that only those who had something they felt they had to live for had any chance of survival. Under the circumstances the chance was slim. But for those without an impelling purpose there was none at all. He concludes that the will to meaning is more fundamental as a human drive than the will to happiness or the will to power.[17]

I do not believe such a meaning can be one which we have, however unconsciously, manufactured for ourselves. On the other hand, it is never possible to be certain of our ultimate significance. It can be seen only after our life on earth is ended. For it too is to be found in the whole, not in the parts. We cannot grasp our vocation as a totality while we are still responding to it. We can only discern it step by step.

Sometimes a line we have been following seems to terminate in a meaningless dead end. We start off in a new direction and leave it behind. Yet later on we may discover that it had its importance after all. Perhaps I may be permitted a personal illustration. For my thesis at Oxford I made a critical edition of two comedies of the Jacobean dramatist Thomas May. Long before I finished it I had lost interest in it. I had decided to do no more graduate work in English, but to go to seminary to prepare for the priesthood. I did not expect that anything I had learned in doing the thesis—such as how to collate sixteenth-century books—would be of future use to me.

Years later I had the opportunity to collate and compare the communion service in the various editions of *The Book of Common Prayer*, starting with those of the sixteenth century. Those researches led to my appointment to the Standing Liturgical Commission of the Episcopal Church, and the opportunity to participate in its revision of the prayer book. The skills learned at Oxford did turn out to have meaning for me.

Such meaning, be it noted, is living meaning. It is not a predetermined logical sequence. No doubt God's loving purpose for each individual is the same yesterday, today, and forever. But he is also working his purpose out. As our paradigm shows, it is constantly being adapted by the responses of the Logos and the Spirit to the responses of creatures. The interrelationship is vibrant and dynamic. So the specifics of God's will are different yesterday, today, and forever. They depend on what happens. Yet so inexhaustible is God's patience and ingenuity that his love can always redeem the situation, whatever the cost to himself.

That concept of reality cannot express the ultimate in terms of truth, goodness, and beauty. The terms are too static. Truth in the hands of philosophers and theologians turns into statements based on definitions. But the ultimate cannot be de*fin*ed because it is not *fin*ite. Reality is not a concept in the mind of God, eternally existing in detail, which he reveals and we discover bit by bit, and which can be formulated into changeless decrees.

Idolatry is the worshiping of humanly conceived ideas, of ideologies, instead of God. All truth that can be formulated by the human mind is but partial truth. When treated as absolute and applied to society it eventuates in injustice and suffering. When applied to God it is blasphemy. We call God ineffable beause we recognize that he transcends any truth that the human mind can grasp.

God is a living being who does not remain fixed long enough to be defined or pictured. We cannot see God and live, not so much because those who see him die—like those who looked on Medusa —but because God dies by being seen. Instead of the living God he becomes just another object of our perception. He can then be confined to human concepts of truth and goodness that we consider infallible doctrines and immutable laws of conduct. In the place of God we erect the idol of an omnipotent moral despot.

After nineteen centuries of Christianity the prophet Nietzsche had to proclaim that such a God (the only God he knew through his Christian upbringing) was dead. Nietzsche was right. Such a God is not the true and living God. Nietzsche then substituted a superman for God. It was an understandable mistake. For the living God is he who became a man in Jesus and who still dares to be man as the vehicle of his self-expression within creation.

God cannot be captured by our concepts of truth and goodness. Nor can he be pictured in terms of static beauty. Harmony is a better word for him. It points to vibrant relationships. That applies to paintings as well as to music. A harmonious composition is one that encourages the eye to explore the whole canvas, yet keeps it from wandering out of the picture. Harmony is action, so it is appropriate to the God who acts. It is a process that both differentiates and unites. Its supreme expression is creation itself, in which every creature is encouraged to achieve its highest potential in relation to itself, to all other creatures, and to God. Such harmony is the fulfillment of love. It is our present goal and our eternal hope.

Chapter 9 / **CONSUMMATION**

Both John the Baptist and Jesus proclaimed that the kingdom of God was at hand. John expected a mighty judge who would consign the wicked to unquenchable fire and gather the good to himself. Judgment, punishment, vindication, and reward were the characteristics of the kingdom. John prepared for it by a baptism of repentance. But though the kingdom was at hand, it had not yet begun to come. It would arrive suddenly with a terrible and final assize.

For Jesus the essence of the kingdom was love. He called men and women to enter it by repentance and faith, but he believed it was already beginning to come on earth through the healing and forgiving love which he was able to bestow on those who responded to his call. That Jesus expected the kingdom soon to come in its fullness and finality seems to me fundamental to his life and teaching. The recognition of that is the great achievement of New Testament scholarship in the past hundred years. But it must also be acknowledged that Jesus' thought and teaching on the subject has been interpreted by the church in the light of Christ's resurrection and the delay of the parousia.

First, it must be noted that, if the integrity of his human experience kept Jesus from perceiving himself to be the Messiah, then he did not expect the final arrival of the kingdom to take the form of his own second coming. He believed the kingdom would be established by the Son of Man, from whom he always distinguished himself. Jesus and those who responded to his call with repentance, faith, and love would be ready to enter it. The failure to respond to him indicated unfitness to enter the kingdom. "For if anyone in this adulterous and sinful generation is ashamed of me and of my words, the Son of Man will also be ashamed of him when he comes in the glory of his Father with the holy angels" (Mk. 8:38).

Second, the judgment is not an assignment of rewards and punishments but a recognition of love. In the allegory of the last judgment (Mt. 25:31ff) Jesus took a familiar eschatological scene to illustrate the points he wanted to make. They would seem to be that the Son of Man will judge all nations. The Jews will not have any favored position. The judgment will be based neither on actions considered morally good or bad that have been performed or avoided, nor on wrongs or injustices that need to be righted. The grounds for commendation will be acts of love that have been so natural and spontaneous that they are hardly noticed. The service of others is not to be performed to get credit for oneself.

The idea of a second coming of Jesus himself arose when the Church, through the resurrection experience, recognized Jesus as the Son of Man. His coming was expected at any moment; indeed, his resurrection was the firstfruits of the general resurrection. It is interesting that Paul, in 1 Thessalonians 4:15ff, puts the emphasis on the meeting of those who have died in Christ and those who are still alive in him with "the Lord in the air. So we shall stay with the Lord forever." Judgment is implied. Those who reject and oppose the kingdom will be destroyed by its coming. But union in love is the main point. The legalistic aspect of reward and puishment is conspicuously absent.

Year after year went by and the expected consummation did not occur. It got harder and harder to live as if it were about to happen, even though one continued to believe theoretically in its imminence. Meanwhile life had to go on and the church discovered resources for that purpose. There was the gift of the Spirit that united Christians to each other in Christ, and the eucharistic fellowship in which they could worship "until the Lord comes" (1 Cor. 11:26). His coming was still expected. But the interval before it was not to be spent just sitting around waiting. Christ's teaching, life, love, death, and resurrection were to be proclaimed so that all men and women, Jews and gentiles alike, might learn of him, repent, and be saved.

Emphasis shifted slowly but surely to the church as an institution in this world that has a function to perform in preparing for the consummation. The organization, structure, and continuity of the fellowship became important. Its teaching had to be clarified and grounded in the words and acts of Jesus. So the tradition developed and the gospels were written. Sacraments were supplied with interpretations and liturgies. Doctrines were defined and morals codified. Heresies were condemned and schisms occurred. The messianic concept was not denied nor the hope of the second coming lost. But the church was more and more considered to be a present anticipation of the final, the eschatological age, in which we are already living in Christ through the gift of the Spirit.

In recent years this has been called "realized eschatology." The phrase has its dangers, which were already manifesting themselves in the New Testament church. In 1 Corinthians 15, Paul seems to be dealing with those who, interpreting Christianity in terms of mystery cults, believed that they were already fully participating in the risen life, and therefore what they did in the body no longer had any significance. Through their initiation into the secret knowledge (*gnosis*) their souls had attained spiritual immortality. Paul insisted that the physical body has to die and be planted in the earth before it can be raised as a spiritual body. Meanwhile one must live and love in the fellowship here.

The continued delay of the parousia led to still another shift in emphasis. Less and less did people expect to live to see its coming. So death became the likely end of life in this world and the church concentrated its efforts on preparing individuals for it. After the mass "conversions" of the Germanic tribes this was not easy. Only minimal cooperation could be expected from most of the secular laity — attendance at Sunday mass, going to confession and receiving communion once a year, and the reception of the last rites at time of death. To a considerable degree they had to be saved in spite of themselves.

The medieval church accomplished this by the treasury of the merits of the saints, applied to individuals through the purchase of pardons, indulgences, and masses for the dead. Protestantism rejected all this, but kept the emphasis on the individual in terms of conversion and assurance of salvation. For the whole church eschatology has become concerned almost exclusively with the death and particular judgment of each person and his or her fears and hopes for the life to come.

Survival
I have already indicated that I find no evidence for a human mind or soul as a separate entity, independent of the body and of a different

substance from it. Rather, with Whitehead, I hold that the self of which we are subjectively conscious exists only in the sequence of subjective aims of our successive actual occasions of experience. There is no subject who has these experiences. A conscious subject is simply an occasion of experience to some extent aware of its process of becoming.

This concept avoids the vexing mind-body problem. When the material world, including our bodies and brains, is conceived as a physical continuum which operates entirely in terms of its own sequence of cause and effect — that is, each event could be, if we knew all the facts, explained without remainder by physical causes — there is no room for a nonphysical mind to influence the material world. The behaviorists would then be right. Our bodies would operate solely in terms of a closed system of causation. Our minds would be epiphenomena with no function in the real world of change.

However simple and convincing this explanation may seem to be, it has one difficulty. Not even the behaviorist really believes it. If he did he would not consciously try to do anything, least of all expound his philosophy. For in doing that he is assuming that his mind is able to affect his body and the material world in a way that communicates with another mind, and that is precisely the process his philosophy declares to be impossible.

The concept I advocate avoids that difficulty because the mind is simply the inner and subjective experience of what we experience objectively as our bodies and their relation to the material world. There are not two distinct substances each with its own process of cause and effect which somehow have to interact. There is but one process of causation that to some degree we both objectively observe and subjectively experience.

Having united body and mind as two aspects of the same phenomenon, those who hold this view are faced with a difficulty in the opposite direction. Does this concept give any possibility of personal survival after death? The usual presupposition of a theory of immortality is that the soul is independent of the body and so can survive it. Even the traditional notion of the resurrection of the body assumes that the soul can leave its physical body behind and either continue in a disembodied state until the general resurrection or receive a spiritual counterpart of the body immediately after death.

But in the concept I have been urging the subject exists only in the succession of subjective aims and becomes itself by organizing the data received from its own and other past occasions of experience, of which the occasion of its own brain is the primary channel. When the brain ceases to function, is there any data in terms of which a subjective aim can operate?

Whitehead never pronounced categorically on whether or not personal survival of death is possible and does not seem to have been interested in exploring the question. David Griffin has considered it and suggests that the subjective aim might be able to receive the necessary data from God himself and other human subjects. He argues that the psyche as a personally ordered series of actual entities is as real as any enduring object. In other words, the continuity of the subject through the subjective aims of its successive occasions of becoming is a reality, even though it exists only in those occasions.[1]

I have pictured this in my paradigm (as probably Griffin would not) by indicating that the previous subjective aim has a direct subjective influence on the next one, an influence not entirely mediated through the body and brain of the previous occasion and the material world. That concept, I believe, is justified by reflection on our experience and it gives the subject more definite continuity without in any way making it independent of the occasions of becoming. If the Holy Spirit initiated another subjective aim immediately after death, it would have enough direct relation to its previous subjective aim to continue as the same subject.

Our paradigm also constantly relates the subjective aim to God through the lure of the Logos. As the person more and more consciously recognizes that call of God and comes to know the God who is calling, again a direct subjective relationship is developed that could continue. The Logos is already providing through his lure the data in terms of which the subjective aim can realize itself while the psyche is still operating in this life. He could go on doing so after the person's death.

It may be that survival depends on the development of this relationship. In defending belief in the resurrection against the Sadducees' denial of it, Jesus quoted Exodus 3:6, where God said to Moses from the burning bush, "I am the God of Abraham, the God of Isaac, and the God of Jacob." Those patriarchs had long been dead by the time of Moses. Yet Jesus said, "He is God, not of the dead, but of the living" (Mk. 12:26f). If God could still call himself their God, they had to be still alive. Jesus was not playing with words. The point is that those who have come into a loving relationship with the living God will enjoy it forever.

Many process theologians are content with an immortality that consists in all human acts, or at least all good human acts, being eternally remembered in the mind of God. They argue that personal survival is impossible and only an unduly exalted concept of individual human importance would expect it.[2] But this disregards the nature of love, which is a subject-to-subject relationship. If we survive only as cherished memories of God, we are destined to become objects of God's (selfish) enjoyment, not subjects eternally united to him in love. It is strange that he commands us to love him in this life, if he intends to terminate that love at death.

Love, I find it more reasonable to think, is the basis of our hope for life everlasting.[3] Negatively, that means that if there is no outreaching love, there can be no survival, for there would be nothing to survive. If a person's whole interest is absorbed in the physical aspects of life, in the body, its sensations and appetites, and in its material possessions and worldly power, when death destroys the access to these things, no data would be available for the subjective aim to use in becoming itself in another frame of reference.

C. S. Lewis illustrates this well in *The Great Divorce*. One of the characters, when met by a friend who has come to lead her into heaven, launches at once into an uninterruptable tirade of complaints. After listening a while the protagonist protests that such "a silly, garrulous old woman who has got into the habit of grumbling" should not be in danger of being lost forever. But his teacher replies, "The question is whether she is a grumbler, or only a grumble. If there is a real woman—even the least trace of one—still there inside the grumbling, it can be brought to life again. If there's one wee spark under all those ashes, we'll blow it till the whole pile is red and clear. But if there's nothing but ashes we'll not go on blowing them in our eyes forever."[4]

Inconsistently, I think, Lewis implies that if there is nothing redeemable, the woman will go to hell. I maintain that if there is enough woman to go to hell, there is enough woman to be saved, and that the persistent ingenuity of God's love will ultimately break through her selfishness. Admittedly, the Bible and the Christian tradition insist on the possibility of hell. I hold that the concept that conscious persons could live forever in torment is incompatible with the love of God. It derives from the excessive moralism of the Judeo-

Christian tradition, the ideas that law-breaking must be punished and that without such a threat laws will not be kept.

Surely that runs counter to the basic principle of Christianity—that we are saved not by law but by faith in God's redeeming love. In the last analysis, we cannot be saved without responding to that love. If we reach the point of self-centeredness where it is no longer possible to love anything other than ourselves and what we have grabbed for ourselves out of the material world, there is nothing left to be saved. The opposite of salvation is not hell but self-annihilation.

Saving faith, then, is a personal response to God. That is the essential element in Christian spirituality. Worship culminates in praise and thanksgving. Our gratitude is not just for benefits received. Above all it is for the giver and his gift is himself. Prayer ascends from the complications of its lower stages of petition and discoursive meditation through the dryness and emptiness of the "cloud of unknowing" to that simple loving union which was so beautifully expressed by the French peasant: "I look at God and he looks at me." No matter how high Christian mysticism may soar it never loses the element of love between two persisting "personal" entities, God and the individul human being.

In this it differs from the two other fundamental types of spirituality. Natural mysticism is either identity with nature, which is considered to be God (pantheism), or the integration of the personality into perfect self-realization. Monistic mysticism is the absorption of the self into the Absolute like a drop of water into the ocean.[5] The distinction is important and seems to involve flat contradictions between the three basic types. Yet I believe all three are valid approaches that eventuate in the same relationship to the same deity. Each tradition has insights and values that must not be lost, for they are elements in the self-revelation of God.

One value of my paradigm is that all three types can be fitted into it, even though our present insights do not permit us to reconcile and integrate them with each other. God makes himself knowable through the natural processes to those who view them in faith. He also is intimately involved in every occasion of becoming, and can be perceived subjectively in the process of self-realization and objectively in the love response to the Logos and the Spirit. Finally, God as the abstract source of all reality is beyond being and nonbeing, personality and impersonality, good and evil, and our ultimate union must be with that Absolute. Yet somehow I still believe even that union must be consummated in abiding love. After all, that is the relationship the Logos and the Spirit have with the Father, with whom we associate the absolute attributes of God.

Afterlife

Were the afterlife, if it exists at all, only a personal relationship between the individual and God, much of what constitutes a human personality would not survive. For that personality comes into being only through its relationships with other humans and with nature itself. It constantly functions in this life in terms of them. Without them, therefore, nothing we could rightly call a human being would persist after death. Data supplied from these sources is necessary to the self-realization of each occasion of human becoming here and hereafter.

In our present experience this data comes primarily through our physical bodies. Even our knowledge of other persons is conveyed largely by means of them. But does it come exclusively in that way? Is there any possibility of direct influence on a human subject by the subjects expressed in other subjective aims?

The systematic investigation of paranormal experience, such as telepathy, which has been going on for some time, is now being taken seriously by some scientists in other fields.[6] The results have not yet reached that degree of objective assurance that makes it safe to put full confidence in them. But they do indicate the possibility of a subject-to-subject relationship that is not mediated through the material world.

Whether or not these exceptional contacts occur, there would seem to be in our ordinary intuitions of other persons, especially those with whom we have intimate bonds, more than can be explained by the knowledge gathered through the senses. Admittedly, their body language expresses more than what they put into words for us, but our insights into their character, their thoughts, their intentions, and their actions frequently surpass what even their unconscious physical postures could have conveyed. Apparently love at least permits direct subject-to-subject contact. If so, such contacts could survive the demise of the body and provide the social data that is so clearly essential to the formation and continuance of human personality, and therefore equally essential to its survival in afterlife.

The possibility of other subjective aims directly influencing the one in process of becoming might also account for an experience reported by many who have had a close brush with death. They claim to have had a rapid review of past events in their lives that was more vivid than a mere recollection of them. Perhaps this was a reliving of the subjective aims of past occasions of becoming.

If, as I am inclined to guess, the afterlife is a passing into a new dimension in which the time we know becomes as static as the three dimensions of space are in this life, then all times would be potentially contemporaneous. From the viewpoint of the fifth dimension, time would become eternity. Hence in that dimension, especially when first entering it, the subjective aims of all one's occasions of experience, not just the last one before death, could influence the process of becoming.

All these potential sources of the data necessary to give substance to that process in the afterlife fit the experiences reported by some of those who have been resuscitated after being clinically dead. Raymond Moody has collected and summarized over a hundred and fifty such reports. He is the first to admit that his pioneering work in this field has not yet reached the point where firm conclusions can be drawn. Still it is interesting to find corroboration of the tentative hypotheses I have made.[7]

The reported experiences include the review of one's own past and contact with other persons known to be dead. Some have tried to explain what happened in terms of being in a new dimension; all have insisted that their experiences cannot adequately be expressed in language designed to fit our space-time continuum.

Most impressive of all is the experience of what is usually described as light, brighter than any known on earth, yet not dazzling. The attractiveness of this light is almost irresistible. Those who are Christians tend to identify it with Christ, though (fortunately) it has none of the features of familiar religious art. But those who have been practicing no religion have the same experience and find it equally attractive.

In its presence the review of their past lives, including their mistakes and sins, meets with no condemnation, but rather an understanding love which enables them to recognize and accept the total experience. In no single instance, Moody insists, was there any judgment or separation of the wicked from the good, with the possible exception that attempted suicides sometimes report a sense of having shirked the full responsibility of life. For those who are turned back from the threshold of full afterlife, the reason when known seems to be the necessity of fulfilling a further obligation of love in this world.

One feature of some accounts needs special mention because at first it would seem difficult to fit into my paradigm. Some persons seem, for a while immediately after death, to hover in the vicinity of their bodies. The body is distinctly visible as an external object and the acts and words of those ministering to it are perceived. In some instances the latter were subsequently confirmed, much to the surprise of those who had done and said them in the presence of what they considered an insensible corpse.

Can this phenomenon be explained without resorting to the hypothesis of an astral body, an immortal soul, or some other entity that could be separated from the body? I think the clue may be that every actual occasion of becoming, including those of the cells and possibly the organs of the body, has a subjective aim. It may be possible, especially if one is functioning in a new dimension, for the subjective aims of parts of the body to influence the afterlife occasions of becoming. Moody seems to indicate that the out-of-body experience occurs most frequently in connection with an accident, such as in an automobile or a mishap on the operating table, and that the person returns directly to the body when the resuscitation procedures are successful.

The other experiences usually occur after the person has passed through a dark passage or tunnel to emerge into the presence of the brilliant light. The relationship of the afterlife occurrences and the previous concepts of what they would be like seems to be ambivalent. On the one hand, the details of the common imagery—the pearly gates, angels with harps, a record of good and evil deeds, Peter as an arbiter or Jesus as the judge—are universally lacking in the accounts. On the other hand, not only do Christians tend to identify the light with Christ, but even the nonreligious persons consider it to be a source of personal love and concern, that is, to have the traditional Judeo-Christian attributes of deity.

The dominance of love in these reports makes them corroborative of a paradigm based on God as a Trinity of three loving divine persons. All is love, understanding, and the hope of a joyous and expanding experience. That fits the need to be lovingly open to subjective influences from God, from other human selves, and from nature, if the subjective aim after death is to have data with which to become itself in an afterlife. This data will no longer be available as the objective influence of the material world channeled through the body which has died. It will be accessible only to those who have learned to open themselves to direct subjective influences through love.

City of God

Love is first experienced in the care that parents and others give us in our infant years. If we continue to encounter it as we move out into the world, it comes through our teachers and schoolmates; our loves, spouses, and children; our neighbors and coworkers; our doctors, pastors, and other counselors.

Love comes to us from others; it is most readily expressed to others. Only rarely do we experience the love of God directly. Still less frequently can we express our love directly to him. The incarnation is basic to our love of God. He came to earth as a man so that he could be known and loved. He comes to us in the men and women of our everyday life so that we can know and love him.

Too easily that truth can become a pious platitude. We love those who love us when they love us—period. "If you love those who love you, what thanks can you expect? Even sinners love those who love them" (Lk. 6:32). Loving the unlovable is the true test of love. The unlovable come in two kinds—the repulsive and the hostile. A friend of mine tells the story of being accosted by a gaunt, toothless man dressed in not-too-clean rags. "Do you love Jesus?" he asked. "I hope so," my friend replied, somewhat embarrassed and deliberately vague, as we tend to be when answering that question. "If you love Jesus," the man continued, "you must love me too." That brings the matter down to earth with a thud.

It is still more difficult to love persons who are hostile to us, who hurt us. They often include those closest to us, and for just that reason. We rub against each other. They irritate us, rub us the wrong way. Most difficult of all is to love when it is we ourselves who are hostile. Many of our enemies are more often made by our selfish rejection of them than, as we try to fool ourselves, by our standing for principles.

The first settler in a western valley had barely staked out his homestead when a migrant came along and asked, "What are the folks like in this valley?" "What were they like where you came from?" asked the first settler. "Awful," was the prompt reply, "I couldn't stand them any longer. That's why I'm moving west." "I'm afraid you'll find the people in this valley the same crummy lot." So the migrant moved on. A while later another migrant came along and asked what the local folks were like. But in answer to the settler's question he replied, "The folks back home were wonderful. I loved them so it was all I could do to leave. But I felt I should strike out on my own." "In this valley," said the first settler, "you'll find the same kind of people. Move in, neighbor."

Other people's attitudes are largely what we make them. This applies to groups as well as individuals. Indeed, the main way we erect barriers of hostility is by rejecting whole classes of people. We hate the rich, the poor, people of another race, color, or nation. Because of the selfishness of our families, and they often are as selfish as we are, we cut ourselves off from them, run away from them, break them up. Because of the sins and injustices of our society, we repudiate it, wash our hands of it, withdraw into a little conclave of like-minded nonparticipants. All the rest are going to hell anyway; so we form a fellowship of the elect, of the saved.

That was not the attitude of the primitive church even though it had to disengage from its contemporary society. It could not exercise any direct responsibility in the state, both because there was no machinery whereby ordinary people could influence the government and because the empire thrust the Christian fellowship outside society by declaring it illegal. But Christians did cooperate as far as possible. They were urged to pray for the emperor and to obey the state and its officials in all the ways they could. The church also welcomed into its fellowship all who responded in faith and penitence to the call of Christ. Regardless of their background, they were joyously received.

When the state is not officially persecuting the church, it tends to dominate it or use it for its own interests. Therefore, as Augustine saw, there must always be a distinction between the city of the world and the city of God. Even were the state to adopt purely Christian principles, which it never has in the past and is not likely to do in the future, its nature and function are different from those of the church.

The state is society organized to operate with some degree of order and efficiency. To achieve this, as long as all members of the society are not fully loving, force must be used and the individual's self-expression restricted. Inevitably force is concentrated in the hands of power groups and there are always some who, because of circumstances beyond their control, are put into a position of oppression and neglect. When the institutional church aligns itself with the state the result is always compromise and the loss of its true vocation to identify with the outcast and poor.

Christian community is based on love not force, on venture not law, on enterprise not duty, on hope not security. So the church must detach itself from the ways of the world. But there is danger in that direction also. Down through the centuries there have been those who, because they found the ordinary Christian life contaminated with the spirit of the world, as it always is, withdrew from it to form a self-contained community. They did not find it easy. Although a group may have come together in the quest of a common ideal, differences in temperament and background make the mutual adjustments required in a tightly knit community extremely difficult. Humble and persistent self-sacrifice is necessary.

If successful, a genuinely loving, hard-working fellowship with a simple, healthy, joyous life style may well result. It can serve as an example and inspiration to others. The danger is that to preserve its integrity it will cut itself off from the world to the extent that it becomes ingrown and has little influence on any except those who enter it. This is the more likely if it considers the world, and even the traditional church, to be irretrievably evil. Admittedly, its isolation may not always be its own fault. Frequently the church itself has driven into schism movements whose original aim was to reform genuine abuses and corruptions in the church.

On the other hand, groups such as the Benedictines and the Franciscans were equally ruthless in their withdrawal from the accepted mores in order to pursue the highest Christian ideals. But they succeeded at the cost of some compromise in remaining faithful to the church itself. They have had a wider and more lasting effect. They did not sacrifice themselves only for their mutual benefit in community. They withdrew not to reject the world but to redeem it. So Christ has been able to use them in his work. "For God sent his Son into the world not to condemn the world, but so that through him the world might be saved" (Jn. 3:17).

To appreciate the analogy of the church as the city of God we must look at the Greek *polis*, or city state. Its citizens were free men, free not only in the sense of being their own masters, but also free from the necessity of engaging in any kind of labor. For the polis was built on slavery. The slave did all the work—the field and household drudgery, the management of the estate and the keeping of accounts, the writing of letters and the tutoring of the sons. Some slaves were, in fact, very learned.

The citizen was free to devote himself to the affairs of the polis, to politics in the widest and noblest sense of the word. He was expected to expend himself and his substance for the common good. The affairs of state were to be debated until, ideally, a comprehensive consensus was reached in which all aspects of the truth were fully integrated. The citizen was to provide such leadership as he was able, and finance, supervise, and direct public works. He was free to give himself unreservedly to the upbuilding and well-being of the community.[8]

Such are also the ideals of the citizens of the city of God. But that polis is built on liberation not on slavery. The freedom, however, is from selfishness and sin instead of from labor. All the citizens are not leisured intellectuals. Every kind of work, with the hands as well as with the brain, is to be significant and creative. If modern machinery were utilized fully, most of the drudgery could be eliminated from agriculture, manufacturing, and homemaking, so that to engage in those enterprises could be an enjoyable expression of human skills.

Instead, our present society rests on an economic form of slavery more dehumanizing than that of the Greek polis. Until this has been removed for all men and women, and work has been made an expression of human dignity, our society cannot be the city of God. So the church must dissociate itself from contemporary culture sufficiently to form a true Christian community of self-sacrificing love. The local fellowship would then be an outpost of the city of God, providing training and mutual support in fulfilling its duties.

Each congregation should be a witness, not only showing by its internal harmony what the city of God is like, but also reaching out to work for the removal of evils from the world around it. Insofar as Christians have learned in community the necessary detachment from possessiveness, self-assertion, and self-indulgence, they are free to strive for the radical reduction of the causes of injustice, despite its costliness to themselves as the beneficiaries of the status quo.

So long as we who are citizens of a democracy have the opportunity and responsibility of contributing to its betterment, we do not have the right to abandon it in despair. The church on earth is always on pilgrimage to the holy city, which can be achieved only by God and in God. Our destination is not of our own making. But to some degree the journey is. The city of God may never fully be consummated in the world at large. Nevertheless, we are called to press on toward it in hope.

Teilhard expressed that hope in his concept of the omega point.[9] He saw that our instant communication, interdependence, and the population explosion are compressing mankind into a single, world-encircling unity that he called the noosphere. Our survival depends on the development of a society of mutual understanding and love. The church as the body of Christ, the new humanity, is the pioneer of this current evolutionary breakthrough.

The corporate fellowship, united in the mind of Christ so that it becomes the second Adam, a social individual, is a good symbol of that development. Its body is made up of persons who retain their integrity as subjects. But they so give themselves in love to Christ and to each other that they can think and act as one. A secular example of such an ideal is the mind of the scientific community which, in spite of linguistic and political barriers, is coordinating its insights and actions to a remarkable degree.

Teilhard hoped that the current pressures themselves would produce the desired unity in love. I am not so optimistic. On the natural level closely integrated societies have been achieved in the beehive, the ant hill, and the termitary. Individuals are programed to perform their varied tasks in the society. It is entirely possible that by breeding and conditioning the same efficiency can be achieved at the human level in a totalitarian state, such as is vividly imagined in Aldous Huxley's *Brave New World* and George Orwell's *1984*.

That would be a union of compulsion not of love. We may go in that direction, especially since the church, divided into competing communions and sects, and selfishly preoccupied with its own survival, gives little evidence of being the body of Christ. Nevertheless, we are called to hope. It is Christ who will unite and coordinate the church if we give him a chance. There are signs today that he is stirring the hearts and minds of men and women to press forward in that great adventure.

Unity

After centuries of rampant individualism the emphasis is now shifting to community. This is discernible in the church, as in other societies. But individualistic piety dies hard. Many still think of the spiritual life as essentially a private relationship with God. Some feel they can dispense with the church altogether. For others it exists to foster and support the individual's quest for God. It is considered to be more or less helpful in providing the needed grace. Beyond caring for its own members and encouraging others to join and support it, it has no other function. It is often, in fact, looked upon as a haven from the harsh realities of the world, a place to go on Sunday to get away from the unpleasantness of the rest of the week, an escape from the world where Christian standards and precepts are not considered to be applicable.

If one believes that the church is the body of Christ in which we are called to participate, it takes precedence over the individual. Of course a person must, by penitence, self-control, and self-sacrifice, surrender to it. We remain free agents making our own response. But that should be to contribute all we have and are to its corporate life, finding and fulfilling our vocation in terms of the integration of the Christian community and its outreach to the world. "The saints [that is, all members of the church] together make a unity in the work of service, building up the body of Christ. In this way we are all to come to unity in our faith and in our knowledge of the Son of God, until we become the perfect man, fully mature with the fullness of Christ himself" (Eph. 4:12f).

The first sphere of that unity is the local fellowship. It is not easy to achieve, however, in many of our congregations. Often they are too large for their members to have real concern and love for each other, especially as they are seldom together during the week. It may be necessary to break up into smaller units, or at least to supplement the large assemblies with neighborhood gatherings for worship and mutual support. Christians need an environment in which they can get to know each other so that they can lift up their hearts in unity as they worship God and uphold each other as they serve the world.

In the other direction, it is important that the local fellowship be integrated into the church as a whole. There are several hindrances to this. Congregations tend to be absorbed in their own affairs, often concentrating chiefly on sustaining and financing their program. They have little to do with other groupings in their own denomination.

A still greater scandal is interdenominational divison and rivalry. The modern ecumenical movement is striving to overcome this. Two mistakes must be avoided. Locally it must not be content with occasional cooperation for little more than social purposes. Officially it must eschew concordats that try to create a semblance of unity by ambiguously worded pronouncements.

There is opportunity today to work toward a more constructive dialogue. Scholarship for the last two centuries has been able to get behind the causes of the disputes that have divided the church. Often it is found that they rested on a false premise which was accepted without question by both parties to the dispute. The problem with false premises is not just that they give one a false conclusion but that they often yield several which form the basis for insoluble arguments. As we get behind them to the more ancient and inclusive interpretation of the faith, it is sometimes possible to find an answer that all can accept.

In the first instance this must be the work of experts in theology and biblical analysis. But the insights of their research should be passed on to the church as a whole. There has been a failure to do that on the mistaken grounds that the laity should be left undisturbed in their simple faith. The result for some has been a fierce loyalty to a very limited, often erroneous, concept of Christianity that cuts them off from other Christians. For others it has led to the abandonment of the church because its teaching is incompatible with modern thought. The fostering of peace where there is no peace has produced divisive ignorance.

It may be quite a while before any major ecumenical breakthrough occurs. Fortunately, the church is not waiting until it has put its own house in order before beginning to dialogue with other great world religions. For I am convinced that we can never grasp the full significance of Christianity or get it into perspective without the help of the other major faiths of mankind. Insights derived from dialogue with them will, in turn, aid in resolving some of our interdenominational disputes.

Foremost among the religions with which Christians need to relate are those that share the Old Testament with us. Both Judaism and Islam have been flourishing for centuries, bringing millions of men and women to God, although they never have accepted our estimate of Jesus' teaching and death. That should remind us that our interpretation of the Old Testament, which prepared the way for him, has not been comprehensive enough to convince others who value that tradition.[10] Dialogue with Judaism and Islam also throws additional light on the significance of Jesus himself. Much of the recent progress that New Testament scholarship has made in understanding his thought and actions has been based on the work of Hebrew scholars and the study of rabbinical writings.

I suggest two other areas in which Judaism can be helpful to Christianity. First is the absolute prohibition against making an image of God, even by the mentioning of his name. This should remind us that theology cannot define or picture God as he is. His relationship to creation, as he reveals it, can be partially described. But God himself can never be conceptualized.

Second, Israel is essentially a people called into being by God. It has survived centuries of persecution, much of it, to our shame, at the hands of Christians, because it has held together as a society centered in God. To that vocation millions of Jews have been faithful to death. The church as the new Israel should have a like cohesion. All too often it has been lost through cultural or ideological divisions or excessive subjective piety. Judaism can help us seek the church's corporate reality in God, where it alone can be found, instead of trying to concoct fellowship for ourselves by compromises and contrivances.

Other quite different channels of God's self-revelation are the religions of the east—Hinduism, Buddhism, Taoism, and the like. Some find in them adumbrations of such Christian doctrines as the Trinity and the incarnation.[11] Others are welcoming them today because they provide contrast to Christianity. The truth seems to be that some of their forms are similar to Christian concepts and others flat contradictions.

More significant, in my opinion, is the difference in tone and spirituality that could serve as a counterbalance to the excessive moralism and pragmatism of western thought. It would be a disaster if these religions were converted to Christianity in a way that caused them to lose their distinctive tenets. No religion has yet achieved the fullness of which it is capable. Christianity needs the criticisms and insights of the great world religions just as much as they need ours and each other's. If they are ever to adopt Christianity, it must be as interpreted by them, not as interpreted to them by us. Their interpretation will both make it compatible to them and enrich our own comprehension of it.

The central problem of dialogue with these religions is the uniqueness that inheres in our claim that God himself, the only God, became a man in Jesus, and that this is a historical fact. There are stories aplenty of a god manifesting himself temporarily in a human form to give some revelation or to accomplish some purpose. But if what Christians claim really happened, it is hard to avoid the implication that this was the supreme contact of God with man that all religions must acknowledge.

Christianity has not hesitated to assert that in the past, and even those who in the interest of dialogue would like to put our faith on a par with the other major religions find it incompatible with the traditional Christian claim. For if God entered history as a man to manifest himself, surely that must be the ultimate revelation. As long as we insist on stating it in terms of revelation the problem is insoluble.

But must we so state it? It has often been pointed out that Jesus taught hardly any doctrine. He lived a life. Insofar as we can recover his teaching it does not differ markedly from the Jewish tradition of his day. Perhaps an exceptional intimacy is expressed in his calling God Abba, but the fatherhood of God was a common Jewish concept. He opposed excessive legalism, but so did the Sadducees. The most I think we can say is that, as no other man, he sensed the nature of and necessity for self-sacrificial love.

He expressed it not in intellectual propositions but by giving himself in service and forgiveness of others and in faithfulness to God. The uniqueness of Christianity lies not in what Jesus taught but in what he did. Redemption not revelation is the keynote of the gospel. Jesus endured suffering, evil, and death, and overcame them by invincible love. Henceforth, suffering can be the means of human liberation and union with God.

Since this is the heart of my position let me pinpoint it once more. God did not need to become man in order to suffer. Hosea is correct in portraying God's grief at having to punish Israel for its sins. God can sympathize with human suffering; he can identify himself with it. He can experience divine suffering, but human suffering he cannot have experienced except as a man. It is his firsthand experience of human suffering that allows us to unite our sufferings with his.

Elie Wiesel, a Jewish survivor of German concentration camps, relates how on one occasion three Jews, two men and a boy, were hanged in the presence of their fellows. The men died quickly, but for more than half an hour the boy hung there struggling between life and death. When one of the prisoners exclaimed, "Where is God now?" Wiesel comments, "I heard a voice within me answer him: 'Where is he? Here he is—he is hanging here, on the gallows.'"[12]

To Wiesel in the depth of his suffering this signified the death of God. It showed that God was unable or unwilling to protect and rescue his chosen people. Their persecutors had destroyed the last vestige of hope for the Jews, as God hung there impotently with them on the gallows.

To the Christian this story has a different significance. We know that God of his own free will did hang on the gallows of the cross. In Jesus the Logos experienced more excruciating agony, rejected by his own people, abandoned by God. But he used it to triumph over evil with forgiving, redeeming love. Because God as man has shared with us the ultimate in human suffering, he can uphold us in our sufferings also, and use them, if we offer them to him, as the means through which his love continues to take away the sins of the world.

That is the objective basis of atonement which no subjective theories that treat it as merely revealing God's love can adequately express.[13] At the same time it avoids those propitiatory transactions by which God's offended dignity is supposed to be appeased. God acts to redeem by experiencing the depths of evil with us in his own human life and death, and overwhelming it by self-oblation. Thus even sin and death are subjected to him and reconciled with him in redemptive love.

When we see the uniqueness of God's action in Jesus as redemption instead of revelation, two things follow. First, it is especially needed in the Judeo-Christian tradition because of the burden of guilt generated by its moralism. It is the specific answer to our particular problem. If other religions come to recognize that problem and begin to suffer its consequences, they too may welcome the redemption accomplished. But it is not for us to thrust it upon them until they feel the need.

Second, because God manifests himself on Calvary in terms of our situation, his revelation of himself to other peoples in terms of their circumstances is not invalidated. Paths up different sides of a mountain vary but they all reach the top. Whether the consummation of all revelation as an integrated whole will ever be achieved in this life I do not know. But the Logos sees it as one truth that conforms with the Father's eternal purpose and is rightly adapted in its various forms.

Ages of Ages

What about the endtime? It is noteworthy that the only apocalypse included in the New Testament has a sort of double ending. Destruction follows destruction until surely nothing is left of this world and there must be a new heaven and a new earth. But no. Before they come there is the millennium in which Christ reigns with all the redeemed right here on this planet. Whatever the author of the apocalypse intended, I see in this the choice that does face mankind today.

It is possible that we shall destroy the earth. A nuclear war becomes daily a more imminent threat as the availability of atomic energy increases. The United States and Russia have lived with the bomb long enough to recognize the futility of using it. But an irresponsible group might make a bomb and trigger a holocaust. Or we can destroy the planet by polluting the atmosphere or the waters to the point where life can no longer exist in them. We can use up natural resources faster than they can be replaced. The side effects of some of our well-intentioned actions may upset the genetic process to the degree that humanity becomes incapable of reproducing itself.

At times it seems as if there was neither the will nor the way in contemporary society to check this headlong rush toward self-annihilation. The demon of bureaucratic technocracy that we have spawned may have grown beyond the point of human control. But perhaps, if enough of us recognize the danger and are willing to sacrifice ourselves utterly, Christ may still be able to use us to overwhelm even that demon with his love. Perhaps someday he can establish a kingdom of love on earth.

Christian hope, however, is not confined to this space-time continuum. If we do not destroy the earth ourselves, it will ultimately come to an end by natural processes. But barring some cosmic or nuclear accident, it is unlikely we shall be alive at the demise of this planet. For us therefore the end of our earthly life will be our physical death. I have indicated why I hope we shall survive it with personal consciousness, provided we are at all capable of love.

The insistence of the Christian tradition that the afterlife begins with a particular judgment is reasonable. A review and evaluation of our life here would seem to be natural on our entrance upon a new one. But I do not believe it will be a legal judgment on and punishment of our sins, or a careful balancing of our good and evil deeds to determine our eternal state, or a purgative process to burn away once for all the dross of our selfishness. Rather, I think we shall be able to see our lives in the light of God's forgiving love.

We shall be aware of our sins, and sorry for the damage they did to others and the rejection of God they expressed. That will not be the selfish sorrow that leads to shame, self-pity, and self-hatred. So much of what we call penitence here is concern primarily with ourselves. I trust that hereafter we can view sin from the perspective of the loving God who grieves with us over the perversity that has both injured others and stunted our own development, but who nevertheless has himself absorbed the evil and continues to offer us the opportunity to reach our potential.

Supermoralists will not like this concept. They feel that the importance of our choices in this life will be lessened if at its end a final, irrevocable, and everlasting verdict is not pronounced. They want our good deeds rewarded and our sins either eternally punished or painfully purged away. On no other grounds, they fear, can perverse human beings be compelled to behave. Penologists know that this approach is mistaken. Penalties neither deter nor reform criminals.

Far more effective is a loving concern that provides the wrongdoer with a genuine opportunity to avoid crime in the future. He must be given another chance based on the expectation that it will be used for honest living. According to our paradigm that is what the Logos constantly does in this life by presenting the lure to our highest potential on each occasion in the light of our past becomings, be they good or bad. Will he not continue to do this in the life to come, with some of the social pressures that foster crime removed?

I do not believe that love pronounces any final verdicts while there is still hope of further growth. For that reason I find difficulty with the traditional concepts, not only of a particular judgment but also of the second coming and the last judgment. I have no doubts about Christ's coming in judgment. But I believe this is a constant, ever-present event. At all times every man and woman, every society, nation, church, religion is being judged by God.

What I find hard to believe is that this will all be wrapped up in some final cataclysmic event. No doubt this planet will eventually disappear. But I do not expect it to terminate in either a spectacular coming of Christ or a last judgment at which all creatures will be fixed forever in their relationship to God and to each other. Such a static situation would be everlasting death not eternal life.

An old hymn assures us that when we get to heaven faith will vanish into sight and hope into delight. I am sorry, but I do not agree. Love, because it is a living relationship between conscious beings, always demands faith and hope. Faith jumps the gap that must remain between persons if they are to have the independence necessary for them freely to give themselves to each other. Hope is the recognition that we are in the process of becoming ourselves and that there still lies before us a higher potential to be achieved.

At no point will we ever exhaust the fecundity of God's creative love. Like Paul, I believe "there are three things that last" (and last forever) "faith, hope, and love" (1 Cor. 13:13). It is true that "the greatest of these is love." But that love is experienced by the lover in response to the call to faith in the beloved, and is lured from glory to glory by the call to hope. Of that consummation there shall be no end as for ages of ages, through men and women united to him in love, God dares to be man.

Abba—Father,
source of love
Logos—Jesus,
lure of love
Ruach—Mother,
womb of love
Triune—Godhead,
abyss of love
Lord God—My God
I love you!

Postscript / The Problem of Evil

As I said on p. 34, it is necessary to consider the different aspects of the so-called problem of evil separately and therefore they are dealt with in various contexts.

1. Natural evil is a misnomer. The violent and destructive forces of nature are a necessary element in a universe of self-determining creatures, especially for it to develop human beings with their capacity for conscious and deliberate love. (See pp. 35-39,43-46.)

2. Human sin, the choice of selfishness rather than love, is the real source of evil. It is a corruption of what God has created. As Dorothy Sayers pointed out, once Shakespeare had written *Hamlet*, it became possible for an actor to play the title role so badly as to create an Anti-Hamlet.[1] Each human sin wrests some aspect of reality from the purpose for which God created it and makes it evil. The accumulation of such evils, as I have suggested on pp. 81-85, can become demonic powers. Actual evil as we experience it is the direct or indirect result of human sin. It is the risk God had to take in order to give mankind the freedom to love.

3. God has not lost. His persistent love can turn evil into good. Man can be redeemed from sin when the suffering that it causes is embraced in love. God does not ask mankind to bear the evil alone. God himself has borne it when the Logos endured in his own human nature the rejection and agony of Calvary. In that way God has assumed full responsibility for the risk he had to take and has suffered its consequences along with man. See especially pp. 116-17, 164-65, 197-98.

It must be recognized, however, that theodicy, the attempt to judge and justify God in terms of human morals, is essentially sinful.

It was the sin of Job, as well as of his comforters. God answered Job from the whirlwind by showing him the sweep of creation, the rational and the irrational, including the ridiculous behemoth and leviathan, survivors of the primal chaos. Faced with the incomprehensible scope of creation, Job, as must all theodicists who demand that God be justifiable in human concepts, repented in dust and ashes.

Notes

If a book is mentioned more than once, subsequent references indicate the chapter (Roman) and note (Arabic) where it is first mentioned and full information is given.

Chapter 1 / **CREATION**

1. The book that made many of us aware of what had been going on in scholarly circles to cope with the problems of traditional thelogy was John A. T. Robinson's *Honest to God* (Philadelphia: Westminster, 1963).

Radical secular theology was a drastic response to this problem. Gabriel Vahanian, *The Death of God* (New York: Braziller, 1961); Paul M. van Buren, *The Secular Meaning of the Gospel* (Macmillan, 1963); Harvey Cox, *The Secular City* (c1965; revised ed., Macmillan, 1966); Thomas J. J. Altizer, *The Gospel of Christian Atheism* (Philadelphia: Westminster, 1966); Thomas J. J. Altizer and William Hamilton, *Radical Theology and the Death of God* (Indianapolis: Bobbs Merrill, 1966); Bernard Murchland, ed., *The Meaning of the Death of God* (New York: Random House, 1967). These theologians were inspired by such religious rebels as William Blake, Kierkegaard, Dostoievsky, Nietzsche, and Kafka. Though the extreme forms of this position have failed to elicit wide support, its criticism of aspects of traditional theology continues to be taken seriously.

Roman Catholic books that face some of these problems are: Leslie Dewart, *The Future of Belief* (New York: Herder and Herder, 1966); id., *The Foundations of Belief* (New York: Seabury, 1968); Eulalio R. Baltazar, *God Within Process* (Paramus, NJ: Newman, 1970); Gregory Baum *Man Becoming* (Seabury, 1970). For more ponderous expositions see the works of Karl Rahner, Edward Schillebeeckx, and Hans Küng.

2. Ian G. Barbour, *Myths, Models and Paradigms* (SCM, 1974).

3. Charles Hartshorne's *The Logic of Perfection* (LaSalle, IL: Open Court, 1962) and *Anselm's Discovery* (Open Court, 1965) contain important reappraisals of the philosophical attributes of God.

4. Dorothy L. Sayers, *The Mind of the Maker* (New York: Harcourt, Brace, 1941; reprinted New York: Living Age, 1956). See also Arthur Koestler, *The Act of Creation* (London: Hutchinson, 1964).

5. Dante, *Paradiso*, last verse.

6. Alfred North Whitehead's *Process and Reality* (Macmillan, 1929) is the full ex-

position of his philosophy. It is best approached, however, through a reorganization of the material into a more logical sequence as in Donald E. Sherburne, *A Key to Whitehead's Process and Reality* (Macmillan, 1966). Other books by Whitehead important for our subject are: *Religion in the Making* (Macmillan, 1926); *Adventures of Ideas* (Macmillan, 1933); and *Modes of Thought* (Macmillan, 1938).

The theological aspect of process philosophy has been developed by Charles Hartshorne. Of particular significance for this book is his *The Divine Relativity* (Yale University, 1948; reprinted with an introduction, 1964).

Ewert H. Cousins, *Process Theology: Basic Writings* (New York: Newman, 1971) gives selections from its literature. A recent exposition is David Tracy, *Blessed Rage for Order* (New York: Seabury, 1975). Two good summaries are: Robert B. Mellert, *What is Process Theology?* (New York: Paulist, 1975); and John B. Cobb, Jr. and David Ray Griffin, *Process Theology* (Philadelphia: Westminster, 1976).

Two other books whose authors do not consider themselves process theologians, but whose thought has been helpful in formulating my own position are: John Austin Baker, *The Foolishness of God* (Atlanta: John Knox, 1970); and Geddes MacGregor, *He Who Lets Us Be* (New York: Seabury, 1976). The title of MacGregor's book comes from the concept of God as the source of being expounded by John Macquarrie, *Principles of Christian Theology* (Scribner's 1966).

7. Charles Hartshorne, *Creative Synthesis and Philosophic Method* (SCM, 1970), p.232. He is speaking of God, not of the Logos in particular. His *Reality as a Social Process* (c1953; New York: Hafner, 1971), p. 169f, relates his concept of God to the Trinity.

8. Henry Nelson Wieman, *Man's Ultimate Commitment* (Carbondale: Southern Illinois University, 1958); Daniel Day Williams, *The Spirit and the Forms of Love* (Harper and Row, 1968); John V. Taylor, *The Go-Between God* (SCM, 1972).

9. Gerald G. May, *Simply Sane* (New York: Paulist, 1977) is a psychiatrist's protest against the concept of an independent self.

10. I find many of these ideas expressed in Austin Farrer, *Finite and Infinite* (Westminster: Dacre, 2nd ed., 1959); *Faith and Speculation* (London: A. and C. Clark, 1967); and *Reflective Faith* (SPCK, 1972). Although he explicitly rejects process theology and expresses his thought through more traditional concepts, I do not think the two positions are irreconcilable.

11. Rubem A. Alves, *A Theology of Human Hope* (St. Meinrad, IN: Abbey Press, 1972), p.94. This is the answer to the contention that communists have to reject God in order to maintain that history is open to the future because "it is impossible to conceive of a God who is always in the process of making himself" (Roger Garaudy, *From Anathema to Dialogue* [New York: Herder and Herder, 1966], p. 95).

Chapter 2 / EVOLUTION

1. For the text of the psalms I use the 1979 Book of Common Prayer rather than the Jerusalem Bible.

2. William Paley, *Natural Theology* (1802).

3. William G. Pollard, *Chance and Providence* (Scribner's, 1958); *Beyond Reductionism*, ed. by Arthur Koestler and J. R. Smythies (London: Hutchinson, 1969); Jacques Monod, *Chance and Necessity* (New York: Knopf, 1971); Don Cupitt, *The Worlds of Science and Religion* (New York: Hawthorne, 1976).

4. Richard H. Overman, *Evolution and the Christian Doctrine of Creation* (Philadelphia: Westminster, 1967), is a Whiteheadian interpretation.

5. The concept that a vital "inside" parallels and informs the whole of the material "outside" of the universe is expounded in various ways by such books as the

following: Henri Bergson, *Creative Evolution* (New York: Holt, 1911); J. C. Smuts, Holism and Evolution (Macmillan, 1926); Samuel Alexander, *Space, Time and Deity*, (Macmillan, 1927); C. Lloyd Morgan, *Emergent Evolution* and *Life, Mind and Spirit*, (New York: Holt, 1931); William Temple, *Nature, Man and God* (Macmillan, 1949); Karl Heim, *Christian Faith and Natural Science* (SCM, 1953); Pierre Teilhard de Chardin, *The Phenomenon of Man* (Harper and Row, 1959); and *The Future of Man* (Harper and Row, 1964).

Bergson considered life a new factor in evolution and Teilhard postulates big jumps at the coming of life and of consciousness. Harry F. Harlow, *The Evolution of Learning*, pp. 269-88 of *Behavior and Evolution*, ed. by Anne Roe and George G. Simpson (Yale University, 1958), argues for a more continuous process.

Whitehead's thought in this area is expounded and developed by John B. Cobb, Jr., *A Christian Natural Theology* (Philadelphia: Westminster, 1965); id., *God and the World* (Westminster, 1969); and Peter Hamilton, *The Living God and the Modern World* (Philadelphia: United Church Press, 1967).

Michael Polanyi's *The Study of Man* (University of Chicago, 1959) and *The Tacit Dimension* (Garden City: Doubleday, 1966) maintain that all human knowledge is shaped and sustained by inarticulate tacit powers that mankind shares with lower forms of life, perhaps with all life. Alister Hardy, *The Divine Flame* (London: Collins, 1966), p. 46, considers the sense of the sacred, the numinous, the supernatural to originate in tacit powers.

6. George G. Simpson, *The Meaning of Evolution* (Yale University, 1967); Bernard G. Campbell, *Human Evolution* (Chicago: Aldine, 2nd ed., 1974); id., *Humankind Emerging* (Boston: Little, Brown, 1976); Ian Tattersall and Niles Eldridge, *Fact, Theory and Fancy in Human Paleontology*, pp. 204-11 in *American Scientist*, vol. 65, no. 2 (March-April 1977).

7. Albert Camus's *The Rebel* (New York: Knopf, 1956) and *The Myth of Sisyphus* (New York: Random House, 1959) impress me as the noblest, most moving, and most tragic of the books of the school of the absurd. The former contains brilliant criticism of both Marxism and traditional Christianity.

8. There have been many recent books on the problem of evil. Among them are: Austin M. Farrer, *Love Almighty and Ills Unlimited* (Garden City: Doubleday, 1961); John Hick *Evil and the God of Love* (Macmillan, 1966); H. J. McCloskey, *God and Evil* (The Hague: Martinus Nijhoff, 1974); David Ray Griffin, *God, Power and Evil* (Philadelphia: Westminster, 1976); Brian Hebblethwaite *Evil, Suffering and Religion* (New York: Hawthorne, 1976). The various aspects of my position are brought together in the "Postscript: The Problem of Evil" p. 203.

9. John Oman, *The Natural and the Supernatural* (Macmillan, 1931), p. 197.

Chapter 3 / **COVENANT**

1. On the Old Testament I have found helpful: G. Ernest Wright, *God Who Acts* (SCM, 1952); Th. C. Vriezen, *An Outline of Old Testament Theology* (Newton, MA: Bradford, 2nd ed., 1958); Martin Noth, *The History of Israel* (London: A. and C. Black, 2nd ed., 1960); Gerhard von Rad, *Old Testament Theology* (Harper and Row, 1962, 1965); John Bright, *A History of Israel* (Philadelphia: Westminster, 2nd ed., 1972).

2. Leonard Hodgson, *For Faith and Freedom* (Oxford: Blackwell, 1956, 1957).

3. Cuthbert A. Simpson, *Early Traditions of Israel* (Oxford: Blackwell, 1948), pp. 433ff, reconstructs the earliest account as Exodus 13:21, 22; 14:5, 6, 19, 20, 21, 24, 27, 28; 15:20, 21.

Chapter 4 / SIN

1. N. P. Williams, *The Idea of the Fall and of Original Sin* (Longmans, 1927). The whole book is important, as are: F. R. Tennant, *The Sources of the Doctrine of the Fall and Original Sin* (Cambridge University, 1903); Dietrich Bonhoeffer, *Creation and Fall* (SCM, 1959); id., *Ethics* (Macmillan, 1965); André-Marie Dubarle, *The Biblical Doctrine of Original Sin* (New York: Herder and Herder, 1964); Piet Schoonenberg, *Man and Sin* (Notre Dame University, 1965); Paul Ricoeur, *The Symbolism of Evil* (Harper and Row, 1967); id., *The Conflict of Interpretations* (Northwestern University, 1974).

2. The blessing of the paschal candle in the Easter Vigil. Its reference, however, is to the greatness of the redeemer, not the maturing of mankind. Unfortunately the passage has been omitted from the form of the blessing given in the 1979 Book of Common Prayer.

3. Shakespeare, *Macbeth*, act 1, scene 7.

4. Shakespeare, *Hamlet*, act 3, scene 1.

5. C. S. Lewis, *Perelandra* (Macmillan, 1944), p. 73.

6. Theodore of Mopsuestia interprets the image of God in man in terms of the analogy of a statue that the emperor erects in a town to remind its citizens of his rule. So it signifies that man is to represent God to the universe in the exercise of his control over it. See Richard A. Norris, *Manhood and Christ* (Oxford University, 1963), p. 42.

7. Martin Buber, *I and Thou*, trans. Walter Kaufman (Scribner's, 1970); id., *Between Man and Man* (Macmillan, 1947); Eric Gutkind, *The Body of God* (New York: Horizon, 1969), p. 78.

8. Peter C. Hodgson, *New Birth of Freedom* (Philadelphia: Fortress, 1976), p. 178. The whole book is stimulating.

9. The logical end of this line of thought was the demand, made by linguistic analysis, that the concept of God must be verifiable by empirical evidence if even the word itself is to have meaning. The contention has been answered sufficiently that the controversy need not be reviewed here. Important among the answers, however, is Ian Ramsey, *Religious Language* (SCM, 1957).

10. Quoted by F. R. Tennant, *The Origin and Propagation of Sin* (Cambridge University, 2nd ed., 1906), p. 82.

11. Thomas Merton, *New Seeds of Contemplation* (New York: New Directions, 1961).

12. The mistranslation of the last clause of Romans 5:12, "all have sinned in Adam," which is the cornerstone of the Augustinian doctrine of original guilt, is rejected by all competent scholars today.

13. C. Wright Mills, *The Power Elite* (Oxford University, 1956).

14. Ernest Becker, *The Structure of Evil* (New York: Braziller, 1968), p. 142. Jacques Ellul's *The Ethics of Freedom* (Grand Rapids, MI: Eerdmans, 1976) is a penetrating and stimulating analysis of our contemporary ills. Its conclusions, however, are unacceptable to one who does not believe in the total depravity of man and the restriction of salvation to those who with true faith consciously accept the lordship of Christ.

Chapter 5 / INCARNATION

1. The classical expression of this is the Formula of Chalcedon, see the 1979 Book of Common Prayer, p. 864.

2. Marshall Boyer Stewart, at The General Theological Seminary, New York, NY.

3. Process theologians are strong on Jesus' humanity: William Norman Pittenger, *The Word Incarnate* (Harper, 1959); id., *Christology Reconsidered* (SCM, 1970); David Ray Griffin, *Process Christology* (Philadelphia: Westminster, 1973). The same emphasis is found in Raymond E. Brown, *Jesus God and Man* (Milwaukee, WI: Bruce, 1967); David E. Jenkins, *The Glory of Man* (SCM, 1967); John A. T. Robinson, *The Human Face of God* (SCM, 1973); and José Comblin, *Jesus of Nazareth* (Maryknoll: Orbis, 1976).

4. Reginald H. Fuller, *The Foundation of New Testament Christology* (Scribner's, 1965).

5. William Porcher DuBose, *The Soteriology of the New Testament* (Macmillan, 1892); John Knox, *The Humanity and Divinity of Christ* (Cambridge University, 1967); Robert C. Tannehill, *Dying and Rising with Christ* (Berlin: Topelmann, 1967); Wolfhart Pannenberg, *Jesus–God and Man* (SCM, 1968), pp. 167ff. Karl Barth, *Church Dogmatics* I/2, also agrees that Jesus took "fallen" nature.

6. The objection to the authenticity of the episode of the Syrophoenician woman on the grounds that it is improbable that Jesus went out of Palestine can be answered: (1) the geographical details may have originated in the tradition or with the evangelists; and (2) Jesus could have met her in Galilee where many Gentiles were living. That the church invented a story that portrays Jesus in such an unfavorable light is hard to believe.

7. John Henry Newman.

8. The New English Bible, margin.

9. Raymond E. Brown, *The Birth of the Messiah* (Garden City: Doubleday, 1977).

10. Joachim Jeremias, *The Prayer of Jesus* (SCM, 1967).

11. James D. Smart, *The Quiet Revolution* (Philadelphia: Westminster, 1969), especially pp. 58ff.

12. Nels F. S. Ferré, *Christ and the Christian* (Harpers, 1958).

Chapter 6 / **REDEMPTION**

1. John Austin Baker [I, 6].

2. The New English Bible.

3. Gerhard von Rad [III, 1], p. 206. See also Simone Weil, *Waiting for God* (New York: Putnam, 1951); id., *Gravity and Grace* (Putnam, 1952).

4. Kazoh Kitamori, *The Theology of the Pain of God* (Richmond, VA: John Knox, 1965); Jürgen Moltmann, *The Crucified God* (Harper and Row, 1974); Dorothee Soelle, *Suffering* (Philadelphia: Fortress, 1975).

5. Reginald H. Fuller, *The Formation of the Resurrection Narratives* (Macmillan, 1971). Other important recent discussions include Willi Marxsen, *The Resurrection of Jesus of Nazareth* (SCM, 1970); Frederick Houk Borsch, *God's Parable* (Philadelphia: Westminster, 1975).

6. Wolfhard Pannenberg [V, 5].

7. Don Cupitt, *Christ and the Hiddenness of God* (Philadelphia: Westminster, 1971).

8. Bonnell Spencer, *They Saw the Lord* (West Park, NY: Holy Cross Publications, c1947), pp. 203ff, gives the details of the process of Paul's conversion as I see it.

9. John A. T. Robinson [V, 3], p. 139, cites an instance, supposedly attested as recently as 1953, of the corpse of a holy man, locked in a closet at his request, that disintegrated within a week. How much credence should be given such accounts I do not pretend to know.

Chapter 7 / MISSION

1. John Macquarrie, *Thinking about God* (Harper and Row, 1975), pp. 125ff.
2. Carl Gustav Jung, *Answer to Job* (London: Routledge and Kegan Paul, 1954; New York: World Publishing Co., 1960), p. 188. But Jung recognized that the doctrine of the immaculate conception makes both Mary's and Jesus' humanity somewhat divine (p. 77).
3. John Hick, ed., *The Myth of God Incarnate* (SCM, 1977), raises important questions, though its answers leave something to be desired.
4. Bonnell Spencer [Vl, 8].
5. Rosemary Ruether, *The Church Against Itself* (New York: Herder and Herder, 1967).
6. Dorothee Soelle, *Christ the Representative* (SCM, 1967).
7. For a Roman Catholic restatement of eucharistic thought see Tad W. Guzie, *Jesus and the Eucharist* (New York: Paulist, 1974).
8. Rupert Brooke, *Collected Poems* (New York: John Lane, 1915), p. 111.
9. The New English Bible. The Jerusalem Bible mistranslates "priest" as "high priest."
10. William Walsham How.

Chapter 8 / LIBERATION

1. Jürgen Moltmann, *Theology of Hope* (Harper and Row, 1965); id., *The Gospel of Liberation* (Waco, TX: Word Books, 1973); id., *The Experiment Hope* (Philadelphia: Fortress, 1975); Carl E. Braaten, *The Future of God* (Harper and Row, 1969); Johannes B. Metz, *Theology of the World* (New York: Herder and Herder, 1969); id., ed., *New Questions on God* (Herder and Herder, 1972); Dorothee Soelle, *Political Theology* (Fortress, 1974).
2. Herbert Marcuse, *One Dimensional Man* (Boston: Beacon, 1964); Roger Garaudy, [I, 11]; Ernst Bloch, *Atheism in Christianity* (New York: Herder and Herder, 1972); Vítězslav Gardavsky, *God is Not Yet Dead* (Penguin, 1973).
3. Rubem A. Alves [I, 11]; Gustavo Gutiérrez, *The Theology of Liberation* (Maryknoll, NY: Orbis, 1973); Juan Luis Segundo, *A Theology for Artisans of a New Humanity*, 5 vols. (Orbis, 1973-1974); José Miguez Bonino, *Doing Theology in a Revolutionary Situation* (Philadelphia: Fortress, 1975); Hugo Assmann, *Theology for a Nomad Church* (Orbis, 1976).
4. Helder Camara, *Church and Colonialism* (New York: Sheed and Ward, 1969); id., *Race Against Time* (Denville, NJ: Dimension, 1971); id., *Spiral of Violence* (Dimension, 1971); anonymous, *Between Honesty and Hope* (Maryknoll Documentary Series, 1970); Camilo Torres, *Revolutionary Priest* (New York: Random House, 1971); Paulo Freire, *Pedagogy of the Oppressed* (New York: Herder and Herder, 1972); Denis Goulet, *A New Moral Order*, (Maryknoll, NY: Orbis, 1974); Enrique Dussil, *History and the Theology of Liberation* (Orbis, 1976). The above deal with Latin America. For a wider view, see: Rosemary Ruether, *Liberation Theology* (New York: Paulist, 1972); Alistair Kee, ed., *A Reader in Political Theology* (SCM, 1974).
5. Frantz Fanon, *The Wretched of the Earth* (New York: Grove, 1963); id., *Black Skin, White Masks* (Grove, 1967); James H. Cone, *Black Theology and Black Power (New York: Seabury, 1969); id., A Black Theology of Liberation* (Philadelphia: Lippincott, 1970); J. Deltis Roberts, *Liberation and Reconciliation* (Philadelphia: Westminster, 1971). In terms of practice: in East Harlem, Bruce Kenrick, *Come Out of the Wilderness* (Huntington, NY: Fontana, 1965); in the Caribbean, Idris Hamid, ed., *Troubling of the Waters* (San Fernando, Trinidad: Rahaman, 1973).

6. The first two quotations have been in The Book of Common Prayer since Cranmer's day. The third is a popular modern revision which, however, the Episcopal Church has avoided in its latest revision.

7. Alan McGlashan, *The Savage and Beautiful Country* (Boston: Houghton Mifflin, 1967); Peter Hodgson [IV, 8].

8. Carl Gustav Jung [VII, 2] is good on the dark side of God.

9. Jürgen Moltmann, *Theology and Joy* (SCM, 1973).

10. G. W. H. Lampe, *The Saving Work of Christ*, pp. 141-53; cf. William Norman Pittenger, ed., *Christ for Us Today* (SCM, 1968).

11. Ernst Käsemann, *Jesus Means Freedom* (SCM, 1969).

12. Joseph Fletcher's *Situation Ethics: The New Morality* (SCM, 1966) is the seminal work on the subject.

13. Michael Harrington, *The Other America* (Macmillan, 1962).

14. The question of whether Jesus was connected with the Zealots is argued pro by S. G. F. Brandon, *Jesus and the Zealots* (Scribner's, 1967), and con by Alan Richardson, *The Political Christ* (SCM, 1973). I think the latter makes the better case.

15. Krishnalal Shridharani, *War Without Violence* (New York: Harcourt, Brace, 1939).

16. Charles A. Reich, *The Greening of America* (New York: Random House, 1970).

17. Viktor E. Frankl, *The Doctor and the Soul*, (New York: Knopf, 1955); id., *Man's Search for Meaning* (New York: Simon and Schuster, 1962); id., *The Unconscious God* (Simon and Schuster, 1975). See also: A. E. Taylor, *The Faith of a Moralist* (Macmillan, 1930); Shubert M. Ogden, *The Reality of God* (Harper and Row, 1966).

Chapter 9 / **CONSUMMATION**

1. This is discussed in detail in David Ray Griffin, *The Possibility of Subjective Immortality in Whitehead's Philosophy*, pp. 39-57 of *The Modern Schoolman*, vol. 53, no. 1 (Nov. 1975). See also John B. Cobb, Jr. [II, 5]. pp. 64ff.

2. See especially Peter Hamilton [II, 5], pp. 112ff.

3. John A. T. Robinson, *In the End, God* (c1950; Huntington NY: Fontana, 1968); Ian T. Ramsey, *Freedom and Immortality* (SCM, 1960).

4. C. S. Lewis, *The Great Divorce* (Macmillan, 1946), p. 70ff.

5. R. C. Zaehner, *Mysticism: Sacred and Profane* (Oxford University, 1957).

6. Alister Hardy, *The Living Stream* (Harper and Row, 1965).

7. Raymond A. Moody, Jr., *Life After Life* (Atlanta, GA: Mockingbird, 1975).

8. Hannah Arendt, *The Human Condition* (University of Chicago, 1958).

9. See, e.g., *The Phenomenon of Man*, pp. 258ff and *The Future of Man*, pp. 21ff and 123ff [II, 5].

10. For an excellent exposition of what Christianity could learn from rabbinical Judaism see "Judaism and Christianity: A Dialogue Refused," pp. 65-84 of Rosemary Ruether, [VIII, 4].

11. See Raymond Panikkar, *The Unknown Christ of Hinduism* (London: Darton, Longman and Todd, 1968); id., *The Trinity and the Religious Experience of Man* (Maryknoll, NY: Orbis, 1973).

12. Elie Wiesel, *Night* (London: Macgibbon & Kee, 1960), p. 82f.

13. Maurice Wiles, *The Remaking of Christian Doctrine* (Cambridge University, 1974), pp. 79ff, gives a good summary of subjective atonement theories.

Postscript / **The Problem of Evil**

1. Dorothy Sayers [I, 4, 1941], p. 101f.

Index of Topics

Index of Biblical References

(Mark)		(Luke)	
7:21	80	12:49	44
7:24ff	90–1	13:4	165
8:30ff	106	13:31ff	102
8:38	180	16:1ff	100
9:7,12	106	16:31	123
9:17f	99	18:8	109
9:30f; 10:29ff,35ff	106	19:1ff	101
10:44f	154, 156	21:31f	110
11:2ff,10	102	22:31	81
11:17; 12:13ff,18ff	108	23:27ff	114
12:26f	183	23:34,39ff	115
12:35ff	92	23:46	116
14:3	102	24:13	102
14:13ff	102, 109	24:22ff,34	121
14:23	119		
14:24	148	JOHN	
14:25	119	1:28	95
14:36	107	2:15	168
15:6ff	113	3:1	102
15:21	114	3:17	191
15:34	107, 115	3:26	95
15:39	106	6	124
15:42ff	125	6:42	92
15:43	102	6:53	148
16:1ff	124	7:41f	92
16:9ff	121	8:44	70
		11:1	102
LUKE		14:6	140
1	93	16:13	13
1:26ff	94	17:4	144
1:44	95	18:15	102
2:22ff	96	19:1ff	113
3:10ff	110	20:1,11ff	125
5:4ff	121	21	121–2
5:10	123	21:15ff	123
6:32	189		
7:41ff	101	ACTS	
7:48,50	163	2:36	86
8:1ff	102	2:38	145
9:28ff	127	6:1ff; 8:1	126
9:31	106	9:7	123
9:49f	99	10:41	120
10:29ff	101	13:2f	134
10:38f	102	13:29	125
11:20,24ff	81	14:23	135
12:8	109	22:9; 26:13f	123